The Emotionally Abusive Relationship

How to Stop Being Abused
and How to Stop Abusing

Beverly Engel

JOHN WILEY & SONS, INC.

I dedicate this book to those
who are willing to confront emotional abuse—
whether it is in their partner or in themselves.

Published by John Wiley & Sons, Inc., Hoboken, New Jersey
Published simultaneously in Canada

The author gratefully acknowledges permission to use an adapted version of material from *Stop Walking on Eggshells: Coping When Someone You Care About Has Borderline Personality Disorder* by Randi Kreger and Paul Mason, © 1998 by Paul T. Mason, M.S., and Randi Kreger. Used by permission of New Harbinger Publications, Oakland, CA. www.newharbinger.com

For general information about our other products and services, please contact our Customer Care Department within the United States at (800) 762-2974, outside the United States at (317) 572-3993 or fax (317) 572-4002.

Wiley also publishes its books in a variety of electronic formats. Some content that appears in print may not be available in electronic books.

ISBN 0-471-21297-0

Printed in the United States of America

10   9   8   7   6   5   4   3   2   1

Contents

Acknowledgments

My deepest gratitude goes to Tom Miller—my editor at John Wiley & Sons—who has steadfastly supported all my book ideas. Thank you for your vision, your patience, your faith in me, and your expert editing.

My heartfelt appreciation also goes to my wonderful agents, Stedman Mays and Mary Tahan who work tirelessly on my behalf. Thank you for all you do for me and for being people of such integrity.

Thank you as well to all those who shared their stories with me. Your willingness to share your pain and your triumphs will no doubt help many people.

Much appreciation also goes to all my clients. I have learned a great deal from working with all of you and this knowledge is reflected in my writing.

Finally, while much of my knowledge of Borderline Personality Disorder and Narcissistic Personality Disorder came from my experience working with clients who suffer from these disorders, professional workshops, such as those led by Dr. James Masterson, helped me tremendously. Books such as *Trapped in the Mirror: Adult Children of Narcissists in Their Struggle for Self* by Elan Golumb, Ph.D.; *Lost in the Mirror: An Inside Look at Borderline Personality Disorder* by Richard A. Moskovitz, M.D.; and *Stop Walking on Eggshells: Taking Your Life Back When Someone You Care About Has Borderline Personality Disorder* by Paul T. Mason, M.S. and Randi Kreger added still further to my growing understanding of these disorders.

Introduction

I wrote this book for several important reasons. First of all, evidence is mounting that emotional abuse is a major epidemic in our culture. At the same time, emotional abuse is the least understood form of abuse. Unlike sexual abuse and domestic violence, there has been very little public education on the subject. Very few people know what constitutes emotional abuse and even fewer understand the consequences of it. Although the number of people who suffer from emotional abuse as children and who either become emotionally abusive themselves as adults or become involved with partners who emotionally abuse them is phenomenal, few people are cognizant of how this form of abuse has deeply affected their lives.

Second, I have a deep and abiding desire to help end the cycle of abuse that characterizes our nation and many others. My hope is that by helping individuals and couples to stop abusing each other, we will raise children who are less likely to pass on abusive communication and behavior to their children and substantially reduce the incidence of child abuse in the future. I have been an advocate for those who have been emotionally, sexually, or physically abused for most of my career as a psychotherapist and an author. My dedication to helping those who have been abused comes from the fact that I myself was emotionally and sexually abused as a child. Many of you reading this book may know me from one or more of my previous books on abuse, especially *The Emotionally Abused Woman, Encouragements for the*

Emotionally Abused Woman, and *The Right to Innocence,* in which I shared some of my own story.

Third, in the ten years since I wrote *The Emotionally Abused Woman* and *Encouragements for the Emotionally Abused Woman,* I have learned a great deal more about the subject, mostly from my continuing work with those who have been emotionally abused. My thinking has changed somewhat from the time I first wrote about emotional abuse, especially concerning the types of people who emotionally abuse their partners. Ten years ago, I, like many authors who have written on the subject of abuse, characterized emotional abusers as monsters beyond redemption. But since that time I have continued to work with those who have become abusive and have gained a great deal of insight and empathy for them. What I have found is that many do not deliberately set out to control, manipulate, or destroy their partners and that most were either emotionally, physically, or sexually abused themselves as children. While books on the subject offer information and strategies to help victims of abuse, few, if any, offer help to partners who become abusive. It is my belief that if we are ever going to stop the cycle of abuse, we must begin to focus on helping the abuser as well as the victim.

Over the years, many women who have read my previous books on the subject have asked me to recommend books for their partners, especially those whose partners have acknowledged their abusive behavior. Unfortunately, it has been difficult to do so. It is my hope that this book will fill the gap and that the information I offer will help men and women who are willing to work toward change.

Another difference between this book and those written by other authors is that I do not assume that the abuser is a male and the victim is a female. While this is still primarily the case when it comes to physical abuse, more and more I am discovering that there are many females who emotionally abuse and many males who are the victims of emotional abuse. Both of these groups of people need help. Females who abuse are often completely unaware that their behavior is harming their partner or damaging their relationship. Males are often unaware that they are being abused or unwilling to admit it out of fear of being ridiculed by others and accused of being less than a man for putting up with it. Nor do I make the assumption that only heterosexual couples suffer from this problem. Gay men, lesbians, and bisexuals all experience emotional abuse in their relationships.

The Emotionally Abusive Relationship will also offer much-needed help to couples who have slipped into a mutually unhealthy style of interacting with one another. I focus a great deal on the dynamics of an emotionally abusive relationship and how partners can work together to resolve their issues. I offer help to both partners and offer strategies to help them work together to stop the emotional abuse in their relationship.

Since I wrote *The Emotionally Abused Woman* I have also discovered that there are a large number of people who are in emotionally abusive relationships because one or both partners have Borderline Personality Disorder (BPD). Some of the primary symptoms of this disorder are frequent emotional outbursts, radical mood swings, unreasonable expectations, and a tendency to blame one's partner for one's own problems—all forms of emotional abuse. *The Emotionally Abusive Relationship* will include information on Borderline Personality Disorder and its effects, as well as a section offering partners of borderline individuals strategies for dealing with the types of emotional abuse they are likely to experience.

Up to ten million North Americans suffer from Borderline Personality Disorder, which seems to occur to a slightly higher degree among gay men and lesbian women. My hope is that the book will also be of interest to those who suffer from this debilitating disorder since many people with BPD feel confused and ashamed by their own behavior. Those who are aware that they have become abusive to their partner and/or children will grow to understand themselves and their behavior better, and this will hopefully help them to work past the stigma of being an abuser. While there are now many books on the subject of BPD, few, if any, address the issue of how to overcome emotional abuse.

It is also true, of course, that people with BPD are also emotionally abused. Their tendency to become involved quickly and intensely often causes them to overlook significant warning signs that a partner is a potential abuser. In my recent book *Loving Him without Losing You,* I focused on helping women (both those who suffer from BPD and those who don't) to slow down and get to know a man before becoming too involved, and I suggested ways to maintain a separate life so they don't become isolated and lost in the relationship—one of the reasons why women stay in abusive relationships. In *The Emotionally Abusive Relationship,* I offer further help for women who need to establish firmer boundaries and develop a stronger sense of self.

A Step-by-Step Program

Most people who are in an emotionally abusive relationship feel stuck, hopeless, and desperate. They want help to understand the dynamics that are going on, but they don't know where to turn. Many have attempted marital or couples counseling but are often disappointed. Most victims of emotional abuse don't realize they are being abused, and many blame themselves for the problems in the relationship. Because emotional abuse can be so subtle, it is extremely difficult for therapists to recognize it during counseling sessions. Recognizing and stopping emotional abuse takes special knowledge and skills that many therapists simply don't have. Couples are often on their best behavior, and even those who are more upfront aren't always able to present an accurate picture of what actually goes on between them. Often it is the person who is being abused who is presented as the identified patient (the one with the problem). Because emotional abuse causes a person to doubt his or her perceptions, and to blame himself or herself for all the problems in the relationship, the abused party often takes on the role of the identified patient quite willingly. The abuser not only goes unrecognized but can also feel bolstered by the counseling experience as his or her perceptions are validated and his or her beliefs are reinforced.

Many television talk shows and relationship gurus continually send the message that resolving relationship issues is merely a matter of learning better communication skills or honoring each other's differences. But if one or both partners are being emotionally abusive, it doesn't matter how hard a couple tries to communicate feelings, how much they attempt to understand the differences between the sexes, and how tolerant they try to be—the problem is not going to go away. In fact, often those who are being emotionally abused become even more confused and doubt their perceptions even more after listening to people who espouse such glib and quick answers. Worse yet, some relationship experts espouse the idea that a person can change simply by deciding they are going to do so. They seem to ignore the fact that behaviors such as being abusive or allowing abuse to occur are deeply ingrained patterns established when we are young. To tell a person they are choosing to be abusive or to be abused is not only insulting but can be extremely damaging.

The Emotionally Abusive Relationship offers the kind of help readers may not have been able to receive in the past through either therapy or other books. In it I offer the same help I offer my private clients. I will present a step-by-step program for working through the unfinished business from the past that has contaminated present relationships. I'll also provide strategies readers can use in their daily lives to help them stay focused on the present, as well as healthy ways to cope with the anger, the shame, the stress, and the insecurities that have propelled them into acting in emotionally abusive ways. For those couples who are willing to stop blaming one another and start taking responsibility for their own patterns, this can mean the difference between separation or divorce and salvaging your relationship.

How the Book Is Organized

The Emotionally Abusive Relationship offers strategies that will help couples no matter what your specific situation. There are separate chapters for the person who is being abused, the abusive partner, and the couple who are abusing each other. If you are being abused, you need to learn how to stop taking in the abusive words, gestures, or behavior of your partner and how to confront your partner when he or she becomes abusive. If you are being abusive, you need strategies to help you catch yourself in the act and find healthier ways to cope with stress, anger, disappointment, insecurity, and shame. If you're part of a couple who emotionally abuse each other, you need to learn how you can work together to stop the abuse. You need to understand your partner's history as much as your own so you can gain empathy for his or her struggles and offer the right kind of support. And you need help in developing a plan of action you can use when you start to get into trouble.

The book is divided into three parts. In Part One, "Identifying and Understanding Emotional Abuse," I explain in detail how emotional abuse poisons and even destroys intimate relationships. I define emotional abuse and describe the various types of emotional abuse that exist. I also explain in detail how most emotional abuse is unconscious and how most people who emotionally abuse their partners are doing so because they themselves were emotionally abused in childhood or in previous relationships.

In Part Two, "Stopping the Abuse," I offer strategies to help couples stop the emotional abuse that is destroying their relationship. I present separate chapters for the abused, the abuser, and the couple who are caught up in an abusive cycle, as well as chapters for those suffering from a personality disorder or those whose partner suffers from such a disorder.

Part Three, "Where Do You Go from Here?" offers information that will help couples and individuals decide whether they can salvage their relationship. It will also offer information on how victims of emotional abuse can recover from its devastating effects and how both abusers and victims of abuse can prevent emotional abuse in the future.

At the end of most chapters, I recommend one or more films. These films illustrate either a type of emotional abuse or a point I am making in the chapter. I encourage you to see these films to help you further understand how emotional abuse affects individuals and couples.

PART ONE

IDENTIFYING AND UNDERSTANDING EMOTIONAL ABUSE

CHAPTER 1

Emotional Abuse— The Destroyer of Relationships

No matter what Tracey does, she just can't seem to please her boyfriend. He complains constantly—about the way she dresses, the way she talks, the amount of time she spends on the phone with her friends—and even though she's taken his concerns to heart and made changes in these areas, he always seems to find something else to complain about. "I love him and I want him to be happy, but I'm confused," Tracey explained to me. "Sometimes it seems like no matter what I do he never seems to be satisfied, and at other times I begin to think that maybe I do things deliberately just to upset him."

Robert's wife isn't speaking to him again. This time it's been two weeks. Although it's happened many times before, it still bothers him immensely. "I feel like a bad boy who is being punished by his mother. It's not just the silent treatment that bothers me, it's the dirty looks, as well."

Over the years, Robert has learned to stay away from his wife and give her time to cool down. "It doesn't do any good to try to apologize or explain my side of the story—she refuses to listen, and often it makes her more angry. When she's ready to start talking to me again, she will—until then, I just have to suffer in silence."

Jason's lover, Mark, is extremely possessive and jealous. "He has to know where I am twenty-four hours a day," Jason complained to me. "He calls me at work several times a day, and if I'm away from my desk, he gets really angry and wants to know where I was and what I was doing. There are several nice-looking men in my office, and Mark is convinced I'm going to have an affair with one of them. It does absolutely no good at all for me to try to reassure him. And he's constantly accusing me of flirting. The worst part about it is that I'm beginning to question myself. I don't think I flirt, but maybe I do without realizing it."

Although Tracey, Robert, and Jason don't realize it, they are all being emotionally abused. The same is true of thousands of other women and men like them. Slowly, systematically, their self-confidence is whittled away, their self-esteem is eroded, and their perception of themselves is distorted—and yet they don't even know it is happening.

An individual or a couple can remain locked in a prison of conflict, humiliation, fear, and anger for years without realizing that they are in an emotionally abusive relationship. They may assume that all couples fight as they do or that all women (or men) are treated as they are. Often, emotional abuse between couples is denied, made light of, or written off as simple conflicts or "love-spats" when in fact one or both partners are being severely damaged psychologically. Even those who realize they are being emotionally abused tend to blame themselves or make excuses for their partner's behavior. Little do they know that by allowing their partner to continue this kind of destructive behavior, they are actually participating in destroying their relationship. Emotional abuse is one of the prime factors in creating dysfunctional relationships and one of the major causes for separation or divorce.

What Is Emotional Abuse?

When most people think of emotional abuse, they usually think of one or both partners belittling or criticizing the other. But emotional abuse is much more than verbal abuse. Emotional abuse can be defined as any *nonphysical* behavior that is designed to control, intimidate, subjugate, demean, punish, or isolate another person through the use of degradation, humiliation, or fear.

Emotionally abusive behavior ranges from verbal abuse (belittling, berating, constant criticism) to more subtle tactics like intimidation, manipulation, and refusal to be pleased. We will take much more in-depth looks at the various types of emotional abuse in the next chapter, but for now, here are some examples of emotional abuse in intimate relationships:

- Humiliation and degradation
- Discounting and negating
- Domination and control
- Judging and criticizing
- Accusing and blaming
- Trivial and unreasonable demands or expectations
- Emotional distancing and the "silent treatment"
- Isolation

Emotional abuse can also include more subtle forms of behavior such as:

- Withholding of attention or affection
- Disapproving, dismissive, contemptuous, or condescending looks, comments, and behavior
- Sulking and pouting
- Projection and/or accusations
- Subtle threats of abandonment (either physical or emotional)

Emotional abuse is not only made up of negative behaviors but negative attitudes as well. Therefore, we need to include the word *attitude* in our definition of emotional abuse. A person who is emotionally abusive need not take any overt action whatsoever. All he or she needs to do is to exhibit an abusive attitude. Here are some examples:

- Believing that others should do as you say
- Not noticing how others feel
- Not caring how others feel
- Believing that everyone else is inferior to you
- Believing that you are always right

So emotional abuse is any nonphysical behavior or *attitude* that is designed to control, intimidate, subjugate, demean, punish, or isolate another person. But there are also some types of physical behavior that can be considered emotional abuse. These behaviors have a name: *symbolic violence*. This includes intimidating behavior such as slamming doors, kicking a wall, throwing dishes, furniture, or other objects, driving recklessly while the victim is in the car, and destroying or threatening to destroy objects the victim values. Even milder forms of violence such as shaking a fist or finger at the victim, making threatening gestures or faces, or acting like he or she wants to kill the victim carry symbolic threats of violence.

How Emotional Abuse Does Damage

The primary effects of emotional abuse on the victim are depression, lack of motivation, confusion, difficulty concentrating or making decisions, low self-esteem, feelings of failure or worthlessness, feelings of hopelessness, self-blame, and self-destructiveness. Emotional abuse is like brainwashing in that it systematically wears away at the victim's self-confidence, sense of self-worth, trust in his or her perceptions, and self-concept. Whether it is by constant berating and belittling, by intimidation, or under the guise of "guidance" or teaching, the results are similar. Eventually, the recipient loses all sense of self and all remnants of personal value.

Abused partners tend either to take on the criticism and rejection of their partner or to be in constant turmoil, wondering things like: *Am I as bad as she makes me out to be, or is she just impossible to please? Should I stay in this relationship, or should I go? If I'm as incompetent as he says I am, maybe I can't make it on my own. Maybe no one will ever love me again.* Ultimately, given enough time, most victims of emotional abuse come not only to blame themselves for all the problems in the relationship but also to believe that they are inadequate, contemptuous, and even unlovable.

Emotional abuse is considered by many to be the most painful form of violence and the most detrimental to self-esteem. Emotional abuse cuts to the very core of a person, creating scars that may be longer lasting than physical ones. With emotional abuse, the insults, insinuations, criticism, and accusations slowly eat away at the victim's self-esteem until he or she is incapable of judging a situation realistically. She may begin to believe that there is something wrong with her or even fear that she is losing her mind. She has become so beaten down emotionally that she blames herself for the abuse.

Emotional abuse poisons a relationship and infuses it with hostility, contempt, and hatred. No matter how much a couple once loved each other, once emotional abuse becomes a consistent aspect of the relationship, that love is overshadowed by fear, anger, guilt, and shame. Whether it is one or both partners who are being emotionally abusive, the relationship becomes increasingly more toxic as time goes by. In this polluted environment it is difficult for love not only to grow but to survive.

At the very least, emotional abuse causes both the abuser and the victim to lose sight of any redeeming qualities his or her partner once had. The more a partner is allowed to degrade, criticize, or dominate her partner, the less she will respect her partner. And the more a partner is emotionally abused, the more he will slowly build up an intense hatred toward his abuser. The disrespect and hatred each partner begins to feel leads to more and more emotional abuse and to each partner justifying inappropriate, even destructive, behavior. Over time, anger can build up on the part of both abuser and victim, and emotional abuse can turn to physical violence.

When emotional abuse is mutual, it becomes a matter of survival, as each partner has to constantly fend off the criticism, verbal attacks, or rejection and shore up enough strength to go on with daily tasks.

As the emotional abuse takes its toll and each partner becomes less and less self-assured, each clings to the relationship even more. A destructive cycle is created—even as the relationship becomes more and more abusive each person becomes more dependent on his or her partner. And as the relationship continues to deteriorate, each partner feels further justified in becoming even more abusive.

Whether you suspect you are being emotionally abused, fear that you might be emotionally abusing your partner, or think that both you and your partner are emotionally abusing each other, this book will help you. If you are uncertain as to whether you are being emotionally abused, you will learn important information that will help you decide once and for all. If you fear that you might be emotionally abusing your partner, you will learn exactly what constitutes emotionally abusive behavior as well as what causes it. And if you think you and your partner are emotionally abusing each other, you'll learn how to stop triggering one another, how to stop bringing out the worst in one another, and how to develop healthier ways of relating to each other.

QUESTIONNAIRE: *Are You Being Emotionally Abused?*

Answer the following questions to help determine whether or not you are being emotionally abused in your relationship.

1. Do you feel as if your partner treats you like a child? Does he constantly correct you or chastise you because your behavior is "inappropriate"? Do you feel you must "get permission" before going somewhere or before making even the smallest of decisions? Do you have to account for any money you spend, or does he attempt to control your spending (even though he has no problem spending on himself)?

2. Does your partner treat you as if you are "less than" or inferior to her? Does your partner make a point of reminding you that you are less educated or that you make less money or that you aren't as attractive as she is?

3. Does your partner routinely ridicule, dismiss, or disregard your opinions, thoughts, suggestions, and feelings?

4. Does your partner constantly belittle your accomplishments, your aspirations, or your plans for the future?

5. Do you find yourself "walking on eggshells"? Do you spend a lot of time monitoring your behavior and/or watching for your partner's bad moods before bringing up a subject?

6. Have you stopped seeing many or all of your friends and/or family since being in this relationship? Did you do this because your partner dislikes them, because your partner feels jealous of the time you spent with them, or because you are ashamed of the way he treats you in front of them? Did you stop seeing friends and family because you are ashamed of the fact that you're still with him, even though you've complained to them many times about the way he treats you?

7. Does your partner usually insist on getting her own way? Does she want to be the one to decide where you will go, what you will do, and with whom you will do it?

8. Does your partner punish you by pouting, by withdrawing from you, by giving you the silent treatment, or by withholding affection or sex if you don't do things his way?

9. Does your partner frequently threaten to end the relationship if you don't do things her way?

10. Does your partner constantly accuse you of flirting or of having affairs even though it isn't true?

11. Does your partner feel he or she is always right?

12. Does your partner seem impossible to please? Does she constantly complain to you about some aspect of your personality, your looks, or the way you choose to run your life?

13. Does your partner frequently put you down or make fun of you in front of others?

14. Does your partner blame you for his or her problems? For example, does he claim it is your fault he flies off the handle and starts

screaming? Does he tell you he wouldn't do it if you didn't make him so mad? Are you to blame for her problem with compulsive overeating? Because she has a drinking problem? Does he blame you for not being able to finish college or fulfill his dream of becoming an actor (author, musician, singer, etc.)?

15. Does your partner feel you are the one who is responsible for all the problems in the relationship?

16. Does your partner's personality seem to go through radical changes? Is she pleasant one minute only to be furious the next? Does he become enraged with only the slightest provocation? Does she experience periods of extreme elation followed by periods of severe depression? Does his personality seem to change when he drinks alcohol?

17. Does your partner tease you, make fun of you, or use sarcasm as a way to put you down or degrade you? When you complain, does he tell you it was just a joke and that you are too sensitive or don't have a sense of humor?

18. Is your partner unable to laugh at herself? Is she extremely sensitive when it comes to others making fun of her or making any kind of comment that seems to show a lack of respect?

19. Does your partner find it difficult or impossible to apologize or admit when he is wrong? Does she make excuses for her behavior or tend to blame others for her mistakes?

20. Does your partner constantly pressure you for sex or try to persuade you to engage in sexual acts that you find disgusting? Has he ever threatened to find someone else who will have sex with him or who will engage in the activities he is interested in?

If you answered half or more of these questions with a yes, you are definitely being emotionally abused. But a yes answer to even a few of the above questions can also indicate emotional abuse. More than anything else, what characterizes an emotionally abusive relationship is a consistent pattern of hurtful, humiliating, and condescending behavior.

Determining Whether You Are Being Emotionally Abusive

As difficult as it is to admit you are being emotionally abused, it is even harder to face the possibility that you might be guilty of emotionally abusing your partner. No one wants to have to face the fact that he or she has lost control in this way and that his or her actions and/or words have caused his or her partner emotional damage. It is much easier to continue trying to justify or rationalize your behavior by telling yourself that your partner pushes you too far or that your partner deserves the treatment you give her. But if you are emotionally abusing your partner, the only way you are going to save your relationship and save yourself is to stop making excuses and admit the truth—first to yourself and eventually to your partner. The first step in admitting this truth is to answer the following questions as honestly as possible.

QUESTIONNAIRE: *Are You Being Emotionally Abusive?*

1. Do you believe you have a right to make most of the decisions in the relationship?

2. Do you insist that your partner do as you say?

3. Do you perceive yourself as being superior to or "better than" your partner (e.g., smarter, more competent, more powerful)? Do you feel you have a right to special treatment or consideration in the relationship because of this?

4. Do you secretly disrespect or even despise your partner because you feel she is weak, inadequate, stupid, or a pushover?

5. Did you deliberately get involved with a partner who would allow you to maintain the dominant role in the relationship?

6. Do you give your partner the silent treatment or withhold approval, affection, sex, or money when he or she doesn't do as you wish?

7. Do you threaten to leave the house or to end the relationship whenever you don't get your way?

8. Do you think your partner and others are just too sensitive and that is why they get their feelings hurt so often by the things you say and do? Do you think your partner should just learn how to laugh at himself instead of taking offense when you tease him?

9. Have you insisted that your partner drop all or most of her friends and outside activities?

10. Have you ever denied doing or saying something just to make your partner doubt her perceptions or her sanity?

11. Do you believe your partner should be willing to have sex with you whenever you are in the mood and that she should be willing to engage in any sexual activity you are interested in exploring?

12. Have you ever threatened to find someone who would have sex with you or who would engage in the sexual activities you want to engage in if your partner doesn't comply?

13. Do you experience frequent mood shifts, sometimes going from loving to rejecting in only a matter of a few minutes? Do you frequently become enraged? Are you often unaware of what causes your moods to change but assume it is something your partner did or didn't do?

14. Do you believe your partner should put other things aside in order to tend to your needs? Do you believe your partner should want to spend all her free time with you, and when she doesn't, do you accuse her of being unloving or failing as a partner?

15. Do you telephone your partner at work or at home wanting reassurance that he is still there and still loves you? If your partner isn't available to talk to you, do you become enraged?

16. Do you question your partner incessantly about her activities when you are apart? Do you want her to account for every minute

of her day? Do you assume she is hiding something if she can't account for what she was doing at any given time? Do you insist she carry a pager or cell phone so you can always get hold of her? Have you ever listened in on his phone conversations without his permission or made visits to his work or the place where he said he'd be just to make sure he is there?

17. Do you insist on being in control of the money in the relationship? Do you insist that your partner ask your permission before spending any money, or have you imposed a budget or an allowance on him? Do you require your partner to account for every penny he spends?

18. Do you expect your partner to always have the same opinions as you? To vote the same way? To like the same activities?

19. Have you ever threatened to hurt or destroy something of your partner's? Have you ever threatened to hurt your partner? Have you ever threatened to hurt your partner's children, family, or friends?

20. Have you ever thrown or broken objects while in a rage at your partner or in an attempt to scare her? Have you ever refused to let your partner leave a room or your home? Have you ever pushed or shoved your partner?

If you answered yes to even one of these questions, it means that you have been guilty of emotionally abusing your partner. This doesn't mean you are a horrible person or even that you should be referred to as an "abuser." We are all guilty of using emotionally abusive tactics on our partners from time to time. This certainly doesn't make it right, however, and you should make a concerted effort to stop this behavior now that you know it is abusive.

If you answered more than five questions with a yes, you have exhibited a pattern of emotional abuse, and this is far more serious. If you want to regain your self-respect and your partner's trust, you will need to become totally honest with yourself and to your partner about your behavior and your attitude toward him or her. Later on in the book, you'll discover the reasons why you have become abusive, and you'll discover other ways of dealing with stress and with the feelings of shame, guilt, envy, and anger that have caused you to be abusive.

Please note: Questions 1 to 5 reflect an emotionally abusive *attitude*. If you answered yes to half or more of these questions, you have an emotionally abusive attitude, and this in itself is experienced as emotional abuse. Even if you answered yes to only a few of the remaining questions, you still have reason to be concerned, because an emotionally abusive attitude often leads to emotionally abusive behavior.

No Monsters Here

Unlike many other books on the subject of abuse, this book is not going to characterize those who emotionally abuse their partners as horrible monsters. First of all, those who become emotionally abusive often do so unintentionally and unconsciously instead of deliberately and maliciously. Their unconscious motivations often come from the same source as partners who put up with emotionally abusive behavior—an abusive or neglectful childhood. This was the case with my client Don.

DON: LIKE MOTHER, LIKE SON

I didn't mean to emotionally abuse my wife. Hell, I didn't even know I was doing it for a long time. I was just treating my wife the way my mother treated me. When I was growing up, my mother smothered me emotionally. She said she loved me so much that she couldn't bear to have me out of her sight. When I got older and insisted on going out to play with the other kids, she acted wounded and told me I didn't love her—otherwise I wouldn't want to leave her all alone. My dad died when I was five, and from that time on, my mom always said I had to be the man of the house. That meant taking care of her needs.

When I decided to get married, I looked for a woman who was very different from my mother—someone who wouldn't try to smother me, someone who had her own life and didn't need me to be there for her all the time. Sherry was just that kind of woman. She was independent and had lots of friends and was involved in lots of activities. But shortly after we got married, I suddenly started feeling threatened by her friends, and I felt abandoned if she decided to do something with them instead of staying home with me. I complained to her that she didn't love me, that if she did she'd prefer to be with me.

As time went on, I became more and more possessive of her and accused her of having an affair. I even started following her when she went out. I began stalking my own wife! It wasn't until she insisted that we get counseling that I became aware that I was being abusive, and I was treating her the way my mother treated me.

Sometimes a person can be aware that he is being abusive and feel horrible about it and yet still be unable to stop. When this person gains some insights as to why he is being abusive, he is often able to begin making significant changes. This was the case with my client Alex.

ALEX: GETTING TO THE REAL REASON FOR HIS ANGER

Alex came to me because he realized his treatment of his wife was becoming more and more abusive, yet even though he tried, he just couldn't stop himself. "I don't like it that I'm so critical of Carol all the time. I hate what comes out of my mouth. I can't believe the things I've said to her—horrible things. I always feel so angry with her, and I don't always know why."

Alex often told himself he was angry with Carol because she couldn't seem to keep a job, and he had to support their family all by himself. He told himself it was because she didn't believe in birth control and so she kept having more and more kids. But while it was true that the financial pressure played a factor, it didn't really explain Alex's need to chastise and degrade Carol all the time. As it turned out, we were both to discover that it went back much further.

Alex's family was very poor when he was growing up. His father used to have to go out of town to find work, and he'd send money home to Alex's mother that was intended to last the entire month. But his mother was an extravagant woman who spent almost the entire amount in the first week on luxury items like chocolate, expensive meats, and alcohol for parties she'd give for her friends. By the end of the month they were always down to potatoes, and sometimes they didn't even have that and they'd go hungry for a few days. Alex had vowed he'd never let his kids go hungry.

During one of our sessions, Alex was talking about his mother when he turned to me and said, "Do you think that's why I feel so angry at my wife? Am I really angry at my mother?" That was, in fact, exactly what I was thinking. Alex and I began working on helping him to release his anger toward his mother.

It is actually quite common for people who were emotionally abused in previous relationships to become abusive themselves in their attempt to avoid being victims.

KAREN: TURNING THE TABLES

Karen was emotionally abused as a child and in her first two marriages. Her second husband became so abusive that Karen almost committed suicide. This brought her into therapy. For two years Karen and I worked on repairing the damage caused by her husbands' and her father's domination and constant criticism. She worked on releasing the repressed anger that she had turned on herself and on being more assertive. Karen left therapy when she became involved with another man, a man who was different from her usual pattern. "This guy is so great. He lets me decide what we are going to do instead of telling me. And he never puts me down. He thinks I'm wonderful just the way I am."

Even though I felt Karen had left therapy prematurely, things were indeed looking good for her. Two months later I received a wedding invitation in the mail. While it seemed a bit too soon, I hoped she was marrying a man who would be good to her.

I received a call from Karen only four months later. She was in tears. Her new husband was threatening to leave her, and she wanted to know if I could see them in couples therapy to help her understand what was going on.

Her new husband, Brett, explained that he loved Karen, but he simply couldn't tolerate the way she treated him. "She orders me around like I'm a child, and she insists on having her way. I'm a very easygoing guy, and I don't have to have things my way all the time, but I would like her to consider my needs sometimes. I know other men in her life treated her badly, but I'm not like those men. I treat her with respect, and I expect her to do the same. I just can't stand her belittling comments any longer."

Karen admitted that she often criticized Brett, but she didn't realize she had become emotionally abusive. "I guess I mistook Brett's tendency to be easygoing as weakness, and for some reason this made me feel like I could get away with treating him badly. My God, I've become my father and my ex-husbands."

Women and men like Karen often go from one extreme to the other—from victim to abuser—in their attempts to achieve some balance in their lives. While many become healthy enough to thwart their attraction to abusive partners, they often choose a person who is unassertive or passive in order to guarantee they will never be abused again. Unfortunately, their own abusiveness is then activated, as it was with Karen.

With a few months of couples therapy, Karen and Brett were able to turn their relationship around. Karen learned to balance her need to not be dominated with consideration for Brett's needs, and Brett learned that he could be assertive with Karen without becoming an abuser himself.

Instead of blaming and shaming those who have become abusive, I believe it is far more important to take responsibility for your behavior and for changing your behavior. This involves exploring your childhood for clues to your present behavior, releasing repressed and suppressed emotions toward what I call your "original abusers," and learning strategies for dealing with anger and stress in more constructive ways.

Ending Emotional Abuse

Sometimes stopping the abuse means walking away from an emotionally abusive relationship. Other times it means that the victim needs to gain enough strength and learn appropriate strategies so that she or he can become more assertive in the relationship. It almost always means that the abusive partner needs to discover and work on those core issues that cause the abusive behavior, and often it means working together as a couple to change the destructive patterns both have created.

Some of you reading this book will, for the first time, discover that you are being emotionally abused. This may lead you to come to the conclusion that you need to end your relationship, and you may, in fact, be emotionally prepared to do so. But many of you will not be prepared to leave the relationship now. It may be that you fear being alone, or you may be afraid you won't be able to make it on your own—you may feel you need to become more financially stable before you can leave. Reading the book in its entirety and completing all the exercises, especially those in the chapters dedicated to victims of emotional abuse, will help you emotionally prepare to leave.

Some of you may feel there is still a chance to turn things around in your relationship. By following the strategies offered in Part Two of the book, especially those about standing up to an abusive partner whenever he or she becomes abusive, I believe you have a good chance of salvaging your relationship. This is especially true if you and your partner are both willing to do your part in changing your negative patterns.

Sometimes it becomes clear that a couple should not stay together, either because they continue to bring out the worst in one another or because the abusive partner refuses to work on changing. When this is the case, partners need to know when it is time to end the relationship and how to do so without destroying each other. The information in Part Three will help with this process.

Each partner needs to understand why he or she is being abusive and/or why he or she is putting up with abuse from his or her partner. Part Two will explain in detail how we develop patterns of behavior based on our childhood experiences—the way our parents treated us and each other—and how we unconsciously repeat these patterns of behavior as a way of trying to resolve early childhood conflicts.

Once you understand the root of your behavior, the next step will be to learn guidelines for how you can go about completing the unfinished business that has created your patterns of unhealthy behavior. Those of you who emotionally abuse your partner need help in working through your feelings of pain, rage, shame, fear, and guilt concerning your own abuse or neglect so you do not continue to repeat the behavior with your partner. If you are being emotionally abused, you need help recognizing the fact that you do not deserve such treatment and understanding why you have tolerated the abuse in the first place.

CHAPTER 2

Patterns of Abuse

Sticks and stones may break our bones,
but words will break our hearts.

ROBERT FULGHUM

The specific types of emotional abuse that we briefly discussed in
chapter 1 are most often combined together to create certain patterns
of abuse. In this chapter we'll explore these patterns in depth and discover why they are the most prevalent types of emotional abuse
between intimate couples. As you read the descriptions, try to keep an
open mind about whether you are on the giving or the receiving end
of these types of abusive patterns.

Domination

To dominate is to attempt to control another person's actions. The person who tries to dominate another person has a tremendous need to
have his own way, and he often resorts to threats in order to get it.
Domineering behavior includes ordering a partner around; monitoring time and activities; restricting resources (finances, telephone); restricting social activities; isolating a partner from her family or
friends; interfering with opportunities (job, education, medical care);

excessive jealousy and possessiveness; throwing objects; threatening to harm a partner or a partner's children, family, friends, pets, or property; abusing a partner's children, parents, or pets in front of her; and forcing or coercing a partner into illegal activity.

ANDREA AND TIM: A NEED TO CONTROL

Andrea's husband, Tim, insisted on having control over all aspects of their lives. He insisted that Andrea turn over her entire check to him as soon as she was paid, and then gave her an allowance for the week to pay for lunches and other incidentals. If Andrea needed to buy something, such as some new shoes or a new dress for a special occasion, she had to ask Tim for the money. She always had to have a good reason why she needed the money, and depending on his mood, he would give it to her or not.

Tim also had to have control over their social life. He chose their friends and which movies and restaurants they would go to. Whenever Andrea tried to assert herself by suggesting a particular movie or restaurant, Tim would act as if she were the controlling one. "You know I hate those girly movies," he'd yell at her. "Why do you keep on insisting we go to them?" That didn't stop Tim from insisting on going to violent action movies, even though he knew Andrea hated them. When they were first married, Andrea tried insisting that she and Tim go to a new restaurant every so often. But once they were seated, Tim would begin to find fault with the lighting, the service, and the food to such an extent that it ruined her evening. Andrea soon learned that it just wasn't worth it to be assertive with Tim, that it was best to give him his own way.

Tim even dictated when Andrea could see her parents. He felt threatened by her close relationship with them and didn't want them "interfering" with their marriage, so he refused to let her see them very often or even talk on the phone with them. If her mother called, Tim would insist Andrea hang up after only a few minutes because he was expecting an important call from work, or he would make so much noise in the background that she couldn't hear what her mother was saying.

Verbal Assaults

Verbal assault includes berating, belittling, criticizing, humiliating, name-calling, screaming, threatening, excessive blaming, shaming, using sarcasm in a cutting way, or expressing disgust toward the person. This kind of abuse is extremely damaging to a person's self-esteem and self-image. Just as assuredly as physical violence assaults the body, verbal abuse assaults the mind and spirit, causing wounds that are extremely difficult to heal. Yelling and screaming is not only demeaning but frightening as well. When someone yells at us, we become afraid that he or she may also resort to physical violence. In her book *The Verbally Abusive Relationship,* Patricia Evans includes the following as forms of verbal abuse: withholding, countering, discounting, verbal abuse disguised as jokes, blocking and diverting, accusing, judging, trivializing, forgetting, ordering, denial, and abusive anger.

KITTY AND ROLAND: THE CASE OF THE POISON TONGUE

Roland was constantly exasperated with his wife, Kitty. "I just can't believe you could have been so stupid," was one of his typical phrases. Others included "Get your head out of your butt" and "What were you thinking?" The insinuation was always the same—that Kitty was incompetent.

These comments started shortly after Kitty and Roland were married. "I do make a lot of mistakes," Kitty explained to me. "I don't blame him for getting impatient with me." Kitty didn't seem to understand that Roland's comments were hurting her emotionally and that every time she made a mistake and was chastised by him, her self-esteem was being damaged. "I try to hide my mistakes from him because I know he's going to tell me how stupid I am when if he finds out," Kitty finally admitted. And she admitted something else as well. "When I'm around Roland, I seem to make more mistakes than usual. I guess it's because I'm so worried I'll goof up that I end up doing it."

Both Roland and Kitty seemed to feel that he had the right to chastise Kitty and call her names, even after I explained to both of them that Roland was actually verbally abusing Kitty. Roland quit therapy shortly afterward, but I continued to see Kitty. As time went by, Roland became more and more abusive, and Kitty began to feel more and more inadequate. Finally, one day Kitty broke down and started sobbing after Roland had said some particularly cruel things to her. This was the turning point for Kitty. She finally recognized she was being abused and how it was damaging her.

Constant Criticism/Continual Blaming

This form of emotional abuse can be included in the verbal abuse category, but I have chosen to make it a separate category because it often occurs on its own, without any other form of verbal abuse accompanying it, and because it can sometimes characterize an entire relationship.

When someone is unrelentingly critical of you, always finds fault, can never be pleased, and blames you for everything that goes wrong, it is the insidious nature and cumulative effects of the abuse that do the damage. Over time, this type of abuse eats away at your self-confidence and sense of self-worth, undermining any good feelings you have about yourself and about your accomplishments.

When a partner overtly criticizes or screams and yells, it is easy to come to the conclusion that one is being emotionally abused, but when your partner puts you down under the guise of humor, it can be extremely difficult to come to this realization. In Ted's case, it took a friend calling it to his attention before he realized his wife was emotionally and verbally abusing him.

TED: THE CASE OF THE STICK-IN-THE-MUD

Ted's wife, Judy, was a fun-loving woman who laughed and joked a lot, loved to socialize, and was always the life of the party. Ted was a rather quiet man, and he found Judy's ease with people refreshing and stimulating. He often told her he wished he could be more like her. So when Judy began to tease him about being an old "stick-in-the-mud" right after they got married, Ted just laughed right along with her. But this was only the beginning. Judy began to make jokes about Ted in front of others: "Please excuse Ted. He forgot to wake up this morning." Ted took this as a gentle reminder that he needed to participate more in conversations, and he forced himself to talk about himself and his interests when they had company. But whenever he did this, Judy would feign a yawn or roll her eyes, signaling to him that he was being boring. Ted would take the hint and go back into his shell. He decided he was better off being a listener and letting Judy be the socializer.

But Judy didn't stop there. She started in on the way he dressed, the way he carried himself, and his general demeanor. She called him "the professor"—teasing him about how conservative and low-key his dress and style were. "Don't you have even one tie with some color to it?" or "How long have you had that suit?" she'd complain when they were going out. "Stand up straight," she'd order. "You look like a tired old man." Most of the time Ted just tried to laugh off Judy's comments, even though he was sometimes deeply hurt by them. Often he took her seriously and, believing that Judy was just looking out for him, he actually made some changes, such as improving his posture and buying some new, more stylish clothes. If anyone would have told Ted that he was being emotionally abused, he would have told them they were crazy. After all, Judy was just trying to help him out.

It wasn't until his hometown best friend, Lawrence, came to visit him that Ted began to recognize he was being emotionally abused. "Lawrence was shocked at how Judy talked to me," Ted told me during our first session. "And he was surprised to see me just taking it instead of standing up for myself. He told me I'd gone from a self-assured, congenial kind of guy to an insecure, withdrawn man he barely recognized. He asked me why I let her talk to me that way. When I tried to explain it was just her sense of humor he said, 'Bullshit, she's putting you down all the time.' I finally had to admit he was right."

Abusive Expectations

When you have abusive expectations, you place unreasonable demands on your partner. For example, expecting a partner to put aside everything in order to satisfy your needs, demanding a partner's undivided attention, demanding constant sex, or requiring a partner to spend all of his or her time with you are all examples of abusive expectations. A partner with abusive expectations can never be pleased because there is always something more you could have done. You are likely to be subjected to constant criticism and to be berated because you don't fulfill his or her needs.

TESSA: WHATEVER FRANK WANTED

Tessa's boyfriend, Frank, was guilty of having abusive expectations of her. This is how she described their relationship during our interview: "From the very beginning of our relationship, it seemed to always be about what Frank wanted. He didn't like me to wear short skirts or too much makeup because he said it made me look like a tramp, and he wanted to be proud of me. So I wore longer dresses or pants and lightened up on the makeup. He didn't like me going out with the girls for a drink after work because he was afraid I'd pick up some guy, so I stopped. He still went out with the guys, mind you, but he said that was different. He said men had to have their freedom, otherwise they'll feel henpecked, and it will destroy the relationship. He wanted me to go straight home after work and wait there until he was finished doing whatever he was doing, and then he'd come over. And of course, he wanted to have sex when he got there. It didn't matter how I was feeling, whether I was in the mood or not—I was supposed to be ready, willing, and able whenever he was in the mood. I guess the worst part of it was that he refused to use a condom. He said he couldn't feel as much. I told him I was afraid of AIDS, but he assured me that we wouldn't get it—that only homosexuals or whores got it. I knew he wasn't right about that, but he refused to wear one so what was I to do? I don't know why I stayed with him so long. I knew he was being unreasonable about a lot of things. I didn't realize that was a form of emotional abuse."

Emotional Blackmail

Emotional blackmail is one of the most powerful forms of manipulation. It occurs when one partner either consciously or unconsciously coerces the other into doing what he wants by playing on his partner's fear, guilt, or compassion. Examples of emotional blackmail include one partner threatening to end a relationship if he doesn't get what he wants and one partner rejecting or distancing herself from her partner until he gives in to her demands. If your partner withholds sex or affection or gives you the silent treatment or the cold shoulder whenever he is displeased with you, threatens to find someone else, or uses other fear tactics to get you under control, he is using the tactic of emotional blackmail.

Threats of emotional blackmail don't have to be overt. In fact, they are often quite subtle. For example, a woman may jokingly suggest that her boyfriend better start paying more attention to her sexually if he wants to keep her. In order to get his wife to do as he wishes, a man may subtly threaten her by saying that it will be difficult to find a new partner who is willing to get involved with a woman who already has two children. Or in order to control his partner, a gay man may remind him of how dangerous it is out there in the world, with AIDS and all.

WILLIAM: THE CASE OF THE BUDDING WRITER

Those who use the tactic of emotional blackmail also utilize guilt in order to get their way or keep their partner in line. For example, my client William wanted very badly to become an author. It was a dream of his since he was a child. But he and his wife had gotten married right out of high school, and they started having kids right away, so he had to go to work to support the family. But at age forty, William had saved enough money and vacation time to be able to take off an entire summer to attend a writer's summer residential workshop back east. I remember vividly the day he bounded into my office with the news that he'd been accepted into the program:

"Do you know how many applications they get every year for their program? Do you realize what an honor this is for me? What a dream come true?" He could hardly contain his excitement as he showed me his acceptance letter. I had never seen him as happy.

But William's happiness was short-lived. By the time I saw him at our next session one week later, William's bubble had burst. "What happened?" I asked, sensing immediately that something was wrong.

"I'm not going to go to the writer's program this summer," he said.

"Why not? What made you change your mind?" I asked.

"Sandy doesn't want me to go. She says that if I can take an entire summer off from work, I should volunteer to watch the kids while she goes on a vacation. She says why should I be the one to be able to get away when she works just as hard as I do as a homemaker? She said I'm being selfish, and I guess she's right."

"You feel it is selfish to want to fulfill a dream you've had most of your life?" I asked.

"Yes, if it means making Sandy unhappy. After all, as she likes to remind me, she was a beautiful woman and could have married a man who made a lot more money than I do. I haven't been able to give her all the things she's wanted. Besides, she'll make my life hell if I go. It's just not worth it."

And so, William turned down the opportunity to go to the writer's workshop and put aside his dreams of becoming a writer. As it turned out, his sense of obligation to his wife was stronger than his willingness to stand up for himself and his needs. As Susan Forward wrote in her book *Emotional Blackmail:* fear, obligation, and guilt are the traits most likely to make us vulnerable to emotional blackmail because they obscure our choices and limit our options to those the blackmailer picks for us.

The following are warning signs that you are being emotionally blackmailed:

- Your partner asks you to choose between something you want to do and him.

- Your partner tries to make you feel like you are selfish or a bad person if you do something she doesn't want you to do.

- Your partner asks you to give up something or someone as a way of proving your love for her.

- Your partner threatens to leave you if you don't change.

- Your partner threatens to withhold money or access to money unless you do something he has requested.

Unpredictable Responses

This type of emotional abuse includes drastic mood swings, sudden emotional outbursts for no apparent reason, and inconsistent responses such as: reacting very differently at various times to the same behavior, saying one thing one day and the opposite the next, or frequently changing one's mind (liking something one day but hating it the next). The reason this behavior is damaging is that it causes others, especially a partner, to feel constantly on edge. You are always waiting for the other shoe to drop, and you never feel you know what is expected of you. Living with someone who is like this is extremely demanding and anxiety provoking—you feel constantly frightened, unsettled, and off balance, and that you must remain hypervigilant, waiting for your partner's next outburst or change of mood.

This kind of behavior is common with alcohol and drug abusers who can exhibit one personality when sober and a totally different one when intoxicated or high. It can also be an indication of mental illnesses, such as bipolar disorder, or certain personality disorders such as Borderline Personality Disorder, which cause a person to have drastic shifts in mood, to have emotional outbursts (sudden anger, overwhelming fear, or anxiety attacks), or to react unpredictably. Finally, it can be characteristic of those who suffer from post-traumatic stress disorder or dissociative disorder, as in the following example.

JENNY: THE TWO SIDES OF LUCAS

Jenny never knew what to expect from her boyfriend, Lucas. At times he could be the sweetest man she'd ever known, bringing her flowers, taking her to romantic restaurants, even writing her poetry. This could go on for months at a time—and then suddenly, one day, for no apparent reason, his mood would shift, and Lucas would seem like a different person entirely. He became extremely quiet and withdrawn and would sometimes even snap at her to get away from him whenever she tried to touch him. If she asked him what was wrong he would tell her "nothing" or that he needed some space. This could sometimes go on for days or even weeks at a time with their barely speaking to each other. Then, once again without notice, Lucas would wake up one day and be his old charming, sweet self. When Jenny tried to find out what had happened, he'd give her a peculiar look and ask, "What do you mean?" as if the last few days or weeks hadn't even occurred.

Constant Chaos/Creating Crisis

Although similar to unpredictable responses in that this type of abuse will cause you to feel constantly unsettled and off balance, it is specifically characterized by continual upheavals and discord. If your partner deliberately starts arguments with you or others or seems to be in constant conflict with others, he or she may be "addicted to drama." Creating chaos provides excitement for some people, especially those who are uneasy with silence, those who distract themselves from their own problems by focusing outward, those who feel empty inside and need to fill themselves up with activity, and those who were raised in an environment in which harmony and peace were unknown quantities. Constant chaos is also characteristic of Borderline Personality Disorder, which we discuss in chapters 8 and 9.

J. C.: Never a Dull Moment

As my client J. C. explained to me, life was never calm around his wife, Wendy. "She's always starting trouble. I don't think I can remember one day since I've known her when she wasn't fighting with someone. If she's not angry with someone at work, she's arguing with one of her sisters or her mother. And I never know what to expect when I come home. There might be a house full of people drinking and carrying on, or she might have gone off somewhere without leaving me a note."

While J. C. was initially attracted to Wendy's drama, it was beginning to take a toll on him. "I don't sleep well at night and I'm always nervous. I've lost my appetite and I keep losing weight. And I know all this drama and chaos isn't good for the kids."

Character Assassination

This involves constantly blowing someone's mistakes out of proportion, humiliating, criticizing, or making fun of someone in front of others, or discounting another person's achievements. It can also include lying about someone in order to negatively affect others' opinion of them and gossiping about a person's failures and mistakes with others. In addition to the pain this behavior can cause an individual on a personal level, character assassination can ruin someone's personal and professional reputation, causing them to lose friends, jobs, or even their family.

SUSAN AND LESLIE: THE CASE OF THE NOT-SO-FUNNY COMMENTS

Susan constantly made fun of Leslie in front of their friends. It all seemed to be innocent enough at first, but after a while Leslie began to question whether Susan's comments were a sign of hostility. "She makes fun of how feminine I am—how I like to cook and decorate the house—that kind of stuff. She calls me her little *hausfrau*. She and most of her friends are real jocks, but I'm not really into sports, and she makes fun of me about that, too. There's always an air of superiority in her comments and that hurts. I've told her about it, but she just tells me not to be so sensitive—the implication being that this in itself is a sign that I'm too 'girlie.' Sometimes when her friends are around, she seems to really get off on making fun of how I dress, especially when she's drinking. I know her friends don't take me seriously because of the way she treats me. I'm sure they've lost any respect they may have once had for me."

Gaslighting

This term comes from the classic movie *Gaslight,* in which a husband uses a variety of insidious techniques to make his wife doubt her perceptions, her memory, and her very sanity. A partner who does this may continually deny that certain events occurred or that he or she said something you both know was said, or he or she may insinuate that you are exaggerating or lying. In this way, the abusive person may be trying to gain control over you or to avoid taking responsibility for his or her actions. This is one of the forms of emotional abuse that is done very consciously and deliberately. It is sometimes used by those who need to discredit their partner in order to get access to his or her money, in order to turn others against him or her, or as a way to justify their own inappropriate, cruel, or abusive behavior. In the movie, the husband needed to make his wife and others think she was insane in order to get access to her money.

VERONICA: JUST "IMAGINING" THINGS

"Sometimes I think I'm crazy," my new client Veronica shared with me. "My husband tells me he loves me, and I really have no reason to doubt him, and yet it often seems to me that he deliberately tries to make me doubt myself. I'll see him flirting with a woman at a party, but when I confront him with it he swears it isn't true. He says I'm just imagining things because I'm so insecure, and he'll remind me that he's a friendly guy to everyone. I start telling myself that it is true, I am insecure, and that he is a friendly person, and pretty soon I start to think I must have imagined the whole thing after all. Is this common? Do people really imagine they are seeing things when it isn't really happening?"

Although in rare cases people do imagine seeing things that aren't happening, in Veronica's case it turned out that her husband had been having numerous affairs during their marriage and that he used gaslighting techniques to keep Veronica off balance and confused.

Sexual Harassment

Normally the term *sexual harassment* is used when referring to sexual coercion in the workplace, but a person can be sexually harassed by anyone, including her partner. Sexual harassment is defined as unwelcome sexual advances or any physical or verbal conduct of a sexual nature that is uninvited and unwelcome. In order to be legally considered sexual harassment, the conduct must be tied to an employment decision, such as hiring or promotion, or it must interfere with work performance or create a hostile environment. But whenever a person is pressured into becoming sexual against her will, whether it is because she does not feel like being sexual at the time or does not choose that person as a sexual partner, it is the form of emotional abuse called sexual harassment. It is also considered sexual harassment to try to force a partner into engaging in sexual acts that she has no interest in or that upset or repulse her. Oftentimes, other forms of emotional abuse go hand in hand with sexual harassment, such as unreasonable expectations, constant criticism, name-calling, and emotional blackmail.

RACHEL: THE CASE OF THE COLD FISH

Rachel's husband, Steven, pressured her constantly to have sex. He not only wanted to have sex every night and every morning, but he would often wake up in the middle of the night with an erection and wake her up insisting she "take care of it." Not only were his sexual demands a form of unreasonable expectations, but even when Rachel complied, he never seemed to be happy. "He'd complain that I wasn't into it enough or that I didn't move the right way. It really was impossible to please him," Rachel shared with me during one of our sessions.

If she refused to have sex with him, Rachel would be bombarded with insults such as "You're a cold fish." This verbal abuse certainly didn't warm Rachel up any. "I don't know how he expected me to want to have sex with him after he'd insult me like that. I have to confess that there have been many times I've just agreed to have sex because it was less painful than being pressured or insulted."

Steven also pressured Rachel to engage in kinky sex acts, many of which repulsed her. When she refused, he'd threaten to find someone who would agree to do the things he wanted to do. This emotional blackmail almost always worked, since Rachel was afraid of losing him. "I know it sounds ridiculous, but as much as I hate all the sexual pressure, I'd hate it even more if he actually went through with it and had sex with someone else. I'd feel like such a failure, like I couldn't even satisfy my own husband. And I guess there's a part of me that believes him when he says I'm cold, because I'm afraid if he went out there and had sex with another woman, he'd find out what he was missing and he'd leave me." As you can see, Rachel has taken on her husband's accusations and insults, and they have affected the way she perceives herself—typical of emotional abuse victims.

Clear and Consistent Patterns

As you read through the above descriptions, you no doubt recognize behavior that you or your partner have been guilty of. Does this mean that your partner is an emotional abuser? Does it mean you are? Does it mean you are in an emotionally abusive relationship?

Yes and no. We have all been guilty of committing some of these behaviors, and we all experience them from our partner on occasion, even though he or she is not generally abusive in any other way. When a relationship is not going well, there is often a great deal of arguing and bickering, and either or both partners may resort to name-calling, criticizing, and other behaviors that they normally would not engage in. The same thing occurs when one or both partners are under a great deal of stress, especially if they are unable to communicate frustrations with their partner in order to receive support and understanding. But there is a vast difference between name-calling or criticizing in the heat of an argument and doing so on a day-to-day basis.

Similarly, even constant complaining is not necessarily emotionally abusive unless it is destructive and the intent is to make one's partner feel bad about herself or himself. For example, a wife who occasionally complains that her husband does not make enough money isn't necessarily being emotionally abusive. But if she constantly tells him he is stupid, lazy, and a failure because he does not make enough money, she is being abusive.

Criticism is not considered emotionally abusive unless:

- It is constant, as opposed to occasional.

- The intent is to devalue or denigrate rather than to simply state a complaint.

- The intent is to dominate and control rather than to provide constructive criticism.

- The person has an *overall* attitude of disrespect toward you, rather than just not liking something specific that you are doing.

For example, if, in addition to complaining, the wife in the above example also gives her husband the cold shoulder whenever he brings his check home, makes disparaging remarks about his low pay to others in front of him, or threatens to leave him if he doesn't find a job that pays more, she is definitely being emotionally abusive. *It is the clear and consistent pattern* of her remarks and actions—her ongoing efforts to demean and control her husband—that makes this wife's behavior emotionally abusive.

Overt and Covert Abuse

A pattern of emotional abuse occurs on both an overt and a covert level. *Overt* abuse is openly demeaning. When the wife in the above example openly complains to other family members and friends that her husband doesn't make enough money and that he's just too weak to ask for a raise, she is being *overtly* abusive.

Covert emotional abuse is subtler than overt abuse, but no less devastating. When the wife gives her husband contemptuous looks when he tells her they can't afford something, when she offhandedly suggests that maybe some other man might buy it for her, she is being covertly abusive.

Intentional and Unintentional Abuse

Many experts would add that another way of deciding if a behavior is emotionally abusive is whether or not it is intentional. In fact, when most clinicians refer to emotional abuse, they usually mean *intentional* abuse. While some partners deliberately use words, gestures, silence, or scare tactics to manipulate or control their partner, many do so without conscious intent. This is particularly true when one or both partners are repeating his or her parents' behavior. For the purpose of clarity, I wish to broaden the definition of emotional abuse even further to include *any behavior or attitude that emotionally damages another person, regardless of whether there is conscious intent to do so.*

Many abusers are totally unaware that their attitude and/or behavior is abusive. This doesn't, however, make their behavior any less destructive or damaging to their partner or the relationship.

Even those who are aware they are being abusive often do so in a desperate attempt to gain a feeling of control in their lives. Add to this the fact that we can all become emotionally abusive given the right circumstances, and we can see that emotional abusers are not necessarily horrible people at all. Most people who emotionally abuse others were themselves emotionally abused and are merely reenacting what was done to them. However, this doesn't make their actions, attitudes, or words hurt any less nor does it make them any less damaging.

Certainly, some people deliberately and maliciously set out to destroy their partner. But most people who emotionally abuse their partner do so either unconsciously or as a way of surviving the stress of an emotional relationship. When our first experiences of intimacy were fraught with fear, abandonment, humiliation, or smothering, we can't help but repeat these behaviors when we become adults and enter into intimate relationships. Most people initially felt love feelings for their partner, otherwise they wouldn't have chosen to be with him or her. But those love feelings can be destroyed by feelings of anger when our hopes are dashed, when our partner fails to meet our expectations, or when we come to feel rejected, betrayed, or abandoned by our partner.

To complicate things, sometimes we become emotionally abusive because we love our partners so much or because we are insecure. This is particularly true of those who "love too much" and those who tend to lose themselves in their relationships. Sometimes our love becomes distorted by our feelings of insecurity and our fear of abandonment. This is the often the case with those who become overly controlling and overly smothering of their partner. Others become emotionally abusive because of their fear of intimacy.

Even intentional emotional abuse is not always malicious. In the heat of passion we are all guilty of wanting to hurt our partner. If our partner has hurt us, we want him or her to hurt, too. We may deliberately say something hurtful even though we know the effect it will have. We may threaten to leave, knowing it will cause our partner to become insecure. Or we may give our partner the silent treatment or withhold affection or sex in the hope that he or she will suffer from our rejection. Although these are all forms of *intentional emotional abuse,* even the most loving person is guilty of these actions from time to time.

Again, it does not become emotional abuse unless there is a clear and consistent pattern.

Malevolent Abuse

There is another form of intentional abuse that is more insidious and far more damaging. I call this malevolent (lethal) abuse. Malevolent abuse is abuse that is not only intentional but deliberately undermining. It is when one partner is bent on undermining or even destroying the other, when one partner is so angry or envious or so full of hate that he deliberately and maliciously sets out to sabotage a partner's success, health, or happiness.

EXERCISE: *Are You Guilty of Malevolent Abuse?*

Although it will be terribly painful to admit, ask yourself the following questions and answer as honestly as you possibly can. Remember, unless you are totally honest with yourself, you cannot save yourself or your relationship.

1. Do you often secretly hope that bad things will happen to your partner? For example, do you hope she will fail at an endeavor, lose a competition, or be rejected when she attempts to join a club?

2. Do you get a deep sense of satisfaction when bad things happen to your partner?

3. Do you sometimes cause bad things to happen to your partner? For example, do you sabotage your partner's friendships by telling people he drinks too much and becomes abusive to you when it is not true?

4. Do you deliberately undermine or sabotage your partner's efforts to gain success? For example, do you hide your wife's keys so she'll be late for an important meeting?

5. Do you deliberately cause your partner to doubt himself or to question his perceptions?

If you answered yes to even one of these questions, you need to take responsibility for your actions by committing to therapy in order to discover why you are so angry with or envious of your partner. When you truly love someone in a pure, uncontaminated way, you desire for that person to be happy and successful. You aren't constantly consumed with envy or a desire to get back at him or her for some real or imagined infraction.

If you answered yes to more than two of these questions, you need to seriously question whether you should be with this person. There may be more hate than love in the relationship, or you may have serious issues from the past that are interfering with your ability to be intimate with anyone. By the same token, if you suspect or know that your partner has at times deliberately tried to undermine or sabotage your success, your friendships, or your happiness, you need to seriously consider whether you should stay with such a person.

While we are all guilty of an *occasional* fantasy of harm coming to our partner or an *occasional* act of sabotage, if there is a pattern of such fantasies or behavior, either on your part or on the part of your partner, you need to seek individual or couples therapy to discover the roots of your anger and negativity toward each other or you need to free yourself or your partner from the clutches of such powerful destructive energy.

RECOMMENDED FILMS

What's Love Got to Do With It? (control and domination)

Gaslight (gaslighting)

CHAPTER 3

Not All Emotionally Abusive
Relationships Are Alike

No one worth possessing can be quite possessed.
SARA TEASDALE

Sometimes individuals or couples become confused about whether or
not they are in an emotionally abusive relationship because their particular relationship doesn't resemble those described by other books
or by other experts on emotional abuse. But there isn't just one type
of emotionally abusive relationship—there are many. I have discovered seven primary types:

1. One partner abuses and the other doesn't.

2. One partner began abusing the other, and the other partner chose to
   retaliate.

3. From the beginning of the relationship, both partners have emotionally abused each other on an ongoing basis.

4. It is not clear who is abusing whom.

5. One partner sets up the other to become emotionally abusive.

6. One partner is abusive due to a mental illness or personality disorder.

7. One or both partners has an abusive personality.

The Seven Types
of Emotionally Abusive Relationships

Type One: One Partner Abuses and the Other Doesn't

Even though I often refer to situations in which some couples become mutually abusive, I certainly don't mean to imply that one-sided abuse does not occur. There are clearly situations in which only one partner actively abuses the other. In fact, when most people think of emotional abuse, this is the type they are thinking of. Although abusers frequently blame their partner for their own problems, often it is the case that their partner has not contributed to the abusive situation in any way.

Typically, the only way a partner has contributed to the abuse is by being too complacent or too understanding. This was the case with Paul and Gloria, the sister of a friend of mine. Gloria is an extremely controlling woman who needs to always have things her way. She orders her husband, Paul, around like a child. On one occasion when she, Paul, my friend Rona, and her husband, Al, were getting in Paul's car to leave after a visit in my home, Gloria insisted that Paul move his seat forward to make room for Al's legs. Paul did so, but it wasn't enough to please Gloria. "Give Al more room," she insisted, "pull your seat up further." Paul complied, even though his legs were practically wrapped around the steering wheel. Once again, Gloria looked in the backseat to see if Al had enough room. It looked to me as if he had more than enough room since there was a space between his legs and the backseat. But Gloria wasn't satisfied. "I told you to move your seat forward," she yelled at Paul, hitting him on the head with the flat of her hand.

This is how Gloria regularly treats Paul. She orders him around mercilessly, and nothing he does is ever right. Her most frequent comments to him are "What's wrong with you?" and "I can't believe you can be that stupid." Paul seems to go out of his way to please her and never seems to get angry at her mistreatment of him. When someone asks Paul a question, Gloria often corrects his answer. "That's not the way it was," she'll snap. "Can't you get anything right?"

Paul never argues with her, never contradicts her. He just smiles sheepishly at whoever is within hearing distance. Often, before he says something, he'll look at Gloria first, as if he is looking for some kind of a sign from her whether or not it is okay to speak. And sometimes I've even seen him start to move in a certain direction and then stop and look around, as if he can't decide which way to go. It is really sad.

Paul is a courteous, caring man, and I see nothing in his behavior to warrant Gloria's treatment of him. While it is true that I don't know what happens behind closed doors in their relationship, it appears as if Paul just puts up with Gloria's behavior, no matter how abusive she becomes. As far as I can see, this is clearly an example of one person emotionally abusing another with little or no provocation.

In situations where only one partner is abusive, the abused partner may be unaware that he is being abused, or he may have tried to get the abusive partner to stop—to no avail. He may put up with the abuse because he is afraid to leave the relationship, because he feels he deserves the abuse, or because he feels he loves his partner too much to leave her. This type of abuse is most often characterized by the following:

- One partner has learned to overlook the unkindness and disrespect of the other.

- One partner is made to feel she is always wrong.

- One partner is made to question his perceptions, opinions, and reactions and to feel that his feelings are wrong.

- One partner blames herself whenever there is a problem in the relationship.

- One partner blames himself for his partner's unhappiness.

- The abusive partner continually denies any responsibility for problems.

- The abusive partner often denies that incidents even occurred.

- The abusive partner controls the interpersonal communication.

Type Two: One Partner Began Abusing the Other, and the Abused Partner Chose to Retaliate

In this situation, one partner may have started the abuse, but the other partner became equally abusive, either as a way of getting back at her partner for his hurtful words or behavior or as a way of defending herself. A partner may put up with abusive treatment for years before retaliating, or she may retaliate as soon as the abuse begins.

I have often heard clients say that they started out adoring their partner, going out of their way to please him and show him love—only to be rewarded with coldness, rejection, dismissive looks, and belittling. After a while, these people become so hurt and feel so taken for granted that they become cold or insulting in return.

In other situations, emotional abuse can occur slowly and in the form of blatant disrespect and character assassination and is returned in kind. This is what occurred between Rebecca and Ken. As Rebecca explained it to me:

> It seemed to happen gradually. It started with Ken making snide comments about how much money I spent on groceries and about not liking my cooking. He'd say things like, "For all the money you spend on food, you'd think we could get a decent meal around here." He even said things like that when we had guests. I tried to ignore him, even though his comments really hurt me.
>
> Then he started treating me like his housekeeper or slave in front of other people. When we had company over, he'd order me around, telling me to get something instead of asking for it. He even started snapping his fingers at me to get my attention. I think that's rude when people do it to waitresses, much less to your wife.
>
> I tried telling him about it, but he just brushed me off, saying I was just too sensitive. Finally, I got tired of trying to explain it to him and started giving him some of his own medicine. When he'd complain about my cooking in front of others, I'd say something like, "Well, it sure doesn't stop you from eating, now does it, Ken? You're getting quite a gut there." He'd laugh along with everyone else, but I knew I'd gotten to him.

It just went on from there. He'd put me down, and I'd find a way to get back at him. It got so we lost almost all respect for each other. There was practically nothing we wouldn't say to each other. I've built up a wall so his words don't even hurt me that much anymore, but in the process I've lost any tender feelings for him. I'm completely turned off to him sexually, and I don't know when the last time was we hugged each other or said something nice to each other. We're more enemies than lovers.

Type Three: From the Beginning of the Relationship, Both Partners Have Emotionally Abused Each Other on an Ongoing Basis

In this type of relationship, both partners have been emotionally abusing each other for quite some time—usually from the very beginning of the relationship. Frequently, the abuse has always been mutual, and the level of abuse is quite equal. This was the case with Roxie and Sam, whom I interviewed for the book:

Sam and I started emotionally abusing each other almost from the beginning. We're both pretty insecure, and I think we do it because we both get hurt so easily. We fell in love right away, and our relationship started out being very intense and passionate. We both got swept off our feet. Our lives totally changed when we got together. We both dropped all our friends and had to be together all the time. But I think it made us too dependent on each other and too vulnerable.

Who knows how it started? I'd say something that hurt his feelings and he'd say something back to hurt mine. He'd brush me off one morning when I tried to make love and so I'd reject him the next time he tried. He'd say he wanted to go see his old friends, and I'd get hurt and go out with my girlfriends and get drunk and come home late just to get back at him. It just goes on and on, and now we don't know how to stop it. We love each other so much but we've hurt each other so much—I'm afraid we're going to either destroy our love or destroy each other if we don't find a way to stop.

In the classic movie *Who's Afraid of Virginia Woolf?*, starring Elizabeth Taylor and Richard Burton, we see this type of relationship played out masterfully. In the very beginning of the movie, we get the impression that Martha, played by Taylor, is a brash, loud, and obnoxious woman who constantly verbally abuses and dominates her husband, George, played by Burton. "What a dump," she complains as they enter their home after a party. "Don't you know anything?" she chastises when George can't remember the name of the movie that Bette Davis used that line in. "Dumbbell," she calls him, and "You never do anything," she taunts him later on.

You can't help feeling sorry for this poor man. Why does he put up with this kind of treatment? we ask ourselves. The more George puts up with Martha's insults and taunting, the more she does it. When George gives her one of his long-suffering looks, Martha chides, "Poor Georgie—put-upon pie." Later on she says, "You make me puke. You're such a simp."

But it isn't long before we see George's true colors. He manages to slide his own insults into the conversation in a very passive-aggressive way. He casually makes a comment about how Martha "brays" at everyone and slips in a quiet comment about her "big teeth." When she asks him to pour her a drink, he cautions her about drinking too much, and then—seemingly on a roll—he becomes bolder and says, "There isn't a more sickening sight in the world than you with too many drinks and your skirt up over your head—your heads, I should say." When she takes a gulp of the drink he says, "My God, you can swill it down." A little later, he says, "There isn't an abhorrent award around that you haven't won."

Before long you realize that these two are very well matched in a sad sort of way. They are certainly equal in the amount of abuse they lavish on each other. We don't know who started it—but we can see that it will be a fight to the death to see who ends it.

While their relationship may seem like a caricature, the truth is that it accurately depicts the sort of emotional dueling that occurs between some couples. It is also not that uncommon for partners to take turns at being emotionally abusive to one another. As one client shared with me, "We went back and forth. Sometimes I was unkind to him and said horrible things, and other times he was unkind to me. It just depended on what was going on in the relationship—who felt the most secure or insecure."

The following questionnaire will help you determine whether you are in this type of emotionally abusive relationship.

QUESTIONNAIRE: *Mutual Abuse*

1. Do you and your partner frequently put each other down with cutting comments, sarcasm, and criticism?

2. Do you bring up each other's past failures and mistakes as a way of putting the other in his or her place?

3. Do you blame each other for your own problems in life?

4. Do you each blame the other for the problems in the relationship?

5. Do you deliberately try to make each other jealous by flirting or talking about how attractive or sexy someone is?

6. Do you frequently complain about each other's behavior?

7. Do you punish each other with the silent treatment?

8. Do you punish each other by withholding affection or sex?

9. Are you constantly competing with each other to see who is the smarter, the more accomplished, the more popular, or the more attractive?

10. Do you use each other's weaknesses and insecurities against one another?

11. Do you attempt to alienate each other from friends and family out of your own sense of insecurity?

Type Four: It Is Not Clear Who Is Abusing Whom

In intimate relationships it isn't always clear who is emotionally abusing whom. Some abusive partners are masters at deflecting blame and turning things around. Some deliberately use the gaslighting technique I described earlier to cause their partner to doubt their perceptions or to begin to think they are insane. And often, one partner is so focused on what she perceives as emotionally abusive treatment from her partner that she is oblivious to the harm she is causing with her own behavior. This is especially true of some who suffer from Borderline Personality Disorder (see chapter 8) since they often perceive themselves as helpless victims—even when their own behavior may have affected or created a situation.

The following case is a good example. When I first began to see Christine and Kyle, it wasn't initially clear who was abusing whom.

During our first session, Christine insisted that her husband Kyle was emotionally abusive. "He is so dismissive and adversarial. He usually thinks my ideas and opinions are silly, and he argues with me about even the smallest things. He constantly disapproves of the way I raise our daughter, and I don't really think he trusts me to be a good mother."

From listening to Christine's perspective on their marital problems, it would seem that she was probably right about Kyle being emotionally abusive. That was before I heard Kyle's side of the story.

"I guess you could call me adversarial if you mean I don't agree with everything Christine says and does. She hates it if I have a different opinion about something. She says I'm not being supportive. For example, she'll complain to me about something a friend did, and I know she just wants me to listen and say something supportive like 'That's terrible that she did that to you.' But I know Christine. I know how critical and judgmental she is of everyone. And I know she can make people really angry. So instead I'll say something like 'I'm sure she was just angry with you. She's been a good friend. I'm sure you two will work it out.' This will make her furious with me, and she'll start yelling at me about how I never take her side—how I'm more like her enemy than her partner. She complains about me so much that I'm beginning to think we shouldn't be together. I've left a few times, but she always calls me at work and begs me to come home. When I hesitate, she threatens to kill herself if I don't."

It was becoming apparent that there was more to the story than Kyle being dismissive and adversarial. This was made abundantly clear the next time I saw them. Christine started explaining to me more about their relationship. Kyle sat quietly and allowed her to finish, but then said that he saw things a bit differently. Christine became very angry with Kyle and said, to me, "You see what I mean? He disagrees with everything I say." When I suggested to Christine that Kyle had a right to disagree with her, she got upset and started yelling about how I had no idea what life was really like with Kyle. She stood up and started pacing the floor, saying things like "Kyle has ruined my life" and calling him a fucking asshole. She turned to Kyle and told him he was such a poor excuse for a man that no other woman would want him.

Kyle seemed to crumble before me. He didn't argue with her or fight back in any way but instead looked down and lowered his head. It was clear that Christine regularly emotionally abused him in this way.

As time went by it became apparent that it was Christine who was being emotionally abusive, not Kyle. In fact, it turned out that due to his emotionally abusive childhood and his subsequent low self-esteem, Kyle put up with behavior from Christine that no one should put up with. Not only did he allow her to degrade him verbally by calling him horrible names and saying terribly demeaning things about him, but he bent over backwards to please Christine, even though she constantly found fault with everything he did. Because he doubted his perceptions, Kyle bought into Christine's constant blaming him for their problems.

As it was with Christine, it is quite common for those with a history of emotional abuse to feel they are being victimized, even when they are the ones who are being abusive. This is true for several reasons. First, many who were emotionally abused in childhood (especially those who were physically or emotionally rejected or abandoned by one or both parents) are extremely sensitive to any perceived rejection or abandonment from others. In Christine's case, whenever someone disagreed with her, she experienced it as rejection. And even though she was extremely critical and judgmental of others, if someone disagreed with her, she interpreted this as criticism.

Second, those who were emotionally abused in childhood or in a previous relationship—especially those who were overly controlled or emotionally smothered—are often extremely sensitive to anything that seems remotely like control, even when they themselves are controlling. To these people, even commitment can feel like emotional suffocation. Therefore, if they constantly create chaos in the relationship, it gives them a sense of freedom from the stifling confinement of intimacy.

Third, one of the most common effects of a history of abuse is hypersensitivity. Those with an abusive past often develop a radar system tuned to pick up any comment or action from others that could be interpreted as being negative. And because they are so used to criticism, disapproval, or negative judgments, they often hear these types of comments from others even when they aren't being expressed, and they act accordingly, often in the extreme. Victims of childhood emotional abuse are notorious for flying off the handle at the least provocation, berating those around them or damaging property.

Type Five: One Partner Sets Up the Other to Become Emotionally Abusive

Sometimes one partner will deliberately set the scene so that his partner will lose her temper and be made to look like the abusive one. At other times it is done unconsciously, as when one partner's behavior is so hurtful or disrespectful that the other person becomes enraged and even out of control. Although there is never an excuse for abusive behavior, when a person is pushed to the limit, it is difficult to not retaliate in kind.

Derrick and Stephanie had been going out for over a year. Derrick, who worked out of town, asked Stephanie to dinner on Friday night. He asked her to call him on his cell phone so he could tell her what time he'd be getting in. Stephanie called at 3 P.M. and again at 4 P.M., but there was no answer. By 5 P.M., when she hadn't heard from him and he still wasn't answering his cell phone, she began to become concerned that he might have gotten into an accident. He never went anywhere without his cell phone. At 7 P.M. she called his cell phone and his home phone, but there was no answer on either. Very worried at this point, she called Derrick's next-door neighbor, who was a friend of hers, and asked if she'd seen him.

The neighbor reported that she hadn't seen his car in the driveway. Stephanie then called his ex-wife to see if he'd called her or been by to see his daughter, which he hadn't.

Stephanie continued to call Derrick's home until after 9 P.M., when he finally answered. "Oh, thank God you're all right," she stammered, relieved to hear his voice. "Where have you been?"

"I'm not going to answer that question," he said defensively. Stephanie tried to explain, "I've been worried sick that something happened to you. Why didn't you call me? Why didn't you answer your cell phone?"

"I forgot it. Why should I have called you?"

"You asked me to dinner, that's why. And you asked me to call you on your cell phone to set the time. I thought you were lying in a ditch somewhere. I was so worried I ended up calling Marcie and your ex."

"You what? Why in the hell did you get them involved? What's wrong with you?"

At this point Stephanie completely lost it. She started yelling into the phone at Derrick: "What's wrong with me? What's wrong with you? You asked me to go to dinner. You asked me to call you, and then you don't even answer your cell phone. What was I supposed to think? You never go anywhere without that damn phone. What else could I think but that you'd been in an accident?"

"I don't have to listen to this. You're acting like some crazy stalker. You scare me." With this he hung up on Stephanie.

Stephanie was enraged. She called him back, but there was no answer. This sent her over the edge. She got in her car and sped over to his house, where she stormed up to his door and pounded on it, insisting that he let her in. It wasn't until Derrick threatened to call the police that Stephanie finally got in her car and drove away.

The next day Derrick showed up at Stephanie's door with flowers in hand, telling her he loved her.

What do you make of this situation? Do you think Derrick was wrong not to call Stephanie? Do you understand why Stephanie acted as she did, since anyone would have been worried? Or do you agree with Derrick that Stephanie was acting like a stalker and had no right to involve his neighbor and ex-wife?

After working with Derrick and Stephanie for several sessions, it became clear that both had some major issues to work on and that both contributed to this scenario. It turned out that Derrick had such an aversion to commitment that he couldn't even commit to a time for their date. He wanted Stephanie to call him just in case he changed his mind and decided not to take her to dinner. By doing this he put Stephanie in a one-down position, which is where he liked to keep her. By not taking his cell phone and not calling her, he deliberately kept her hanging. He was finally even able to admit that he sometimes deliberately tried to make her angry so he'd have an excuse to distance himself from her.

Stephanie's part in this situation was that she continued to go along with Derrick's games. When he asked her to call him on his cell phone, she should have refused and instead tried to pin him down to a definite time for their date. If he was unable to set a time, she should have declined the date. But Stephanie is very needy and afraid to be alone and was therefore willing to go along with Derrick in order to get the good things he sometimes gave her—attention and affection.

While it was understandable that she would become worried, by calling his neighbor and ex-wife she crossed a boundary, and Derrick had good reason to be angry with her. Instead of sitting with her anxiety, Stephanie took action, but her actions were inappropriate. She was acting more like a mother than a girlfriend by trying to track him down.

Type Six. One Partner Is Abusive Due to a Mental Illness or Personality Disorder

Colin hated to get up in the morning. He knew that he would immediately be greeted with accusations and complaints from his wife.

She goes over the same things every day. How I'm not making enough money for us to save for our retirement. How afraid she is that she'll end up being a bag lady starving on the streets. It doesn't matter how much I assure her that we have a good retirement plan and that by the time we retire there will be plenty of money for us to live comfortably—it never reassures her. Then she'll start in on the same old song and dance about how I tricked her into marrying me—how I led her to believe I had more money than I did and how I didn't really love her but just saw her as a sex object. I've heard these same accusations every day for over twenty years, and it doesn't matter what I say. I can tell her I didn't mean to imply I had more money than I did, that she made some assumptions because of the car I drove and the profession I'm in. I can tell her that I did and do love her with all my heart and that it doesn't matter to me if we ever have sex again (which, by the way, we hardly ever have), but it doesn't ever do any good—it's like pouring water into a bucket that has a hole in it. It may quiet her for a few minutes, but before I know it she's onto something else—I need to fix something in the house, I said something to someone that hurt her feelings—it goes on and on. Thank God I get to go to work or I'd hear it all day long—which is exactly what happens on the weekends. She follows me from one room to another, crying, yelling, throwing one accusation after another at me. I end up feeling like a prisoner in my own home. I don't know what to do.

There is really very little Colin can do. His analogy of a bucket with a hole in it is actually quite profound, because it describes a particular personality disorder to a T. From everything Colin described, it sounds like his wife suffers from obsessive thoughts brought on by Borderline Personality Disorder, which we will discuss in later chapters. Colin needs to come to terms with the fact that he is being emotionally abused and that his wife needs professional help.

Type Seven: One or Both Partners Has an Abusive Personality

Some individuals have what can be considered to be an "abusive personality." Although they can be somewhat charming at times and can sometimes manage to put on a false front in public when it is absolutely necessary, their basic personality is characterized by:

1. A need to dominate and control others

2. A tendency to blame others for all their problems and to take all their frustrations out on other people

3. Verbal abuse

4. Frequent emotional and sometimes physical outbursts, and

5. An overwhelming need to retaliate and hurt others for real and imagined slights or affronts

They insist on being "respected" while giving no respect to others. Their needs are paramount, and they show a blatant disregard for the needs and feelings of others.

These people wreak havoc with the lives of nearly every person they come in contact with. They verbally abuse their coworkers or employees, they are insulting and obnoxious to service people, they are controlling and domineering toward their children, and they constantly blame others when something goes wrong. When this type of person becomes intimately involved with a partner, there is absolutely nothing that partner can do to prevent abuse from occurring. Their only hope is to get as far away from the person as possible.

RECOMMENDED FILM

Who's Afraid of Virginia Woolf?

CHAPTER 4

The Patterns That Begin in Childhood: Why We Abuse and Why We Take It

The events of childhood do not pass,
But repeat themselves like seasons of the year.

ELEANOR PARJEON

No one consciously chooses to become a victim of emotional abuse, particularly from the one they love. And few people consciously set out to emotionally abuse another human being, especially someone they care about. So how did you get where you are today? Why are you in an emotionally abusive relationship? Why did you begin to emotionally abuse your partner or to be emotionally abused by your partner? Why are you and your partner emotionally abusing each other?

In this chapter you'll find the answers to these questions. You'll also learn how we develop certain unhealthy patterns of behavior at an early age, patterns that can follow us all our lives until we begin to understand them, interrupt them, and trade them in for healthier ones.

If you are in an emotionally abusive relationship, it is very likely that you were emotionally abused as a child. This may sound like an extreme statement, but believe me, it is not. The truth is, few people put up with emotional abuse as an adult unless they were abused as a child. And nearly every person who becomes emotionally abusive has a history of such abuse in childhood.

EXERCISE: *Were You Abused or Neglected as a Child?*

Often we grow up thinking that the way we were treated was normal and to be expected, when in fact it was abusive or neglectful. Emotional abuse is sometimes so innocuous and leaves such invisible scars that many people do not realize they were emotionally abused as a child. Emotional abuse of children includes all the following categories. Make a note of each type of abuse you experienced.

- Physical neglect—when a parent does not feed a child enough food or provide the basic necessities such as clothing, shelter, or medical attention if needed

- Emotional neglect or deprivation—when parents don't take an interest in their child, do not talk to or hold and hug their child, and are generally emotionally unavailable to their child. Alcoholic parents, in particular, are often neglectful of their children's needs

- Physical abandonment—when parents leave a child alone in the home or car for long periods of time or do not pick their child up at a designated time and place

- Verbal abuse—constantly putting a child down, name-calling, being overly critical

- Boundary violation—not respecting a child's need for privacy, such as constantly walking in on a child in the bathroom without knocking, entering a child's bedroom without knocking (especially an adolescent's room), going through a child's private belongings as a regular habit (not as a way of monitoring a troubled child's behavior)

- Emotional sexual abuse—when parents create an inappropriate bond with their child or use their child to meet their own emotional needs, the relationship can easily become romanticized and sexualized

- Role reversal—when a parent expects a child to meet his or her needs; to, in essence, parent *them*

- Chaotic abuse—being raised in a family where there was very little stability but instead constant upheaval and discord

- Social abuse—when parents directly or indirectly interfere with their child's access to his or her peers or fail to teach their child essential social skills

- Intellectual abuse—when a child's thinking is ridiculed or attacked and she or he is not allowed to differ from the parent's point of view

The Repetition Compulsion

One of the most significant patterns established by those who were emotionally abused in childhood is based on what is called the "repetition compulsion"—an unconscious drive to repeat the same type of abusive relationship we ourselves experienced as a child in an attempt to accomplish a new outcome. The repetition compulsion compels us to transfer our longings, conflicts, and defenses from the past onto the present in an attempt to undo the past. It drives us to relive the same story over and over again in the hope that this time the ending will be different.

As Judith Viorst, the author of *Necessary Losses,* so eloquently put it: "Whom we love and how we love are revivals—unconscious revivals—of early experiences, even when revival brings us pain.... We will act out the same old tragedies unless awareness and insight intervene."

Our patterns may take different forms, but ultimately the source of the pattern is the same. Unless and until we become aware of the source of our pattern, we are destined to repeat it over and over throughout our lifetimes. For example, let's say that your mother was very unaffectionate and rejecting of you. Each time you reached out to her for love or comfort she rebuffed you by telling you she was too busy or too tired to attend to you. If you persisted or became upset at her rejection, she made fun of you, called you a crybaby, or accused you of being overly demanding.

When you grew up, you may have ended up getting involved with a partner who treats you the same way your mother treated you. No matter how much you beg, cajole, or demand, you just can't get her or him to pay attention to you. Or in a kind of self-fulfilling prophecy, you may become so demanding in your relationships that you force your partners to reject you, thus turning them into your mother.

Or you may have become very much like your mother in your relationships—remaining aloof, distant, and withdrawn from your partner and withholding support and attention. If your partner complains, you accuse her or him of being selfish and demanding.

If you are male, you may have played out your rage at your mother by emotionally or even physically abusing your partner later on. If you are female, you may have swallowed your rage toward your rejecting mother and turned it inward against yourself, becoming deeply depressed in the process. You may have become the classic passive, submissive "wife," allowing her partner to completely control and dominate her.

To a large extent, the repetition compulsion explains why, if one of your parents was verbally abusive to you, you will tend to be verbally abusive to your partner (and/or your children). If one or both of your parents was controlling and domineering, you will tend to treat your partner (and/or children) in a controlling and domineering way. And if one or both of your parents was extremely critical and judgmental, you will tend to be the same. This is how emotional abuse, like other forms of abuse, gets passed down from one generation to the next. In far too many cases, we unfortunately do become our parents—in spite of our best efforts to the contrary.

My Story

This was certainly true for me. Raised by an extremely distant, unaffectionate, critical, and judgmental mother, I vowed to be more loving and more accepting of others. From early on I seemed to be the antithesis of my mother. I was gregarious and outgoing, so much so that it embarrassed and astounded my uptight mother. As I got older I prided myself on my ability to accept and include people, no matter what their religion, race, or economic background (my mother was extremely prejudiced and a bit of a snob). So afraid was I of becoming emotionally abusive like my mother that I tended to be passive in my relationships with men. I agreed with whatever they said and went along with whatever they wanted to do. But unbeknownst to me, I had become emotionally abusive, in spite of myself. Due to the fact that I was very insecure, I became extremely jealous and possessive. I needed constant reassurance and often accused boyfriends of not loving me. I had frequent emotional outbursts, especially if I was drinking (my mother abused alcohol). Even though my behavior could be described as emotionally abusive, I had no idea. In fact, I saw myself as the victim in most of my relationships. No one ever treated me well enough or loved me enough.

Through the help of therapy I became more secure, less jealous, and had fewer emotional outbursts. But the shocker came many years later when I discovered, while writing my book *The Emotionally Abused Woman,* that I had become as critical and judgmental as my mother.

JANINE: THE CASE OF THE WOMAN WHO BECAME INVOLVED WITH MEN JUST LIKE HER FATHER

The repetition compulsion can also work in the opposite way. Instead of becoming your abusive parent, you may have become involved with him or her. We've all heard the phrase—"he married his mother" or "she married her father." Unfortunately, this is often based on truth. If your mother was verbally abusive to your father, you may have married a woman who is verbally abusive toward you or your children. If your father was domineering and controlling, you may tend to get involved with men who dominate and control you.

My client Janine is involved with a man who has turned out to be very much like her father, although she was not able to recognize this until I pointed it out. It often takes a third party—such as a therapist or close friend—to help us recognize our patterns, even though they are blatantly clear to others. Janine's father seldom had time for her. He spent most of his time away from home, and when he was there, he would lock himself up in his study. Janine longed to spend time with her father and felt that there must be something wrong with her since her father didn't want to be with her. She became very critical of herself, thinking that maybe if she would just do better in school or if she could converse with him about interesting things, or if she were prettier, he would love her more. And so Janine began a lifelong pattern of self-criticism and perfectionism. If someone was rejecting or unkind to her, instead of becoming angry with them, she became angry with herself.

Janine's father was also a charming man. Even though he ignored his daughter and wife a great deal of the time, when he did spend time with them it was somehow easy for them to forget this. He made Janine feel like she was the only person in the world, doting on her, fulfilling her every need, laughing at her jokes, showering her with affection. He'd take her to the park for the day and take her to a lavish lunch at a fancy restaurant, treating her more like a date than like his daughter. But often the very next day, he'd announce he was going out of town, and Janine and her mother wouldn't see him again for a few weeks. He'd come home, lock himself in his study, and the whole cycle would start all over again.

This continued all through Janine's early childhood. Then one day a woman called on the phone and told her mother that she was Janine's father's girlfriend. It turned out that he had been having an affair with the woman for several years, and she finally got tired of his false promises to one day leave his wife and be with her. When his wife confronted him with it, Janine's father continued to lie to his wife, insisting that the woman was making it all up because she was trying to get back at him for rejecting her. He was so convincing that his wife actually believed him, until the woman showed up at her door with photographs proving they had, in fact, been together.

All through her twenties, Janine got involved with men who were unavailable yet charming, just like her father. She blamed herself when they were too busy to be with her, thinking that she wasn't pleasing them sexually or wasn't interesting enough. Little did she know she was getting involved with men like her father in a futile attempt to resolve the conflicting feelings she had toward him.

Janine's latest boyfriend is almost an exact replica of her father, and their relationship is an obvious reenactment of what happened between Janine's mother and father. Marshall works nights and weekends, so Janine is often alone and lonely. She wishes his schedule were different so he could spend more time with her, but she tries to understand. For the first eight months of their relationship, unbeknownst to Janine, Marshall continued seeing another woman. When Janine discovered this she was devastated, but Marshall was able to charm his way out of the mess and convince her that he would never lie to her again. Then one day Janine discovered that Marshall had never really broken up with his ex-girlfriend. She was devastated. She started crying and couldn't stop. Suddenly she realized she was repeating the exact scenario her parents experienced. "You could have rewound the tape to twenty years before. I was acting the exact way my mother acted the day she found out my father had another woman. I even found myself yelling at Marshall, 'Pack up your bags and get out of here,' just like my mother had yelled at my father."

Since the repetition compulsion is an unconscious process, like Janine, many people are often unable to recognize their patterns. Many of us discover that we end one emotionally abusive relationship only to find ourselves in a similar one the next time. On and on it goes, and yet we are often blind to what is happening with us. We may begin to see that our partners tend to treat us in similar ways, but we often explain this away by generalizing that "all men" or "all women" are such and such. Or, we blame ourselves. "There must be something I do to cause all these men to treat me this way, but I can't figure it out," one client shared with me recently. "Either that or I wear some kind of a sign that says, 'It's okay to treat me like shit.' I just can't figure it out."

Although you may, in fact, send out messages that cause abusers to spot you a mile away—an issue we'll discuss later—the point is that it isn't your fault. You are desperately—albeit unconsciously—attempting to find someone like your emotionally abusive parent so you can replay the relationship and get it right this time. It's as if your unconscious mind is saying, "If I can only do things differently this time I'll get my mother (or father) to stop abusing me," or "If I can just be patient enough and loving enough, I'll get my father (or mother) to love me." It doesn't matter to your unconscious mind that your partner isn't really your parent but only someone who acts or looks like him—it feels the same, and that's the important thing.

The Core of the Compulsion— an Abusive Childhood

The information and exercises in this section will underscore the fact that an abusive childhood lies at the core of your current situation. While some of you may be more resistant to understanding this truth than others, try to be as open as you can to the possibility.

QUESTIONNAIRE: *Childhood History*

1. Did your mother tend to be distant or aloof toward you as a child?

2. Was your mother unable to take care of you when you were an infant for any reason (illness, absence)?

3. As a young child, were you adopted, placed in a foster home, or sent to live somewhere outside the family home?

4. Did either of your parents die when you were a child?

5. Did your parents divorce or separate when you were a child or adolescent?

6. Do you feel you were deprived of physical affection as a child?

7. Do you feel that your emotional needs such as being listened to, being encouraged, or being complimented were not met as a child?

8. Did your parents neglect to provide you with adequate supervision, leaving you alone for long periods of time in your home or car?

9. Did your parents seem to be too busy to bother with you? Too busy to teach you about life, ask about your homework, or talk to you about your feelings?

10. Was one or both of your parents excessive drinkers or alcoholics, and/or did either of your parents use drugs?

11. Was one or both of your parents extremely critical or domineering?

12. Did you find that it was difficult to please one or both of your parents, or did you get the impression that no matter what you did, your parents would never approve of you?

13. Was either of your parents extremely possessive of you, not wanting you to have your own friends or activities outside the home?

14. Did either of your parents treat you as a confidante or seek emotional comfort from you?

15. Did either of your parents ever physically abuse you?

16. Did a parent or other authority figure ever sexually abuse you?

17. Was either of your parents emotionally incestuous with you—either by looking at you in a sexual way, asking you inappropriate sexual questions, walking around half-dressed or naked in front of you, or expecting you to meet their emotional needs, such as taking the place of an absent partner?

18. Was a sibling ever emotionally incestuous or sexually abusive toward you?

19. Did you ever run away from home?

20. Did you ever feel so enraged with one or both of your parents or siblings that you seriously wanted to kill him or her?

If you answered yes to questions 1 to 5, you experienced *abandonment* as a child. Physical and emotional abandonment are, beyond a doubt, the most profound prerequisites for becoming both a victim and an abuser. Experiences of abandonment in childhood cause profound insecurities and fears and set you up to be insecure, jealous, and possessive in your relationships.

If you answered yes to questions 6 to 9, you experienced *neglect* as a child. A physically or emotionally neglected child grows up to either feel that his needs are unimportant or spend the rest of his life insisting that others meet the needs that were not met by his parents.

If you answered yes to questions 10 to 14, you were *emotionally abused* as a child. A yes to question 10 indicates that your parents were likely too preoccupied with alcohol or drugs to be available for you, or that there was chaos in the family caused by their alcohol or drug use. A yes to questions 11 and 12 indicate that you were overly criticized, dominated, or controlled by one or both of your parents. An affirmative to question 13 indicates one or both of your parents was overly possessive of you; this is a form of emotional abuse. A yes to question 14 indicates one of your parents saw you more as a parent or a partner than as a child.

If you answered yes to questions 15 to 18, in addition to being emotionally abused, you were either physically or sexually abused or subjected to emotional incest.

If you answered yes to questions 19 and 20, your home life was likely severely emotionally, physically, or sexually abusive.

EXERCISE: *Your Childhood Experiences with Abuse*

- Make a list of the negative ways you were viewed and treated by your parents (or other significant caretakers).

- Write about how you feel this affected your intimate relationships.

Abusive Styles of Parenting

Even after reading some of the descriptions of emotional abuse and completing the above questionnaire and exercise, you may still be uncertain as to whether you were emotionally abused as a child. The following descriptions of abusive styles of parenting may help you become more clear about this.

The Abandoning, Rejecting Parent

This is the most devastating form of emotional abuse to a child. Parents can abandon their children physically (leaving them at home alone, having them wait in the car for hours at a time, forgetting to pick them up at the movies, or, because of divorce, leaving the house and seldom seeing them again) or emotionally (being emotionally unavailable to their children, depriving their children of the necessary attention, affection, and encouragement they need).

Often this neglectful, inattentive treatment by a parent can be especially devastating since the child is likely to assume it is somehow her fault or that she is simply unlovable. Parents who escape into alcohol, drugs, sleep, television, or books also abandon their children because they are essentially not there for them emotionally. This is what my client Jean shared with me: "My mother watched television all day long. When I came home from school, she was too wrapped up in her programs to ask me how my day was or what I learned at school. The only way to connect with her was to sit down beside her and get involved with whatever it was she was watching. So that's what I'd do sometimes, even though I might not even like the show. It was my way of feeling a little contact with her. Mostly, though, I'd just go in my room and listen to my music and do my homework."

Many fathers, while physically present in the home, are passive or not actively involved with their children. This is how Stacey described her relationship with her father: "I never knew who my dad was and he never knew me. He'd come home from work and announce that he was too tired from working all day to talk to us. Then he'd get a drink and go into the den. We wouldn't see him until dinner, and then he was distant and unreachable. If we shared anything with him, he'd just nod and then look back down at his plate. He ate as fast as he could and then went back to the den for the rest of the night."

The Possessive Parent

The possessive parent wants to dominate, control, and emotionally consume her child. Possessive mothers begin when their child is an infant, holding him so close he feels suffocated, being overprotective of him, often refusing to allow others to hold him or take care of him, When her child reaches the age where he wants to begin exploring the world separate from his mother, the possessive mother feels threatened. Either out of fear of her child getting hurt or a need to cling to her child to meet her own emotional needs, she discourages her child's natural need to explore. This behavior may continue throughout childhood, with the parent feeling jealous of anything and anyone that threatens to take away her child. She may discourage her child from making friends by always finding fault with each of her child's playmates. Instead of loosening the reins a little as her child becomes older and more mature, she may become even stricter, insisting on knowing where her child is at all times and enforcing rigid curfews.

When a child begins to take an interest in dating, the possessive parent, especially the possessive father, may become particularly threatened and may either forbid his child from dating or attempt to make her feel that no one is good enough for her or that no one will want her. Some fathers have a particularly difficult time when their daughters reach puberty because they are overwhelmed and confused with sexual feelings toward them. A father who is unable to manage his incestuous feelings toward his daughter may become especially adamant about forbidding her to date and about not allowing her to wear clothes that are the slightest bit revealing.

Some parents' possessiveness comes from a need to protect their child from harm. For example, mothers who were sexually abused as children may become overprotective of their daughters, and fathers who got into trouble with the law or who got a girl pregnant may overreact by restricting their sons' freedom. Fathers who were promiscuous or who used women sexually may assume that every boy who dates their daughter is going to behave in the same way.

Other parents don't want their child to grow up because they want them to be available to take care of their parents' needs. Often these parents did not get their needs met when growing up, and they may now expect their children to parent them. Still others may become too attached to their children because they are widowed or divorced or because their spouse is not meeting their needs. When a parent treats his or her child more like a friend or confidante, this can be a form of emotional incest.

The Domineering, Controlling Parent

This type of parent attempts to dominate and control their children, dictating every aspect of their lives including how they speak, how they act, how they dress, and whom they associate with. Often under the guise of "teaching" or "correcting" their child, their real motivation is to dominate their children completely. Although they may tell themselves and their children that they are doing it for their own good, these parents often need to feel in control over others in order to feel powerful and important. Often raised by overly controlling parents themselves, they are often ventilating the anger they could not express to their own parents.

Others may be motivated more by fear than anger. Some parents fear that if their children are allowed more freedom, they will be hurt in some way. They believe that by holding their children close to them they can protect them from danger. Unfortunately, they don't realize that in the process, they are depriving their children of the benefits of learning by making their own decisions and mistakes. Overly fearful parents can rob their children of their natural curiosity and sense of discovery of the world and take away their spontaneity.

Some overly controlling parents are also very authoritarian. They believe strongly that children should always obey their parents, that they should follow certain rules of behavior, and that their authority should never be questioned, no matter what. When a child breaks a rule or disobeys, this type of parent usually believes they have a right to punish their child in any manner they please, including severe physical punishment.

Domineering parents will often try to control not only their children but their spouse as well. They behave in inflexible, even cruel ways, expecting everyone in the family to bow down to them and do as they say. This type of person often erupts in violence when someone in the family dares to question their authority or to act independently.

The Hypercritical Parent

Hypercritical parents find fault in almost everything their child does—the way he talks, the way he looks, the way he interacts with others, his schoolwork, his choice of friends. A hypercritical parent will be quick to point out what their child did wrong or has left undone. Their child can never be polite enough, thoughtful enough, smart enough, or attractive enough to please them. They focus a great deal of negative attention on their child, often keeping a hypervigilant, critical eye out, assuming that the child is going to do something wrong at any moment. Instead of focusing on what their child has done right or what he has been able to accomplish, an overly critical parent will be quick to point out what their child did wrong or has left undone.

This type of parent may be overly critical of all their children or may single out one particular child to pick on. This may be because this particular child reminds the parent of himself, his spouse, or an abusive parent. In some cases, a parent may be misogynistic—meaning that he or she has a hatred, disrespect, or distrust of females. When this is the case, a parent may only be critical of his or her female children.

Critical words to a child are as painful and damaging as being physically hit. They are verbal slaps in the face. Usually, critical words are accompanied by threats, name-calling, and yelling. This verbal abuse can be especially damaging. Insulting names echo in a child's mind over and over again until he comes to believe he is indeed stupid, selfish, lazy, or ugly, and that in fact, that is *all* he is.

Along with criticism from a parent comes the threat of the loss of that parent's love. Children are totally dependent on their parents, and so a hypercritical parent continually threatens his or her child's sense of security. This, in turn, has a tremendous effect on a child's developing sense of self. This continual criticism can be so emotionally damaging to a child that it may take a lifetime to overcome.

A child looks to his parents for approval, acceptance, and validation. If he doesn't get this approval but instead receives mostly criticism, he grows up believing that there is something inherently wrong with him. And since a young child's life is centered around his parents and what they think of him, their opinion of him will influence how he sees himself, how he assumes others see him, and how he views other authority figures (e.g., as critical, threatening, or accepting). Extreme criticism coming from a parent can severely damage a child's self-esteem and can destroy a child's self-confidence, especially if he doesn't have anyone else close to him to encourage him and build up his confidence.

When a child's parents are hypercritical of her, it causes her to be extremely critical of herself, overly sensitive to what others think of her, hypersensitive to even constructive criticism from others, and critical of others. She may then act this out in her adult relationships by choosing a partner who is critical and then take to heart everything her partner says, just as she did with her parents. Or, she may become so sensitive to criticism that she is unable to listen to anyone's suggestions or feedback. She may choose a partner who allows her to be the one in control, and she may mercilessly criticize him on a daily basis.

The Power of Unfinished Business

No matter how hard we try, we can't seem to escape our parents' influence on us. For example, sometimes we consciously go out of our way to find partners who are the opposite of our parents. But in an odd way, this only proves how much power they have over us. This is how it works: You may have been attracted to your partner out of a desperate need to get what you didn't get as a child. If you are a woman, you may have chosen a partner who seemed to be very caring, protective, helpful, and supportive because your father was never available to you when you were a child. Unfortunately, what you experienced as protectiveness in your partner may have turned out to be dominance, what you initially thought was concern and guidance turned out to be control and possessiveness, and what seemed to be support for your position against your family or friends was a ploy to drive a wedge between you and everyone else you had once been close to so your partner didn't have to share you with anyone. While you may not have ended up with your elusive father, you ended up with someone just as bad, and it was your unfinished business with your father that led you there.

If you are a heterosexual man or a lesbian and your mother was cold and unloving, you may be attracted to detached, unemotional women because you experience them as a challenge. If you can get such a woman to warm up to you, if you can even get her to love you, it is a success indeed. Unfortunately, your success is short-lived. You may get such a woman to marry you or to be your partner, but you can't change her basic personality. That means that day in and day out you are forced to experience the old wounds of rejection and abandonment. The more your old wounds are opened up, the angrier you become, until you can't distinguish between the old wounds and the new, your original abuser and your new one.

Those of you who have become abusive were also likely to be attracted to your partner out of a similar desire to undo or redo the past. If your father physically and emotionally abused your mother, you may have felt concerned for and protective of her. You loved her deeply and wished you could rescue her from her plight. When you grew up, you found that you continued to feel protective of women and that you were attracted to "damsels in distress"—those women who always seemed as if they needed to be rescued from something. You may have ended up marrying such a woman but found that you began to despise her weakness and her tendency to be victimized. You realized she was too weak to ever leave you, so you knew you could get away with anything—including treating her poorly, calling her names, and looking at other women in front of her. The more she let you get away with, the less you respected her, until finally you began to verbally and emotionally abuse her.

Your Original Abuser

Your original abuser is that person or those people who seem to have had the most influence on you with regard to how you behave in relationships. While you may have been emotionally, physically, or sexually abused by several different people when you were a child or adolescent, there are probably one or two of these abusers who stand out in your mind. An original abuser is not always the first person to have abused or neglected you but the first person to have caused significant, lasting damage to you by their abuse or neglect. More than likely your original abuser was one or both of your parents, since parents have a far more profound effect on our lives than anyone else, but an original abuser can also be another significant caretaker or a sibling.

EXERCISE: *Discovering Your Original Abuser*

The following exercise will help you discover whom your original abuser or abusers were.

1. On a piece of paper, make a vertical line down the center of the page. Choose one of the abusers from your childhood and make a list of this person's characteristics, using one-half of the page to list the person's positive characteristics and the other half to list the negative ones.

2. If you have more than one abuser, follow the same procedure for each person.

3. On another piece of paper, list the positive and negative characteristics of your current partner.

4. Compare the lists of your childhood abusers with the lists you made of your current partner. Do you notice any similarities between the lists? If you do, circle them.

5. Is there one childhood abuser who has many of the same characteristics as your current partner? If so, this person is likely to be your original abuser.

Another Pattern: Victim or Abuser?

Why is it that some people who were emotionally abused as children become abusers while others tend to become victims of abuse? Earlier in this chapter I wrote that no one chooses to be either an abuser or a victim of emotional abuse. What I meant by this statement is that no one *consciously* chooses either of these roles. But if you grew up in an abusive household or environment, you did in fact choose one of these roles, albeit on an unconscious level.

Growing up in an abusive household taught you that there are only two types of people in the world—victims and abusers. Let's say that your father emotionally and physically abused your mother. Given the fact that your primary role models, your mother and father, presented to you only two options, you likely chose the role that seemed less repugnant to you. Your thinking would have been something like this—"I'm never going to be a victim like my mother (or an abuser like my father). Given the two choices, I'd rather be an abuser (or victim) than a victim (or abuser)." In most cases this decision would have been an unconscious one.

How did you decide which role to take on? If your father abused your mother and you identified strongly with your father, as most boys and some girls do, you likely chose the role of the abuser. You probably tended to take on your father's way of thinking and acting and blamed your mother for the abuse. Your thinking would have been something like this: "If she'd just keep her mouth shut, or if she wouldn't antagonize him, he wouldn't hit her."

If you strongly identified with your mother, as most girls and some boys do, you likely chose the role of the victim. Your thinking would have been, "I never want to be like my father. He's a monster." You may have become very afraid of your own anger out of a concern that you would lose control like your father. This may have prevented you from standing up for yourself or defending yourself with others, thereby setting you up to be a victim.

If your father abused your mother for many years and you saw that your mother was unable to leave him in spite of her suffering, you may have determined that it is hopeless to try to get away from an abuser. If you are female, you may have even come to believe that to be female is to be a victim.

On the other hand, having witnessed your mother taking abuse from your father for a long time and refusing to leave, you may have lost respect for her. You may have come to believe that she was weak or even that she somehow "liked" the victim role. If you are female, this may have caused you to become determined to never be a victim like your mother. If you are male, it may have caused you to feel that the only way to avoid being a victim is to be an abuser.

Anger In, Anger Out—
Male and Female Patterns

Men and women tend to react to experiences of childhood abuse and neglect very differently, partly due to cultural conditioning and partly due to biological hardwiring. Male children are still given more permission to feel and express anger than female children, and girls are given far more permission to cry, while males are viewed as being weak if they do so. This sets the stage for women to be more inclined to suppress or repress their anger and for men to suppress or repress their feelings of fear and sadness. While men tend to act out their anger, women internalize their anger and become self-effacing or even self-destructive.

When another person hurts a man, either physically or emotionally, he will tend to lash out at that individual, either verbally or physically. "You hurt me so I'll hurt you." When a woman is hurt, however, it is not so simple. By the time they have gone through the acculturation process, most women have long since given up the natural instinct to retaliate directly. (Some researchers believe that females are also biologically wired to avoid anger and to instead work toward peaceful solutions.)

In addition, if something goes wrong in his environment, a man tends to look outside himself first for the cause of the problem. According to research, this tendency is based partly on the male biological tendency to take action (versus introspection) and partly on the male ego, which encourages him to blame others and not take responsibility for his actions.

Conversely, if something goes wrong in her environment, a woman will tend to look inside herself for the cause of the problem. Most women are far more inclined to blame themselves for a problem than blame someone else.

This explains why more males tend to become abusive, while more females tend to become victims of abuse. Because a woman is more inclined to question and blame herself when there is a conflict with her partner, she is more inclined to give in during an argument or to become confused as to exactly what her role was in the conflict. This, coupled with the typical female need to keep the peace, will encourage her to compromise and sacrifice in relationships when she shouldn't.

Because women tend to turn their anger inward and blame themselves for problems in their relationships, they tend to become depressed and their self-esteem is lowered. This, in turn, causes them to become more dependent and less willing to risk rejection or abandonment if they were to stand up for themselves by asserting their will, their opinions, or their needs.

Men often defend themselves against hurt by putting up a wall of nonchalant indifference. This appearance of independence often adds to a woman's fear of rejection, causing her to want to reach out to achieve comfort and reconciliation. Giving in, taking the blame, and losing herself more in the relationship seem to be a small price to pay for the acceptance and love of her partner.

As you can see, both extremes—anger in and anger out—create potential problems. While neither sex is wrong in the way they deal with their anger, each could benefit from observing how the other sex copes with their anger. Most men, especially abusive ones, could benefit from learning to contain their anger more instead of automatically striking back, and could use the rather female ability to empathize with others and seek diplomatic resolutions to problems. Many women, on the other hand, could benefit from acknowledging their anger and giving themselves permission to act it out in constructive ways instead of automatically talking themselves out of it, blaming themselves, or allowing a man to blame them. Instead of always giving in to keep the peace, it would be far healthier for most women to stand up for their needs, their opinions, and their beliefs.

RECOMMENDED FILMS

This Boy's Life (a young boy's triumph over an abusive childhood)

Radio Flyer (a poignant story of a young boy who was physically and emotionally abused by his father)

Angela's Ashes (shows how abuse is passed down from one generation to the next)

Now, Voyager (shows how a woman overcomes the effects of a domineering, controlling mother)

PART TWO

STOPPING THE ABUSE

CHAPTER 5

Action Steps
for Those Being Abused

*Nobody can make you feel inferior
without your consent.*
ELEANOR ROOSEVELT

In this chapter those of you who are being abused will learn what you can do to stop the abuse in your relationship. While the optimum situation would be for both you and your partner to commit to working on your relationship together, often abusive partners refuse to admit they are being abusive and are unwilling to seek help, even in the form of reading a book such as this one. This does not mean that there is no hope for your relationship, however. In many cases, the abused partner can be the one who stops the abuse. This is not to imply that you are to blame for the abuse or that you "cause it" or "ask for it" in any way. Nor does it mean that you can change the abuser. He or she is the only person who can do that. But it does mean that in some situations, changing your behavior may encourage the abuser to change his or her behavior, or at the very least modify it.

This may sound unbelievable to you. "What can *I* do to stop the abuse? I've tried everything and nothing works." Although I'm sure you've tried everything you could think of to make your partner stop abusing you, there are some specific things you may not have considered that may discourage your partner from continuing to treat you in an abusive way.

You have much more power than you realize. What may have been standing in the way of you getting in touch with this power is your personal history—a history that no doubt robbed you of your self-esteem and feelings of personal power. Once you come to terms with your past, first by discovering what aspects have contributed to your present situation and then by following the steps outlined in this chapter, you will be able to regain your power and, with it, the determination never to be treated in an abusive way again.

Although this chapter is specifically designed for those who are being abused, I encourage both partners to read it. In many cases, both partners have been emotionally abusive to one another, and so the chapter may actually apply to both. But even in cases where only one partner is being abused, the abusive partner can gain a tremendous amount of empathy for his or her partner by reading this chapter, and this newfound empathy can make the difference between continuing the abuse and stopping it.

This chapter consists of the following eight-step program for those who are being emotionally abused:

- Step One: Admit to yourself that you are being emotionally abused and acknowledge the damage you've experienced because of it.

- Step Two: Understand why you chose an abusive partner.

- Step Three: Understand why you have put up with the abuse.

- Step Four: Understand your pattern and work on completing your unfinished business.

- Step Five: Confront your partner on his or her abusive behavior.

- Step Six: Pay attention to your feelings.

- Step Seven: Take your power back by setting and enforcing your boundaries.

- Step Eight: Continue to speak up.

This program has been used successfully by many of my clients throughout the years. By following this program, many found that the incidence of abuse decreased or even ended. In those cases where abuse continued, the program helped my clients to gain the necessary strength and resolve to walk away from the relationship. The understanding they gained concerning the reasons why they chose an abusive partner also helped them to avoid future abusive relationships.

Of course, most of my clients continued therapy, and this certainly helped them as well. I encourage those of you who can afford therapy to seek this outside help. You will benefit greatly from the insights and support you will receive. But for those of you who cannot afford therapy and who are willing to put a great deal of time and effort into understanding yourself and your patterns, I am confident you can experience many of the same results my clients have experienced.

Many of the steps can be completed in a relatively short amount of time and offer immediate results. Others offer long-term solutions, meaning that it may take months and even years to complete them. Both the long-term and short-term steps are necessary if you are going to stop the emotional abuse that is destroying your self-esteem, your sense of self, and your relationship.

For the most part, I recommend that you follow this program as it is presented and that you complete each step before going on to the next. You'll find that while some steps are rather difficult, the strength and insights you gain from having worked on a previous step will make each subsequent step a little easier. There will be several times, however, when you can move on to the next step without having fully completed a previous one. For example, Step Four—Understand your pattern and work on completing your unfinished business—will take a great deal of time, so it is perfectly fine (and in fact recommended) that you move on to Steps Five and Six while still working on Step

Four. This may also mean that you will end up working on several steps at one time.

The Program

Step One: Admit to Yourself That You Are Being Emotionally Abused and Acknowledge the Damage You've Experienced Because of It

This step is crucial. If you are ever going to stop the emotional abuse you have been experiencing, you must become very clear that you are, in fact, being emotionally abused. If you are still confused about this, please refer back to chapter 2 and reread the descriptions of emotional abuse. Unless you are absolutely certain that you are being emotionally abused, your partner can talk you out of it, make you question your reality, or even turn things around on you and blame you for your own abuse.

Even after you feel you are clear about being abused, you may go through periods of time when you once again doubt your perceptions or when you tend to minimize the abuse or the negative effects it has on you. For this reason it is also important that you admit to yourself just how much damage your partner's behavior has caused you. One of the best ways to do this is to put it down on paper. Putting things down in black and white makes them more real and harder to deny later on.

EXERCISE: *Your Abuse Journal*

1. Begin by writing down all the incidents of emotional abuse that you can remember. Take whatever time is necessary, but write down all the details, including what abusive tactic your partner used and how it made you feel. If there has been a great deal of abuse or if you have been with your partner for a long time, this exercise may take quite some time. *But every hour that you spend writing about your experiences is an hour of healing.* You need to face what has happened to you, and you need to allow

yourself to feel all the emotions you've suppressed and re-pressed. Of course, you won't be able to remember every single incident, especially if your partner has an abusive personality and his or her behavior and attitude is constantly abusive. But do try to recall the major incidents and the feelings you had because of them.

This writing process will undoubtedly bring up a great deal of pain and anger, and you may feel tempted to stop before you have completed it. If this occurs, remind yourself that you have been in denial for a long time and that these feelings are a necessary part of the process of coming out of denial. The more you allow your-self to feel all your emotions surrounding the abuse, the more you will step out of denial and the closer you will be to recovering from the damage inflicted on you by your partner.

2. Review what you have written, paying particular attention to the way each incident caused you to feel. Using these feelings as your guide, make a list of all the ways the abuse has damaged you (i.e., lowered my self-esteem, caused me to doubt my per-ceptions, made me feel stupid).

3. If at all possible, share your writings with a therapist, members of a support group, or a close friend. This process will bring you further out of denial. Once you've shared what happened to you with someone else, it will be far more difficult to pretend it never happened, and you deserve the support and empathy that someone close to you can provide.

If you can't afford therapy, are not in a support group, and don't have a close friend that you feel you can trust with this information, you may wish to share part of your story on one of the chat lines devoted to emotional abuse. Check the back of the book for web addresses for some of these chat rooms. You may also wish to share your writings or your story with me, either by mail or e-mail.

If your partner has been reading the book along with you and has been willing to admit to the abuse, it may be safe for you to share your journal writings with him or her. Although it will be painful to your partner, it may be just what she needs to come out of denial more completely and it may cause her to feel empathy for you for the first time.

If you haven't yet broached the subject of emotional abuse with your partner, I suggest you ask him to read this book before offering your journal writings to him. Reading the book will prepare your partner for your journal writings. Otherwise it could come as a complete shock and force him to deny any truth written there. He could accuse you of making things up or of being insane, or he might even become physically abusive.

If your partner has refused to read the book along with you and has steadfastly denied abusing you, it is probably not a good idea to share your journal writings with her. She could use your writings against you in some way, or she could become violent. Sharing your personal writings can also expose your vulnerability, and at this point, that is probably not a very good idea. Why give an abusive partner any more ammunition to use against you? Of course, it is possible that reading your journal writings could shock your partner into facing the truth about herself, but think it over carefully before taking this risk.

4. Continue to keep a log of each and every time your partner emotionally abuses you or attempts to do so. You can do this by recording each incident or by listing the following categories and simply making a check beside each one every time an incident occurs:

- My opinions, thoughts, suggestions, and feelings were disregarded or ridiculed.
- My partner gave me the silent treatment.
- My partner withheld affection as a punishment.
- My partner ridiculed or insulted me.
- My partner made fun of me in front of others.
- My partner called me names.

- My partner yelled at me.

- My partner kept me from socializing with my friends or family.

- My partner threatened to leave me unless I did as she said.

- My partner threatened to hurt me unless I did as he said.

- My partner accused me of things I didn't do.

- My partner threw things at me.

- My partner damaged or destroyed my things or things in the house.

In addition to logging each incident, make sure you write about your reactions to each incident and how you are now feeling about yourself and your relationship. This will help you keep your thoughts clear, when and if your partner tries to confuse you or to make you doubt your perceptions. For example:

> When Justin yells at me the way he does, I feel very frightened. I'm not sure what he'll do next, if he'll end up losing control and hitting me or even beating me up. I know I should leave, but in some ways I'm even afraid to do that because I'm not sure what he'd do if I did leave.

> Amanda is constantly telling me not to do something. At first I thought she must be right—that there were a lot of things wrong with me, that I just didn't know how to behave in a relationship. But now I'm beginning to understand that I'm not always wrong and that it is Amanda who has the problem with relationships. She always has to act like the parent or the one who is in charge. I'm getting really tired of feeling dominated by her.

> I've noticed lately that when I'm with Matt I almost always end up feeling confused about my feelings and perceptions. I'll offer an opinion about something in the news, and he'll say, "Is that really what you think, or did you just hear someone else say that?" Or I'll tell him I'd like to do something like going to a certain movie or museum, and he'll say, "I thought you didn't like that kind of

movie," or "The last time we went to that museum, you didn't like it." For the longest time I questioned whether I contradicted myself all the time and thought maybe he knew me better than I know myself. But now I'm beginning to realize that he questions me all the time to keep me off balance. It's his way of maintaining control.

Keeping such a log will help you come out of denial and stay out of denial. You may not be prepared to leave your relationship, but at least you will be forced to be honest with yourself about what kind of a relationship you are in.

Step Two: Understand Why You Chose an Abusive Partner

At this point you have hopefully made the connection between your past and your present. After reading chapter 4 and completing the exercises there, you now know who your original abuser was, and you hopefully recognize how and why you chose a partner who is similar to this abuser. The repetition compulsion is a powerful motivator and explains to a great extent why you chose your partner. But there are other reasons as well.

If you were abused or neglected in any way as a child or if you grew up in an alcoholic or tremendously dysfunctional household, you are carrying the emotional scars of your childhood with you today. The abuse, deprivation, or neglect that you suffered damaged your self-esteem, causing you to underestimate your abilities and desirability. It has more than likely caused you to have difficulties with closeness and intimacy in your relationships. Because of these aftereffects, you may have felt that your choices for a romantic partner were limited and that you had to become involved with those partners who chose you, as opposed to being the one to choose a partner. In other words, you may have thought you had to take what you could get.

If you were a victim of emotional, physical, or sexual abuse as a child, you may have been an easy target for abusive partners when you became an adult. Because survivors of childhood abuse generally have a great deal of shame and suffer from low self-esteem, they feel no one will want them. When someone does pay attention to them, they are grateful, and their gratitude and vulnerability may blind them to any obvious signs of abusiveness, a need to control or dominate, or a tendency to be possessive.

Those with low self-esteem often become involved with partners who mirror their own image of themselves. For example, if your father constantly put you down and told you you would never amount to anything, you likely grew up doubting your own abilities. Or if your mother had no time for you and rejected you constantly, you may feel so bad about yourself that you don't feel you deserve to be loved. Therefore, when a partner comes along who echoes your parent's image of you or who mirrors your own image of yourself as unlovable, you may find this person extremely comfortable to be around. As one client told me, "I felt comfortable with her right away. It just felt right standing beside her." The reason it felt so "right" was that it was familiar—his new partner was very much like his mother and ended up treating him in similar ways.

EXERCISE: *Your Reasons for Choosing*
             an Abusive Partner

Make a list of the reasons why you chose an abusive partner. Due to your low self-esteem, you may feel you didn't choose at all— that you just allowed yourself to be chosen and took what you could get. If this is the case, list low self-esteem as one of your reasons. Remember to list the repetition compulsion, since it surely was a factor. Your list will not be complete unless you have at least three items listed.

Step Three: Understand Why You Have Put Up with the Abuse

While each step in my program is difficult, many people feel that this step is the most difficult. This is because it requires complete and utter self-honesty—the type of honesty that can be excruciatingly painful. While many of you may not have realized you were being emotionally abused, you no doubt did know that you were being mistreated. No one wants to look at why they would allow someone to mistreat them. It's embarrassing and humiliating to admit that you would allow yourself to be treated so poorly and even more degrading to admit that you have stayed with someone even after you realized you were being emotionally abused. No one wants to view themselves as a victim or as someone with such low self-esteem that she would put up with unacceptable behavior. But the truth of the matter is that you have allowed yourself to be a victim, and you did allow someone to treat you in unacceptable ways. Some of you allowed the abuse to occur for only a short time, while most people reading this book have allowed it to happen for months or even years.

Emotional abuse does not continue unless the abused partner allows it. So why do so many women and men allow their partners to emotionally abuse them? Once again you need to look to your history for the answers. Someone who was emotionally abused in childhood usually cannot conceive that another, entirely different kind of relationship is possible. They learned how to behave in intimate relationships both from the way they were treated by their parents and from the way they observed their parents treating one another.

A previous history of emotional abuse can also make it difficult to stand up to an abuser. When someone accuses a partner of being selfish, inconsiderate, lazy, or even crazy, instead of standing up for themselves, those who were abused as children often think to themselves, "Maybe what he's saying is true. I am selfish. My mother used to tell me all the time that I only think of myself." To make matters worse, many victims are convinced that they are at fault and therefore do not perceive themselves as abused. Having been continually blamed by their parents, they are used to taking on the blame.

Often, emotional abusers blame their partner instead of taking responsibility for their own problems, and this can cause the partner to doubt her or his perceptions to such an extent that she or he is unable to recognize the reality of the situation. (A previous history of emotional abuse may have already caused the partner to doubt her or his perceptions.)

Many people stay in abusive relationships because they are afraid to be alone. This is probably the most common reason why people put up with abusive behavior from their partner. Whether they are aware of it or not, many, many people stay in abusive relationships because of this fear. Being alone is so uncomfortable, so frightening to some people that they will put up with almost anything in order to avoid it. Those who were left alone as children often feel like being alone is a punishment or proof that they are unlovable. This is particularly true of those who were severely neglected as children. Those whose parents did not respond to their cries when they were infants and toddlers and who were left all alone to cry themselves to sleep often panic at the very thought of being all alone.

Those who have felt alone most of their lives are reluctant to end a relationship, no matter how abusive it becomes. As my client Nicki shared with me:

My father left us when I was only three years old, and so my mother had to work every day to support us and I had to stay with babysitters all the time. By the time she picked me up at night, there was just enough time to eat before we went to bed. I always felt so alone, almost like an orphan. I didn't have any siblings, and we had no family close by. I dreamed all my life of having my own family one day. I spent my twenties all alone in a big city, dating one guy after another. It wasn't until I was thirty-one, when I met my husband and fell in love, that I found out what it was like to not be alone. Finally, I was going to have the family I always dreamed about. Even though it certainly wasn't ideal—Richard started complaining and criticizing me soon after we got married—it felt so good to know I wasn't alone, that he was always there for me. And he was. Richard can be very supportive when he wants to be. We've been though a lot of difficult times together—like the birth of my daughter Heather. It took us several years to get pregnant, and I had to have a cesarean. The thought of leaving him—of starting all over again—of being alone again at this time in my life is overwhelming. I just don't know if I can do it. No matter how bad about myself he makes me feel, being alone feels even worse.

Some people try to avoid being alone because it leaves them without a sense of identity—a sense of knowing who they are—or with a horrible feeling of inner chaos or inner emptiness. This may account for the frantic and often impulsive effort on the part of many abuse victims to avoid being alone at all costs. For example, borderline individuals are dependent on others for cues as to how to behave, what to think, and how to be since they have not developed a strong sense of self. When they are alone they may feel like "there is nothing to me," and they often experience panic, crushing boredom, and dissociation. If this seems to describe you, be sure to read chapters 8 and 9.

Others actually believe they deserve to be treated poorly. While most people aren't consciously aware that this is their motivation for staying in an abusive relationship, it is actually quite common. Adult survivors of childhood abuse and neglect often blame themselves for whatever happens in their adult relationships. This misdirected blame originates in their childhood since children who are neglected or abused almost always blame themselves for their parents' mistreatment. Children have an investment in perceiving their parents as all good. To face the truth about her parents' neglectful or abusive treatment would cause the child to feel angry with her parents, to feel separated from her parents, and to face her aloneness. Therefore, it becomes much easier to blame herself for her parents' behavior and to convince herself that, "If I only hadn't done such and such, he wouldn't have gotten so mad at me," or "She doesn't love me because I'm a bad kid."

Children who are raised in an emotionally healthy environment are able to develop what is called *object constancy,* meaning they perceive of their parents as both good and bad—"Sometimes my mother can be nice, and other times she can be mean." Along with object constancy, these children develop the awareness that they are indeed separate from their parents—"When my mother is mean, it may not have anything to do with me." These children grow up into adults who aren't likely to blame themselves for their parents' problems or mistreatment nor for anyone else's problems or mistreatment. But those children who are emotionally abused or neglected seldom develop object constancy and never truly separate from their parents. They tend to continue blaming themselves for their parents' problems and mistreatment as well as the problems and mistreatment of those close to them. If a partner mistreats them, they blame themselves. After all, they deserve to be mistreated because they are bad people.

Others feel they deserve to be treated poorly because they feel they are worthless, inferior, or inadequate. For example, those who were sexually abused as children or raped as young adults often feel like damaged goods or blame themselves for the abuse—"If I would have obeyed my parents, it wouldn't have happened"; "If I hadn't gone to that party ..."; "If I hadn't worn that short skirt ..." Those who were sexually abused more than one time are particularly prone to blaming themselves—"Why does this keep happening to me? I must be asking for it in some way." This self-blame, and the shame that ensues, causes those who were sexually abused to feel less than others and to believe that they deserve any poor treatment that comes their way.

Still others believe they deserve to be abused because they feel guilty for real or imagined transgressions in their past. For example, those who have mistreated others in the past often feel that they deserve to be mistreated in kind.

When Earl was growing up, he bullied and harassed his sisters mercilessly. "I took all my anger at my parents out on them. I saw them as being weak like me, and I hated them for it. The more they took my abuse, the more I dished it out. The more I dished it out, the more I hated myself for it, but I just couldn't stop. I knew I was hurting them like my parents had hurt me, and I felt terrible about it. My oldest sister told me that she even had to go to therapy because of it. So now, when my wife goes into a rage and tells me what a horrible person I am, there's a part of me that believes her. And there's a part of me that figures I deserve anything she can dish out."

EXERCISE: *Why You Stay*

There are many other reasons why victims of emotional abuse continue to stay in unacceptable, even dangerous, relationships. I've listed the most common below. Note which statements apply to you:

- My partner told me it was my fault, and I believe her.

- I'm afraid I am as unlovable (unattractive, stupid, irritating) as he says I am.

- I'm afraid no one will ever love me again like she does.

- I'm afraid of my own anger or my own potential to be abusive (it's better to be the victim than to be the abuser).

- I don't want to leave him all alone.

- I'm afraid of what he will do if I try to leave.

- I don't want to take the kids away from him.

- I'm afraid I can't make it on my own financially.

PERSONALITY TRAITS THAT SET ONE UP FOR ABUSE

There are specific personality traits and characteristics that predispose one to becoming a victim of emotional abuse. For example, those who doubt themselves—their intellect, their opinions, their perceptions—often gravitate toward people who seem to be extremely sure of themselves. Whereas a more self-assured person might find a know-it-all offensive, self-doubters are actually comfortable with such a person and may even choose him as a partner. They find it far easier and more comfortable to depend on their partner's certainty than to have to deal with their own uncertainty. Unfortunately, know-it-alls tend to think they know what is best for their partners and that they have the right to insist that their partners do as they say. It is often only a small step from being a know-it-all to becoming a tyrant.

The following is a list of the personality traits that set one up for emotional abuse:

- A strong desire to avoid confrontation

- A tendency to pretend things are better than they are

- A tendency to feel responsible for others

- A tendency to blame oneself for problems in a relationship

- A fear of being alone
- A tendency to doubt oneself, including one's perceptions
- A tendency to make excuses for another's behavior
- A tendency to be naïve about others and to believe that love makes one a better person

Once you understand why you have put up with the abuse, you can begin to forgive yourself and free yourself from the clutches of your past.

Step Four: Understand Your Pattern and Work on Completing Your Unfinished Business

In order to break your pattern of becoming involved with abusive people, you must first recognize your pattern. For example, when you look back on your previous relationships, do you recognize the fact that many of your partners were very similar in terms of temperament, personality characteristics, and possibly even physical characteristics? If you are having difficulty seeing the parallels, the following exercise may help:

EXERCISE: *What's Your Type?*

1. On a piece of paper, draw two parallel lines dividing the page into three columns.

2. In the first column, make a list of the behaviors and personality traits of your current partner. Include such things as not very smart, lazy, brilliant, quiet, dependent, loud, loyal.

3. In the second column, make a list of the traits and behaviors of your previous partner.

4. In the third column, make a list of the traits and behaviors of your partner before the previous one.

Take a look at your three lists and notice any similarities among the three partners. Circle the words that seem to be repeated. Notice that while you may describe the men or women in different terms, their basic personalities may be similar. For example, you may have described one partner as charismatic and another as charming, but you are actually describing the same personality type.

Most people discover that there are striking similarities between all their partners. While the faces and bodies may change, the personalities remain the same. If you find this to be true, this is a key to your pattern. It is not a coincidence that you have chosen partners with similar personalities and behavioral traits. The chances are very high that you have done so in an attempt to complete your unfinished business with an original abuser.

5. Now compare your lists to your work from chapter 4 on discovering your original abuser. Do you find that your partners all share personality traits that are similar to those of your original abuser? Again, be flexible in your analysis. There will obviously be some differences, but look for the possibility that you may have described the same behavior or personality traits in slightly different ways.

6. If you don't see any similarity between your past and current partners and your original abuser, or you have been unable to discover who your original abuser was, complete this part of the exercise. On another piece of paper, make a vertical line down the center of the page. In the first column, describe your father; in the second, describe your mother. Now compare this sheet with the page where you listed your last three partners' characteristics in three columns. The chances are very high that there are significant similarities between your partners' characteristics and one or both of your parents' characteristics. If this is true, it is likely that one or both of your parents is your original abuser, whether you tend to perceive them in this way or not.

Sometimes those who have completed this exercise realize that they have made sure they were not with a partner who is like one or both of their parents. Instead, they've chosen partners who are the exact opposite. This is often an even stronger indication that one or both of their parents was their original abuser.

Now that you've discovered the origin of your pattern, in order to break it, you must complete your unfinished business. This includes all the following:

- Admit to yourself that you were neglected, abandoned, or abused by your parents (or other caretakers). This may be difficult for you to do, but it is essential if you are going to be able to break your pattern. The simple truth is you would not be in an emotionally abusive relationship if you didn't have a prior history of abuse or neglect.

- Acknowledge to yourself that you have unresolved feelings of anger, pain, fear, and shame because of this neglect or abuse. As a victim of emotional abuse, you are probably out of touch with your feelings a great deal of the time. You are likely accustomed to repressing your emotions, ignoring or minimizing your pain, and hiding how you really feel from yourself and others. You may be afraid to explore the feelings that are hiding under the surface for fear of being overwhelmed by them or of your emotions creating havoc in your life. In reality, you have more to be concerned about if you *don't* express them. The more you repress and suppress your emotions, the more likely it is that they will burst out of you when you least expect them. Also, it is often because you have held in your emotions that you are attracted to people who freely express theirs— including abusive partners. This is particularly the case with anger—it is as if your partner is acting out your feelings of anger for you.

EXERCISE: *Your Body Memories*

Even when we unconsciously repress our emotions, our bodies remember them. These memories are called *body memories.* Your body holds memories of what it was like when you were a child, how it felt when you were neglected, criticized, and rejected. It remembers the pain and anger with stiffness, muscle constrictions, and tension.

1. On a sheet of paper, describe any body sensations you are aware of right now as you read this material.

2. See if you can assign the name of an emotion to each bodily sensation. For example: "I am aware that my shoulders are tense. I think this tension comes from fear."

3. Write about an incident in your childhood in which you felt this bodily sensation and the corresponding emotion. For example, "I remember tensing my shoulders when my mother would criticize me."

As you continue to bring back memories of your childhood, your body will react naturally, reminding you of what you survived. Pay close attention to your body's messages, and allow the natural physical reactions to occur.

- Find safe and constructive ways to release these suppressed and repressed emotions. Many people do not feel safe allowing themselves to cry or to release their anger, especially when they are all alone. They fear they will "go crazy," or that their emotions will never end. If this is your situation, I encourage you to seek the support of a professional psychotherapist or to join a group for survivors of emotional abuse. Because our bodies hold repressed anger, it can be especially helpful to release your anger physically, but for some, this is particularly threatening. It may help if you ask your body how it would like to express the anger. Your body will tell you what you need to do if you pay attention. You may need to hit, to kick, to throw things, or to scream. There are many methods for releasing anger in constructive ways. They include:

  1. Write a letter to your original abuser that you do not send. Include everything you've wanted to say, holding nothing back.

  2. Talk out loud as if you were having a conversation with your original abuser.

  3. Yell into a pillow.

  4. Tear all the pages out of an old telephone book.

5. Stomp on old egg cartons or squash aluminum cans.

6. Lie on your bed and have a childlike temper tantrum by thrashing your arms and legs.

- Confront (either directly or indirectly) those who abused or neglected you in childhood. If you feel you can confront your original abusers directly without endangering yourself or others, by all means do so. Many people find that an indirect confrontation is more advantageous, either because their original abuser is too sick and old or is still abusive or because they have tried confronting directly in the past without positive results. For these and other reasons, most people choose to confront indirectly by using one of the following techniques:

1. *Letter writing.* Write down everything you've always wanted to say, making sure you include the following points: (1) what the abuser did to anger/hurt you; (2) how it damaged you and influenced your life; (3) what you want from the abuser now (i.e., an apology, better treatment). After you've completed the letter, you can decide whether you want to send it to your original abuser.

2. *Imaginary conversation.* Pretend you are talking to your original abuser and tell him or her exactly how you feel. Don't hold anything back. You may want to pretend that the person is sitting in a chair across from you (many survivors find that it helps to put a picture of the person in the chair).

Confronting your original abuser, even if it is an indirect confrontation, will allow you to take back your power and prove to yourself that you are no longer going to allow him or her to frighten or control you.

- Resolve your relationship with your original abuser. Resolving your relationship with your parents (or whoever your original abuser was) is one of the most important steps you can take to break your pattern of being abused. All the work you have done so far—admitting you were abused, releasing your anger, and confronting your original abuser—are all necessary in order for you to resolve your relationship. In addition, you may also need to follow these suggestions:

1. If you continue to be too dependent on your parents (or grandparents or sibling), begin making your own decisions and relying less on them for guidance and feedback. This may also involve severing any financial ties you have with your parents that may be keeping you in a dependent relationship with them and from gaining the confidence of knowing you can take care of yourself.

2. If you have parents who continue to be overly controlling or smothering, let them know (in a nonblaming way, if possible) that you are no longer comfortable with the old pattern of relating. Once you have done this, you will need to maintain your position and your boundaries despite any threats or manipulation from them.

3. If your parents continue to be abusive—either emotionally, physically, or sexually—you need to confront them about their unacceptable behavior or temporarily separate from them in order to gain enough strength to confront them.

4. If you have been estranged from your parents for some time, you may need to consider gradually reestablishing the relationship on your own terms.

GET SUPPORT

Completing your unfinished business will take work, determination, and, preferably, the support and guidance of a therapist or other group members who are going through a similar process. If you have not already sought out the help of a professional therapist or joined a group for victims of abuse, I suggest you do so. You're going to need all the support and guidance you can get, and depending on your circumstances, you may need more than this book can offer.

Step Five: Confront Your Partner on His or Her Abusive Behavior

It's very likely that you've already spent many hours trying to understand your partner's behavior, explaining to your partner why you are upset, or trying to figure out what went wrong in the relationship, only to discover that none of these methods were effective in stopping the abuse. Some of you have also discovered that the strategies of trying to reason with your partner or just complaining about his behavior have not been effective. You must begin to respond to his inappropriate or unacceptable behavior in a new way—a way that will make an impact on him. The following strategies will help you respond in such a way. I suggest you practice or role-play these strategies with a friend or counselor before you try them with your partner, especially if you tend to become overwhelmed, frightened, or tongue-tied when he or she is being abusive. If you don't have someone with whom to practice, you can put an empty chair in front of you and imagine that your partner is sitting in it. This will help you get over some of your fears about confronting him or her and will make you more confident about what you want to say. The following suggestions will further prepare you for your confrontations:

- Be sure to speak clearly and firmly. Hold your head up high and look directly into your partner's eyes.

- Make sure your feet are firmly planted on the ground, whether you are standing or sitting.

- Take a deep breath before beginning your confrontation and make sure your eyes are clear and that you are in the present. (Often emotional or verbal abuse can trigger childhood memories and catapult you into the past.)

There are two ways to confront. You can sit down with your partner and have a talk with him about the fact that he is being inappropriate or disrespectful toward you, or you can call him on his behavior or attitude the next time he is abusive. The way you choose to go about confronting your partner will have a lot to do with the status of your relationship. If you and your partner are still emotionally close a great deal of the time and are still able to communicate with one another over most issues, approach number one—a serious discussion—may be the best choice. This approach will be especially effective if you have not confronted him on his abusive behavior in the past. If, on the other hand, you have confronted him before and he has ignored you or insisted that you are making too much of it, then you may need to try the second approach and confront him whenever he commits the abusive behavior. This is also the best approach for couples who have grown distant and noncommunicative.

If you are in a relatively new relationship and have begun to see warning signs of emotional or verbal abuse, a serious discussion with your partner is probably the best approach. Many people are simply unaware that their behavior is abusive. If he is young or has little or no experience in a long-term relationship, he may simply be repeating one or both parents' behavior without being aware of how it affects his partner. Even if a person has been in previous relationships, their past partners may have put up with the abuse without saying anything or may have blamed themselves for their partner's behavior, never realizing that they were being abused.

Your decision whether to choose approach one or two may also have to do with whether your partner is a person who has abusive behavior or someone who is an abusive person by nature. If he or she simply has some bad behaviors, approach number one may work well to help him become more conscious of how his behavior affects you. But if he has an abusive personality, approach number two will work better since reasoning with him will not likely be effective.

APPROACH NUMBER ONE—THE SERIOUS DISCUSSION

Tell your partner that you have something important to talk to him or her about and that you'd like to set up a time to do so. Make sure you choose a time that is good for both of you and a time when you will not be distracted by the kids, the television, or the telephone. In fact, it is best to unplug the phone and turn off all distractions when you have your talk. If she becomes curious or anxious and wants to have the talk immediately, make sure you are in the right frame of mind before giving in to her request. If you are not prepared to have the talk, simply assure your partner that while the discussion is an important one, it can wait for a more appropriate time. If you feel you are unable to talk to her at all, write her a letter.

I suggest you begin by telling your partner that you have been unhappy with some of the ways she has been treating you or speaking to you. If this is the first time you've brought this up, let her know that you care about her but that the way she treats you is affecting the way you feel about her and that you are afraid it will ultimately destroy the relationship. If you have tried talking to her about this before, remind her of this. Let her know that you haven't noticed a change on her part and that this is unacceptable to you.

If she seems open to what you are saying, tell her you appreciate her willingness to work on the relationship, and ask her if she'd like some examples of the kinds of behavior you are talking about. At this point you do not need to define the behavior as emotionally or verbally abusive. It will be difficult enough for her to hear your examples without being accused of being abusive. Don't be surprised if she makes excuses or becomes defensive. This is understandable. But don't allow the discussion to turn into an argument. If she begins to accuse you of making things up, imagining things, or trying to create problems where none exist, say something like the following: "What you are doing right now is an example of the kind of behavior I have been talking about. You are negating my experience and making accusations. Please stop." If she gets angry and becomes verbally abusive, say, "You are being verbally abusive. Stop it right now."

Tell your partner that from now on you are going to let her know when her behavior has become offensive to you and that you hope she will cooperate by being open to these reminders so that she can begin to change her behavior.

APPROACH NUMBER TWO—CONFRONTING AT THE TIME

If you choose to tell your partner by confronting him the next time he is abusive, the following suggestions will help:

- *Speak up.* The very next time your partner says something that is abusive or treats you in an emotionally abusive way, immediately say to him, "I don't want you to talk to me that way (or treat me that way). It is abusive (or inconsiderate or disrespectful). I don't deserve to be treated that way."

    This will no doubt get his attention. He is likely to be startled by your response and may even be at a loss for words at first. But be prepared for an argument, excuses, and even anger. He may tell you that he didn't do any such thing, that you made him say what he said, or that he treated you as he did because of your behavior. This leads us to the next step.

- *Don't argue; just stand your ground.* If your partner defends himself by making excuses or blaming you, don't get caught up in the argument. Stand your ground by repeating the exact words you said before, "I don't want you to talk to me like that (or treat me like that). It is abusive and I don't deserve to be treated that way."

- *Be prepared for silence.* Instead of arguing, some partners will completely ignore you when you confront them about their behavior. This is itself disrespectful and abusive. In essence he is saying to you, "You're not even important enough for me to listen to or respond to." Don't let him get away with it. If he gives you the silent treatment, say, "Ignoring me and giving me the silent treatment is also emotionally abusive (or inappropriate, unacceptable, or disrespectful), and I don't appreciate it. I deserve to be heard and for my words to be honored."

- *Offer information if requested.* If your partner seems genuinely surprised by what you have said and sincerely asks you for more information about what you meant by it, by all means offer it to him. You can explain that you discovered through reading this book that you are being emotionally abused by his behavior. If he seems genuinely interested, give him the book to read, and/or suggest you seek counseling together.

Time will tell whether your confrontation has had an impact on your partner. Often such confrontations enable an abusive partner to recognize the inappropriateness of her behavior and to understand that her behavior is hurtful to her partner and is having a negative effect on her relationship. When these realizations are made, people do sometimes change. Even those who are aware that they are being abusive sometimes stop their abusive behavior when they discover that their partner realizes he is being abused, states he will no longer allow it, and means what he says.

It is also possible that your partner may have been testing you to see just how much she could get away with. As I've mentioned earlier, some partners lose respect for their mates when they allow abuse to occur. By speaking up and letting her know you will not tolerate such behavior, you may not only stop the abusive behavior but also gain back your partner's respect.

On the other hand, some people deliberately look for partners they can dominate and control or someone who will be a scapegoat for their anger. If your new partner is such a person, your confrontation will tip him off that you are not the kind of partner he is looking for, and he may choose to move on. If this is the case, you are better off without him.

Whether this confrontation and your continued attempts to confront your partner's abusive behavior are effective or not, your efforts will not be in vain. By continuing to confront your partner on his or her unacceptable behavior, you will affirm in your own mind that you do not deserve to be treated in these ways. This will, in turn, help raise your self-esteem and help you take one step closer to ending the relationship. In the future you will know that you can recognize emotional abuse when it occurs and that you can respond appropriately.

Step Six: Pay Attention to Your Feelings

Sometimes emotional abuse is so subtle that it can occur before you get a chance to stop it. It can be a certain look, a particular tone of voice, or even a pregnant pause. Paying close attention to how you are feeling when you are in your partner's presence will alert you to when your partner is beginning to get abusive. This will help you to catch him in the act before he gets too carried away.

Notice when your stomach begins to get tight or when you feel a sinking sensation in your stomach. Notice any mood changes on your part. For example, if you have been feeling cheerful and light and you suddenly feel depressed or anxious, try to remember what your partner just said to you or whether she just gave you a certain look. You may have been a victim of a put-down without realizing it, or his attitude toward you may have been condescending. The same can be true if you had been feeling confident and spontaneous but now feel insecure and are now guarding your words.

Step Seven: Take Your Power Back by Setting and Enforcing Your Boundaries

No one gives you power; you must take it. Most people reading this book had their personal power taken from them as children when they were neglected or abused. As a result, most have either continued to relinquish their power to others or have developed a false sense of power over others as a way of compensating. If you are being emotionally abused, you have given your power over to your partner. Now it is time to take it back.

You began to take your power back by admitting that you are being emotionally abused and by confronting your partner about his abusive behavior. Now you need to take one step further and convince yourself that you don't deserve to be mistreated. You must begin to recognize that no one has a right to have power over you and that no one has a right to dictate how you should think, feel, or act. You are an adult and are therefore equal to all other adults, including your partner. Your partner is not perfect and is not your superior, and therefore, he or she does not have a right to criticize or judge you.

EXERCISE: *Putting Things into Perspective*

Make a list of your partner's faults, shortcomings, personality defects, and inadequacies. This is not about judging your partner or "taking someone else's inventory" as they say in twelve-step programs. It is about you taking an honest look at who your partner really is so that you can begin to recognize that he or she is not superior to you. He has problems and inadequacies just like everyone else and therefore has no right to sit in judgment of anyone else or to tell anyone else how they should run their lives.

SET BOUNDARIES AND LIMITS

One of the best ways of taking your power back is to set and enforce your boundaries. Many of you may be quite familiar with the concept of boundaries; for those of you who are not, here is a brief overview of exactly what boundaries are and how to set them.

Boundaries separate us from other people. There are physical boundaries and emotional boundaries. Your skin is an example of a physical boundary since your skin creates a physical barrier that separates you from all other living and nonliving organisms. We also have an invisible boundary around our body that is often referred to as our *comfort zone*. Our comfort zone varies depending upon the situation. For example, you are no doubt much more comfortable allowing a friend to stand close to you than you would a stranger. And even though most people would be comfortable allowing their partners to stand or sit extremely close to them, a person who has been abused by a partner might prefer his or her partner to remain at a more comfortable distance.

An emotional boundary usually takes the form of a limit. We all have limits as to what feels appropriate and safe when it comes to how others treat us emotionally. What may feel fine to me may feel uncomfortable to you. But unless you tell me you are uncomfortable, I will never know, and I will continue treating you in a manner that is uncomfortable to you. This doesn't help either one of us. If you allow someone to emotionally abuse you, you are not honoring and protecting your boundaries, and you are also participating in the erosion of your relationship. Protecting yourself sets a necessary limit for both you and your partner, and this in turn protects the relationship.

Emotional abuse is essentially a boundary violation. A boundary violation occurs when someone crosses the physical or emotional limits set by another person. All relationships, even our most intimate ones, have limits as to what is appropriate. When someone crosses the line between what is appropriate and inappropriate, whether they do it knowingly or unknowingly, that person has violated our boundary.

Boundary violations may be accidental or deliberate. A person can violate your boundaries out of ignorance, malice, entitlement, or even out of kindness. But no matter how or why it occurs, a boundary violation is still harmful.

Most of us begin a relationship thinking we have certain limits as to what we will or will not tolerate from a partner. But as the relationship progresses, we tend to move our boundaries back, tolerating more and more intrusion or going along with things we are really opposed to. While this can occur even in healthy relationships, in abusive ones partners begin tolerating unacceptable and even abusive behavior and then convince themselves that these behaviors are normal and acceptable, and they believe their partner when he or she tells them they deserve such behavior.

EXERCISE: *Establishing Your Boundaries*

In order to set your boundaries, you need to know what they are. Only you can decide what you will and will not accept in your relationship. The following sentence-completion exercise will help you become aware of your limits and to establish or reestablish your boundaries.

- Spend some time thinking about specific behaviors that you are no longer willing to tolerate from your partner. Refer back to chapter 2 to remind yourself of the different types of emotional abuse.

- With these behaviors in mind, complete the following sentence: I will no longer allow my partner to _____.

Continue writing the stem of the sentence and completing it until you have included every abusive, inappropriate, or disrespectful behavior you can think of.
Examples:

I will no longer allow my partner to make fun of me, make sarcastic comments to me, or to verbally abuse me in any way.

I will no longer allow my partner to make me doubt my perceptions.

COMMUNICATE YOUR LIMITS AND BOUNDARIES

Your partner needs to know you have limits and boundaries. Otherwise, you continue to give up your power and control and, in essence, give him permission to abuse you. In order to establish your boundaries, you will need to communicate them by clearly stating what you will and what you will not accept from your partner. For example:

- "It is no longer acceptable to me for you to invade my privacy. That means I do not want you listening to my phone conversations, opening my mail, or going through my drawers."

- "I will no longer accept you criticizing and correcting me. I am not a child, and I don't expect to be treated like one."

Setting your boundaries also includes stating any changes you intend to make in the way you behave or react in the relationship. For example:

- "I am no longer going to ask your permission to go places or to buy something. I am an adult and can make these choices on my own."

You don't have to explain or justify why you will no longer allow your partner to treat you in a certain way or why you are going to behave differently. They are your boundaries, and that is all there is to it.

Be prepared for any number of reactions. If your partner is simply guilty of a few bad habits, she may be very willing to honor your limits. Although she may initially try to argue with you, explain to you why her behavior is justified, or act like she doesn't understand; in time you may see her making an effort to respect your wishes. She may fall back into the offensive behavior from time to time, but overall you will recognize some changes.

If, on the other hand, your partner is hostile toward you, he will probably take offense at what you are saying and may tell you he can say or do anything he chooses. He may ignore you, act as if it is a joke, tell you you are a controlling bitch, or yell at you.

If he is a control freak, he will be very threatened by your assertions because he will recognize the fact that he is losing control over you. He may try to sabotage your efforts by denying that he ever treats you that way and insinuate that you are crazy. He may tell you that you don't know what you are talking about, or he may counter with complaints of his own.

Also be prepared for your partner to test you to see whether you will change your mind. Don't allow her to talk you out of your boundaries or to question your reasons for maintaining them, and don't allow her to manipulate you into feeling guilty about setting them. The more you are consistent and don't back down, the more it will become clear that you mean what you say.

Step Eight: Continue to Speak Up

After you have done the work of stating your boundaries, you will need to make sure they don't continue to be violated. In order to accomplish this, you must bring each and every violation to your partner's attention as it occurs. This will, of course, be very difficult. It will require that you pay attention to what is going on in your relationship moment by moment and that you respond immediately to any sign of abuse. You may be afraid of making him angry or of starting a fight. You may be tempted to let something go because you don't want to ruin a perfectly nice evening. But in order for your boundaries to be respected you must be consistent and bring up each violation immediately. Otherwise your partner will take your silence as permission to continue the behavior.

State your grievance in a direct, nonblaming way. There is no need for name-calling, and you should avoid making statements using the words *you, always,* and *never,* such as, "You always make fun of me in front of your mother," or "You never listen to my point of view." Instead, simply state your grievance using *I* statements such as "I've asked you to stop making fun of me and you're doing it again. Please stop it," or "I would like it if you'd listen to my point of view instead of waving me away like that."

Often the clearest and most effective message is simply to say, "Stop it!" This firm response will let your partner know you will not tolerate any abuse.

Don't back down, and don't apologize for bringing up the issue. There is no need to argue about what you've said. If he defends himself, listen to what he has to say and then state, "You have the right to your point of view, but I am going to stand by what I've said. I don't like to be treated that way."

Boundary violations can be healed in the moment if you tell your partner that she has violated a boundary and she immediately apologizes for it and assures you she will not do it again. Unfortunately, this doesn't happen very often. Your partner is likely to become defensive, to act insulted, or to deny that she violated your boundary. This should not discourage you from bringing up offenses, however. While she may deny the violation at the time, after thinking it over she may realize what she has done and try harder to honor your boundaries. Plus, you need the practice in standing up for yourself and asserting your limits. Over time, you may be surprised to see subtle and not-so-subtle changes taking place in both of you.

If, on the other hand, your partner continues the offensive behavior, you will need to speak up again. If you stay silent or back down, your words of confrontation will mean nothing. Your partner will assume you were just spouting off before and that she doesn't need to take you seriously.

At times you will need to back up your words with action. This doesn't mean you threaten to end the relationship every time your partner does something that is offensive or each time he becomes abusive. If you've decided to work on your relationship, you can't go throwing that in his face or threaten to do something you're unwilling or unable to really do. Threatening to leave if he doesn't shape up can be a form of emotional blackmail, and unless you are willing to carry out the threat, it will weaken your words and your position. Setting a limit is different from a threat. When you threaten with something like "If you ... I will ...," you are manipulating. When you set a limit by saying something like "I will not accept ..." or "I don't want you to ... ," you are merely stating a fact.

REMEMBER THAT YOU HAVE CHOICES

An important part of taking back your power is to realize that you have choices. If you have told your partner that it is unacceptable to you for him to continue to make fun of you in front of his mother and he continues to do so, you have the choice to stop going with him to his mother's house. If he continues to wave you away when you try to express your point of view, you can get up and walk out of the room. If your firm "Stop it" does not stop your partner from verbally or emotionally abusing you, you can always leave. It doesn't matter whether you are at home, at a restaurant, or at a friend's house.

Always carry enough money with you so that you can call a cab if you need to leave an uncomfortable situation. Carry phone numbers of friends and family just in case your partner ever leaves you stranded. Plan ahead to make sure you have someplace to go in case you need to leave your home. All these steps will provide you with a sense of control over your own life and strengthen your determination never to be abused again.

Specific Advice and Strategies

Here is some advice and strategies to use for specific forms of emotional abuse:

- *Gaslighting:* Because you have begun to doubt your sanity, intellect, or perceptions, it is essential that you focus on knowing yourself and trusting yourself. No one knows you as well as you know yourself. While you may sometimes become confused about your feelings and motives, you are the only one who lives inside your skin, and you are the only one who can figure yourself out. No one has the right to try to read your mind or to determine what your "real" motives are. As long as you believe that your partner is superior to you or that he knows you better than you know yourself, he will always have power over you.

- *Criticism:* Most people do not realize they are as critical as they are. They may be repeating the pattern of being critical that their parents modeled, and they may even be repeating the very same criticisms that they were given when they were children. For this reason, some people have had success with using the word "Ouch!" every time their partner is critical. Others have told a critical partner that they will only allow one criticism a day or one criticism a phone call—whatever applies.

- *Criticism in the guise of "teaching":* When you confront your partner with his behavior and he gives you an excuse like "I'm just being honest" or "I'm just trying to help you," tell him that he doesn't need to take on the responsibility for your life, that you are an adult who is fully capable of taking care of yourself.

RECOMMENDED FILM:

Sleeping with the Enemy (an excellent portrayal of an emotionally abusive relationship)

CHAPTER 6

Action Steps for the Abusive Partner

Unable to get our own way, often we settle for trying to prevent other people from getting their way.

SHELDON KOPP,
What Took You So Long?

In chapter 4 we explored some of the reasons why you became emotionally abusive to your partner. In this chapter we are going to take an even closer look at the factors that have contributed to your abusive behavior and explore ways for you to stop the abuse once and for all. I will present alternative ways of dealing with the emotions that cause you to abuse—namely fear, anger, pain, and shame. For those who only occasionally abuse, I offer strategies to help you become aware of the triggers that precede an abusive episode. And for those who have developed a more pervasive attitude and way of behaving that is emotionally abusive, I will offer you information that will help you get to the core of your abusiveness so that you can begin to extinguish it.

In either case, it is very important for you to know that you have within yourself the power to change. I know, because I did so. It wasn't easy. It took all the strength and will that I possessed. It also required my willingness to be completely honest with myself and to step back and observe myself more objectively.

Just as I encouraged those who are abusive to read the previous chapter, I encourage those who are being abused to read this one. By gaining more understanding about why your partner becomes abusive, you will be far more able to offer the support he or she will need in order to stop the abuse and to view your partner as a wounded person instead of as a monster. This doesn't mean that it is your responsibility to help your partner to change—only your partner can make the commitment and take the steps necessary to change.

The following seven-step program has proven successful for many of the clients I have worked with who have abusive behavior. At the end of the chapter, I also offer strategies for specific types of abusive behavior.

- Step One: Admit to yourself that you are emotionally abusive and acknowledge the damage you've done.

- Step Two: Understand why you abuse.

- Step Three: Understand your pattern and work on your unfinished business from the past.

- Step Four: Admit to your partner that you have been emotionally abusive.

- Step Five: Apologize to your partner and work on developing empathy for her and for others.

- Step Six: Learn and practice ways to identify and constructively release your anger, pain, and stress.

- Step Seven: Identify your triggers and false beliefs.

It is important that you follow this program as outlined since each step will prepare you for the next. Step Three—Understand your pattern and work on your unfinished business from the past—will be an ongoing process and need not be completed before moving on to the next steps.

The Program

Step One: Admit to Yourself That You Are Emotionally Abusive and Acknowledge the Damage You've Done

This will not be an easy task. No one wants to admit that he or she has been emotionally abusive. No one wants to admit that because of his emotionally abusive behavior, his partner and his relationship have suffered. And certainly, no one wants to admit that his behavior has actually damaged someone he loves. But if you can't admit these truths to yourself, you will not be able to save your relationship and, even more important, save yourself.

You aren't expected to do this without help, however. Throughout this chapter I will offer you information and strategies that will make admitting your abusiveness a lot easier than it would otherwise be. I can offer you this information and these strategies partly because of my extensive work with others who became abusive and partly because I have been in your shoes.

Even though you may know in your heart that it is true—that you are emotionally abusive—admitting it to yourself may cause you to feel such overwhelming guilt and shame that you find yourself repeatedly pushing the truth away and going back into denial. It may make it easier to face the truth once and for all if you understand the emotions of guilt and shame.

Many people think that guilt and shame are the same emotion, but in fact they are not. When we experience guilt, we usually fear punishment, but when we are punished or have made amends to the person we have harmed, the guilt is resolved. When we feel shame, on the other hand, we fear abandonment. In theory, we feel guilty for what we *do* and we feel shame for what we *are*. But in reality, the feelings of guilt and shame overlap. Most of us do tend to feel guilty if we do something we consider to be wrong, but we can also feel shame for being the kind of person to do such a thing.

Guilt can be a lot easier to deal with than shame. Although the experience of guilt can be very painful, as mentioned above, once we have admitted our offense and apologized to those we have harmed, our feelings of guilt tend to diminish. Shame is a different matter. Those who feel ashamed of themselves because of a wrongdoing may become depressed and even suicidal. This is because shame can obliterate our self-esteem and strip us of any sense of pride we once had in our accomplishments and ourselves. We often feel suddenly exposed as our carefully built self-image is stripped away. We want to hide from what we experience as the critical eyes of others.

Shame, the First Hope of Healing

We are told that shame is the painful feeling of being a flawed human being and that therefore it is an unhealthy emotion. But this isn't necessarily true. First of all, all emotions are natural and are therefore healthy; second, shame can be a message that we are failing to be who we were meant to be. Shame can be the first hope of healing. As noted author Lewis B. Smedes stated in his book *Shame and Grace,* "If we feel like flawed persons, it may be because we are in fact flawed."

Shame can expose us to parts of ourselves that we have not recognized before and to parts of ourselves we have been reluctant to acknowledge. In this way, it can help us to know ourselves on a very deep level.

There are two kinds of shame—healthy shame and unhealthy shame. Healthy shame is a reminder that we are less than we ought to be and less than we want to be. If we can still feel shame, it is because we are healthy enough to feel uncomfortable about our shortcomings. Those who feel shame for their less-than-noble natures should feel grateful that they still have the ability to feel it.

Unhealthy shame (or false shame) differs because it has no basis in reality. It is false because, unlike healthy shame, it is not a signal that something is wrong with us. It is unhealthy because it kills our joy and saps our energy and creative powers. Smedes explained it this way: "It is a shame we do not deserve because we are not as bad as our feelings tell us we are."

The fact that you emotionally abused your partner does not mean that you are a total failure as a partner or as a person. Nor does it take away from all the good things you have said and done for your partner and for others. What it means is that your behavior has harmed your partner (and possibly others) and for this you are responsible. Feeling healthy guilt and shame about what you've done is good in the sense that it will remind you of the changes you need to make in yourself and the work you have ahead of you. Allowing yourself to be overcome by a "shame attack" in which you begin to feel all bad, a complete failure, or completely worthless will not only drag you down but will sap you of any motivation to change.

The next thing that will help you to admit that you have been emotionally abusive is to understand how and why you became abusive. The following step will help you with this.

Step Two: Understand Why You Abuse

In chapter 4 you learned about how those with a history of neglect, abandonment, and/or abuse tend to either become victims or abusers— often mimicking their parents' behavior. This no doubt helped you understand yourself better, but there is even more that you need to learn about emotional abuse and those who abuse before you can completely understand why you became abusive. Up until now we've focused primarily on the effects of *emotional* abuse on children and how they carry this damage forward into their adult relationships. But sexual abuse and physical abuse can also set a person up to become emotionally abusive.

THE CONNECTION BETWEEN EMOTIONAL AND SEXUAL ABUSE

Daniel was what some people call a "rage-aholic." He frequently became enraged at the slightest provocation and would begin to yell and scream. Most often, he became enraged at his wife.

"I felt terrible about it, but somehow I just couldn't stop myself. She'd say something or do something, and all of a sudden I'd lose it. She's a very good woman and certainly doesn't deserve this kind of treatment. I'm surprised she's stuck it out with me as long as she has."

This is what Daniel shared with me when he first started seeing me for therapy. He had recently had memories of being sexually abused as a child, and he sought therapy to help him manage his flashbacks and overwhelming feelings of self-destructiveness since the memories had come up. As it turned out, his uncle and his grandfather had raped Daniel over a period of several years. While Daniel certainly was angry with his uncle and grandfather, he was even more enraged with his mother because he felt strongly that she knew it was happening and did nothing to stop it. He had one memory of his mother actually coming into the room and catching his uncle in the act. He also remembered his uncle doing it again many times and often when his mother was in the house.

At first, Daniel felt confused and bewildered by his mother's behavior. "How could my own mother refuse to help me? Why didn't she stop it? What kind of a mother was she?" he agonized over and over. But soon his confusion turned to rage. "I hate her. I never want to see her again as long as I live, and she better be happy for that because if I ever see her, I'll probably kill her!"

It's quite common for victims of sexual abuse to feel more anger toward what is called "the silent partner"—a mother, father, or other adult who does not intervene while a child is being abused—than they do the perpetrator of the crime. This is true for several reasons:

1. It often feels safer to focus anger on the nonoffending parent than it is to feel anger toward their abuser.

2. We expect parents—mothers in particular—to protect their children. Mothers who do not, especially those who put their own needs ahead of their child's, elicit tremendous anger in all of us.

3. Male children tend to lose respect for mothers who put up with abusive behavior from men or who allow men to abuse their children.

It is also quite common for male survivors of sexual abuse to take out the anger they feel toward their mothers on their female partners. It wasn't long before Daniel figured out that this is exactly what he had been doing with his wife all those years. "I took all my anger out on my wife. I hated my mother so I hated all women."

THE CONNECTION BETWEEN EMOTIONAL ABUSE AND PHYSICAL ABUSE

Jared was physically abused by his father during most of his childhood. He remained deathly afraid of his father even into his teens, when he could have physically overtaken him. "He just had this power over me. I couldn't stand up to him, and I hated myself for it. The only way I could get away from his grasp of control was to move out—which I did at sixteen. I left home and haven't talked to him since."

Unfortunately, it was not so easy to leave behind the damage the abuse had done on Jared's psyche. For years he had been verbally abusing his wife. This is how he explained it to me.

"Whenever I got angry at someone, especially another man, I'd be too afraid to express it directly toward them. So instead I'd silently fume until I got home, and then I'd take it out on my wife because she was safe. The truth be told, I was really a coward. I was afraid to stand up to a grown man just like I'd been afraid to stand up to my father. I hated myself for my cowardice and so I hated my wife, too. I'd think to myself, what's wrong with her? How could she be with someone like me?"

THE CHARACTERISTICS OF THOSE WHO BECOME ABUSIVE

It is also important to realize that abusive people tend to have certain characteristics that can predispose them to becoming abusive. These characteristics include:

- A strong desire to remain in control

- A tendency to blame others for your own problems

- Difficulty empathizing with others or an inability to empathize with others

- A tendency to be jealous and possessive

- A tendency to be emotionally needy

Do you recognize yourself in this description? If you are honest with yourself, you will probably realize that you have most, if not all, of these characteristics. But instead of just condemning and blaming yourself for this and becoming overwhelmed with shame, begin to recognize these as symptoms of your problem—symptoms that you can do something about. Let's take a close look at each item.

- *A strong desire to remain in control.* Why do you need to be in control? More than likely, it is because for much of your life you felt so out of control. Children who are emotionally, physically, or sexually abused have no control over what is happening to them. They are ordered around, put down, criticized, and shamed. They have their emotional and physical boundaries violated constantly. It is a common reaction for survivors of any type of abuse to overcompensate for this loss of control by becoming overly controlling and domineering themselves. Some consciously think such thoughts as "No one is ever going to control me again," but usually the decision is an unconscious one. Many deliberately choose partners they can control; others are unaware that they are attracted to those who allow them to be in control of the relationship.

- *A tendency to blame others for your own problems.* Many who were abused as children, especially males, cope with their abuse by utilizing a form of denial called "identifying with the aggressor." When a young child refuses to acknowledge to himself that he is being victimized but instead justifies or minimizes the behavior of the abuser, he will often grow up to be very much like the abuser, behaving in the same abusive ways.

  Once he has become abusive, a person will have even more investment in denying reality. If he were to acknowledge his own behavior and the devastating effect it has on others, he would also open the door to remembering and acknowledging his own victimization—something that seems just too painful to do. Therefore, he blames the victim for her own victimization, thus avoiding any responsibility and any recognition of his own abusive behavior.

  Another reason abusers tend to blame others is because they have a tendency to view themselves as victims. Because of this victim mentality, their perception is faulty. No matter how much they are hurting someone else, they can only seem to recognize how much they themselves have been hurt.

A car accident is a good analogy. Let's say that you rear-end someone at a stop sign. By all rights, you are the one who is considered at fault legally. But when you see the damage to your front grill, you become outraged at the other driver, telling him that he shouldn't have stopped so long at the stop sign. At that moment it doesn't matter to you how much damage you did to the other person's car, nor do you seem to comprehend the fact that you are the one who caused the accident in the first place. All you know is that your car is damaged and that is all that is important to you. This type of thinking is typical of those who abuse. Due to their own experience of abuse or neglect, they remain forever stuck in the role of the victim, only able to see the harm done to them by other people, completely oblivious to any harm they themselves cause others.

Another reason why those who abuse have a tendency to blame others for their own behavior is the psychological defense mechanism known as projection. The way this works is that as a defense against facing a quality about ourselves we dislike, we project this quality onto someone else.

- *A difficulty with or an inability to empathize with others.* Partly because they remain stuck in the victim role and their perceptions are impaired, those who were neglected or abused as children are often unable to empathize with others or to put themselves in the other person's shoes. In particular, those who were neglected as children often become aggressive and cruel toward others primarily due to this lack of empathy. The ability to emotionally understand the impact of their behavior on others is impaired. They do not understand or feel what it is like for others when they do or say something hurtful. Indeed, adults neglected as children often feel compelled to lash out and hurt others—most typically someone they perceive to be less powerful than themselves. One of the most disturbing elements of this aggression is that it is often accompanied by a detached, cold lack of empathy. They may show regret (an intellectual response) but not remorse (an emotional response) when confronted about their aggressive or cruel behaviors.

Empathy is a learned skill. Children from healthy, functional families usually learn how to empathize from their parents, either overtly or by watching their parents interact with one another. Children who were neglected, abandoned, or abused often come from unhealthy, dysfunctional families in which there are no positive role models for learning empathy and parents do not take the time to teach their children how to empathize with others or even teach them the importance of empathy.

- *A tendency to be jealous and possessive.* This tendency stems from feelings of insecurity and low self-esteem. It only makes sense that if you were neglected, abandoned, or abused as a child, you will tend to be insecure. Children need nurturing, acceptance, and stability in order to gain a sense of security in themselves and in their environment. When they don't receive this, they try to gain security from others, particularly their partner. When that security is threatened by real or imagined circumstances, they will react by tenaciously trying to hold on to their partner.

- *A tendency to be emotionally needy.* This characteristic is also caused by feelings of insecurity and low self-esteem. When a child's emotional needs were not met, he or she remains hungry for the nurturing, the acceptance, and the positive feedback that he or she didn't receive at the hands of his or her parents. When that child grows up and enters an adult relationship, all those unmet needs resurface. We want our partner to give to us what we didn't get as a child, and we become angry, hurt, and demanding when he or she is unable or unwilling to do so. Even though it is unreasonable to expect our partner to make up for what we didn't get as a child, we expect it anyway, and this expectation can lead to serious relationship conflicts. Partners feel put upon and pressured to fulfill our needs and even those who try gradually become more and more resentful when they come to realize that our needs are never-ending. We become more and more angry and more and more demanding as time goes by, until our expectations become abusive.

At the same time we are emotionally abusing our partner with our demands and unreasonable expectations, we feel victimized. Since we believe it is our partner's role to make up for what we didn't get as a child, we feel cheated and unloved.

Sadly, nothing our partner does will ever be enough. No amount of reassurance, no amount of sacrifice on our partner's part will fill up the empty places inside of us. We need to begin filling up the emptiness ourselves. We must begin to meet our own unmet needs.

In addition to these characteristics, the following is a list of other personality traits that predispose one to become abusive:

- Poor impulse control

- Low self-esteem

- Fear of abandonment

- Repressed anger

- A tendency to objectify others in order to avoid being affected by the suffering of others

- High levels of stress and high arousal levels

Step Three: Understand Your Pattern and Work on Your Unfinished Business from the Past

In chapter 4 we discussed how we create patterns in our relationships based on our childhood experiences. If your mother or father was cold and detached, you may have a tendency to become attracted to partners who tend to be aloof and distant, or you may have gone to the other extreme and became attracted to partners who are emotionally effusive and possibly even emotionally smothering. If one or both of your parents were controlling and dictatorial you may have followed their example and become domineering yourself. Whatever your pattern, it is important that you recognize it for what it is and that you begin to come to terms with it. This means that you are able to clearly see just how and why your pattern was formed and the role it plays in your becoming emotionally abusive.

You may resist the idea that it was the neglect or abuse by one or both of your parents (or other caregiver) that set you up to become abusive. Ironically, those who become abusive often have a more difficult time admitting they were neglected or abused than do those who are being abused. As mentioned earlier, many who become abusive do so because they identified with the aggressor. While it is natural to want to protect your parents, if you do so at the expense of your own healing and recovery, you are giving your parents even more power over you.

Understanding your pattern is one thing; changing it will be something else. In order for this to occur, you will need to work on your unfinished business. The following is a brief overview of what "completing your unfinished business" will entail:

1. Acknowledge the anger, pain, fear, and shame that you feel as a result of the neglect or abuse you experienced as a child. Those who were abused or neglected as children often become disconnected from their emotions as a way of surviving what were sometimes intolerable situations. Those who become abusive as a way of coping are particularly prone to becoming desensitized to their feelings. For this reason, it may be difficult for you to recapture these lost feelings and make them your own. But if you are to recover from your childhood and put an end to your abusive behavior, this is exactly what you must do.

   The first emotion you need to access is your anger. While you may have no difficulty becoming enraged with your current partner, your anger toward your original abuser may be buried deep inside you. Fortunately, you can use your current anger to help you access your repressed and suppressed anger from the past. Although you may not associate your tendency to be angry with what happened to you as a child, you will need to work on making this all-important connection.

EXERCISE: *Making the Connection*

• The next time you become angry with your current partner, think of a time when one or both of your parents (or other caretakers) treated you in a similar way.

• How do you feel when you remember this incident? Angry? Ashamed? Afraid?

After you have acknowledged your anger about what was done or left undone to you as a child, you will need to move beyond your blame and resentment. One way to do this is to realize that underneath your anger lies sadness, and that to get past your anger you must allow yourself to feel and express this sadness. This will likely be even more difficult than getting in touch with your anger. You have likely built up a wall to protect yourself from these vulnerable feelings, and it will take safety and effort to bring these walls down.

EXERCISE: *Cocooning*

An excellent way of providing yourself with the necessary safety is to take a day off once in a while to "cocoon"—to sleep in, to write in a journal, to read novels, and to watch movies. If you aren't always pushing yourself to perform and be strong, it will be easier to let your guard down. And sometimes we need to "prime the pump" by watching sad movies about abused kids in order to remind ourselves of how bad it really was. I've recommended some movies at the end of the chapter that work really well for this purpose.

If you are having difficulty allowing yourself to feel sadness for the abused or neglected child that you were, I encourage you to reach out for help. A professional psychotherapist will work with you to bring down the walls in a safe, supportive environment.

2. Find safe, constructive ways to release your anger and pain concerning your childhood abuse (see pages 135–139).

3. Confront your abuser or abusers (not necessarily in person) with your anger and pain (refer to information in this chapter).

4. Resolve your relationship with your abusers in some way.

   While healthy, constructive anger can be your way out of your past, blame keeps you stuck in it. Many people have difficulty moving away from blame and toward forgiveness. They insist they need an apology or at the very least an acknowledgment of the fact that they were hurt or damaged before they can forgive. Although apologies can be tremendously healing, an apology or acknowledgment are not always forthcoming, especially in cases of parental abuse or neglect. Holding on to your anger and blame will not only keep you stuck in the past, but it will imbue all your present and future relationships with hostility and distrust.

   While not everyone can forgive his parents for their mistreatment of him as a child, many in recovery feel this is the only way to truly move on. Allowing yourself to acknowledge and release your anger in constructive ways is the first step. The next step is to develop empathy for those who hurt you. For example, by learning more about your parents' background, you may come to understand why they treated you as they did. Many of us know very little about the forces that shaped our parents' lives. If this is your situation, I urge you to spend some time discovering more about your parents' histories. Others, including myself, have gained empathy for those who harmed them by recognizing that they, too, have hurt people in similar ways.

The repetition compulsion can work in another interesting way: there is a spiritual aspect to our attempt at undoing our past. Our need for closure concerning our parents is so profound that we will go to any length to gain it. Sometimes closure can only be accomplished by acknowledging the damage done by our parents and releasing our anger, other times it can only be achieved by forgiving them. I was enraged at my mother for many years. I expressed this rage in many ways—often directly toward her. I fought with her, I stayed away from her for long periods of time, and I worked on my anger in therapy. But I wasn't able to gain closure with her—I wasn't able to forgive her and get on with my life. Forgiveness only came when I recognized how much I had become like her. The insights I received from noticing our similarities provided me with the empathy toward her I had been lacking. This empathy led to forgiveness. As bizarre as this might sound to some, I believe I would have never been able to forgive my mother if I had not become abusive myself.

Step Four: Admit to Your Partner That You Have Been Emotionally Abusive

While it is difficult to admit to yourself that you have been emotionally abusive, admitting it to your partner may seem impossible. This is especially true for those who have difficulty admitting when they are wrong. If you are a proud person who finds it hard to acknowledge when you've made a mistake and who covers up any weakness or vulnerability with a mask of bravado, admitting that you've been abusive may be the hardest thing you ever have to do.

Isn't admitting it to myself enough, you might ask? *Since I'm working on stopping my abusive behavior why should I have to tell my partner about it? She'll see the end results; isn't that all that's important?*

Admitting to your partner that you have been emotionally abusive will serve several purposes. First of all, it will help you continue to come out of denial. Dealing with the fact that you've been abusive can be so painful and so shame-inducing that you may constantly be tempted to minimize the damage you've caused or talk yourself out of facing up to it. By admitting it to your partner, you make it harder to deny it in the future.

You also owe it to your partner to admit that you have been emotionally abusive. She's been suffering from the effects of your behavior for some time now, and she may or may not realize it is abusive. If she doesn't understand that she has been emotionally abused, she deserves to know. She needs to be able to put a name to what she has been enduring, and she needs to be able to stop thinking she's crazy or that she's been imagining it all along. She needs to know so she can get some help for the debilitating effects of the abuse. Even if she has known she was being emotionally abused, she needs you to admit it to confirm her feelings and perceptions. And in many cases, she may need confirmation so she can stop blaming herself for all the relationship problems and for your abusive behavior.

Finally, you need to admit that you've been emotionally abusing your partner because you need to take responsibility for your actions. Don't hedge. Don't minimize. Owning up to your behavior and taking one hundred percent responsibility for it will be good for your self-respect and your soul.

How should you go about admitting your abusiveness? I suggest you do it as directly and in as straightforward a manner as possible. Don't beat around the bush; don't just try to slip in into the conversation casually. Admitting that you have been emotionally abusive is an important step for you and for your partner, so give it the respect and significance it deserves.

Tell your partner you have something important to tell her or him or make an appointment to talk when you won't be distracted. Face your partner and look her directly in the eyes if you can. If you find that this is just too hard to do, write her a letter. Whether you tell your partner or write it in a letter, make sure you include all the following:

- A clear statement acknowledging that you have been emotionally abusive

- Specific examples of your abusive behavior or attitude

- A statement of regret and remorse for your abusive behavior or attitude and a promise to work on changing

Be careful that you don't blame your partner in any way for your own behavior. Take full responsibility for your actions. You may explain to your partner why it is that you feel you became abusive, but you still need to acknowledge that it is you and you alone who is responsible for your behavior and for changing your behavior.

Believe me, I know this will be difficult. But it is beyond a doubt the single most important step you can take in your own healing and the healing of your relationship. It is also the most loving, unselfish thing you can do for your partner, and it will help her tremendously in her own recovery.

Step Five: Apologize to Your Partner and Work on Developing Empathy for Her and for Others

In the previous step, you were asked to acknowledge to your partner that your behavior has sometimes been abusive. The next step is for you to apologize for that behavior. Apologizing to your partner for your abusive behavior or attitudes will not only be healing for her, but for you as well.

EXERCISE: *Develop Empathy*

Before you can give a meaningful apology to your partner—an apology that will be truly healing to both of you—you must first develop some empathy for your partner.

1. Start by imagining how your partner must have felt when you treated her the way you did. Do you think she felt hurt? Angry? Afraid? Disappointed?

2. Now think about the effects your abusive behavior had on your partner's self-esteem. Can you understand how your words or actions damaged her self-image?

3. If you denied responsibility for certain actions or tried to make your partner doubt her perceptions, can you imagine how this would have affected her?

4. If you continually tried to control or dominate your partner, can you understand how trapped she must have felt?

5. How do you imagine it must have felt to live with you? Can you imagine how hopeless she must have felt at times? Can you imagine how much she must have hated you and hated herself for not being able to leave you?

If you have difficulty putting yourself in your partner's place, don't get discouraged. Keep trying. The more you work on it, the more empathy you will develop. Here are some suggestions to help you:

- Ask her to tell you how your behavior affected her and really listen, no matter how difficult it is.

- Try pretending you are your partner and talk out loud about how the situation affected you.

- Write about the situation from your partner's point of view.

HOW TO GIVE A MEANINGFUL APOLOGY

A meaningful apology consists of what I call the three *R*s of apology—regret, responsibility, and remedy. Unless all three of these elements are present, the other person will sense that something is missing in your apology, and he or she will feel shortchanged. Let's take a look at each element in more detail:

- *Regret—a statement of regret for having caused the hurt and damage to the other person.* This includes an expression of empathy toward the other person, including an acknowledgment of the hurt and damage that you caused the other person.

  Having empathy for the person you hurt or angered is the most important part of your apology. When you truly have empathy, the other person will feel it. Your apology will wash over him like a healing balm. If you don't have empathy, your apology will sound and feel empty.

- *Responsibility—an acceptance of responsibility for your actions.* This means not blaming anyone else for what you did and not making excuses for your actions but instead accepting full responsibility for what you did and for the consequences of your actions.

- *Remedy—a statement of your willingness to take action to remedy the situation.* This takes place either by promising not to repeat the action, promising to work toward not making the same mistake again, stating how you are going to remedy the situation (e.g., go to therapy), or making restitution for the damages you caused.

Apologizing to your partner for abusing her can be insulting unless you offer reassurances such as "It will never happen again because I'm now aware that my behavior is abusive," "I know where my abusiveness came from, and I've learned more constructive ways of releasing my anger and stress," or "I'm going to work on stopping my abusiveness by going into therapy."

Step Six: Learn and Practice Ways to Identify and Constructively Release Your Anger, Pain, and Stress

One of the main reasons why you have become abusive is that you do not know how to handle your anger, pain, and stress. In order to prevent future abuse you must find constructive ways of releasing pent-up anger and pain and coping with stress.

ANGER

Anger is at the core of most abusive behavior. Even though you may not be aware of it, you are more than likely still angry at your parents or others who neglected or emotionally, physically, or sexually abused you as a child. Because you haven't acknowledged your anger or learned to deal with it in constructive, appropriate ways, it lies dormant inside you. This repressed or suppressed anger is triggered when your partner or others do something that reminds you of how you were treated as a child. For example, if your partner doesn't ask your opinion about whether she should do something but goes ahead and does it without talking to you, you may believe your feelings are not being considered or that others are controlling your life, just as you felt as a child. You may or may not be consciously aware that this is why you are angry. All you know is that you feel ignored or controlled, and so you lash out at your partner for making you feel this way. You accuse her of not caring about you, of being selfish, or of being controlling. You may punish her by giving her the silent treatment. Or you may insist that in the future she has to ask you before she decides to do something (thereby becoming controlling yourself).

Differentiating between healthy and unhealthy anger. Many people think of anger as a negative emotion. But anger in and of itself is neither a positive nor a negative emotion. It is the way we handle our anger—what we do with it—that makes it negative or positive. For example, when we use our anger to motivate us to make changes in our life or to make changes to dysfunctional systems, anger becomes a very positive emotion. But when we express our anger through aggressive or passive-aggressive ways (such as getting even or gossiping), it becomes a negative emotion.

Another way to differentiate between healthy and unhealthy anger is to determine whether your anger is appropriate to the situation or irrational and excessive. There are distinct disadvantages to excessive, irrational anger. These include:

- Others usually react negatively to it.
- It frequently increases frustration rather than releasing it.
- It causes you to lash out at others, including those you love.
- It can lead to antisocial acts.
- It can cause you to become obsessed with people and to become paralyzed with anger.
- It leads to more anger.

EXERCISE: *Take Charge of Your Anger*

You are the only one who can manage your anger. Begin by becoming an expert about your personal anger reactions. Answering the following questions will be a good start:

1. What causes you to feel tense or agitated? Think back to specific situations that caused you to feel agitated or angry in the recent past. Do you see a pattern?
2. What situations tend to trigger angry reactions?
3. What are your beliefs and perceptions about how others should or should not treat you?
4. How do you typically express your anger?
5. What do you gain or lose from expressing your anger in this way?

EXERCISE: *Discover the Belief under Your Anger*

The next time you become angry at your partner ask yourself the following questions. For example, if it makes you angry when your partner talks on the phone with a friend or family member, ask yourself:

- *Why does this make me angry? Am I angry because I feel ignored? Because I want my partner's undivided attention?* Is it upsetting to hear her laugh with her friend because you don't ever hear her laugh that way with you?

- *What am I feeling under the anger? Am I feeling hurt? Afraid? Guilty?* Using the above example, perhaps you are feeling hurt because she doesn't laugh like that when she is with you. Maybe this frightens you because it makes you think she isn't really happy with you and she's going to leave you. Or maybe it makes you feel guilty because you know you give her a hard time and you realize she isn't very happy with you. Or perhaps you feel hurt because her talking to someone else for long periods of time makes you feel you are not important to your partner. You don't get to spend much time with her, and you wish she'd tell her friend she would talk to her later.

- *Does it remind me of anything from the past?* Maybe you're angry because it reminds you of how your mother used to spend hours talking with her friends on the phone or around the kitchen table instead of paying attention to you. Or maybe it isn't that literal. Maybe it just reminds you of all the times your mother was busy doing something else besides being with you (e.g., going to bars, spending time with your stepfather).

- *What is the belief that caused the anger?* Is it the belief that if your partner really loves you, she should prefer to spend time with you? Or do you believe it is rude for your partner to interrupt her time with you to talk on the phone with someone else?

EXERCISE: *Anger Journal*

Start keeping a log or journal in which you record each incident that occurs that causes you to feel tense, agitated, or angry. Whenever possible, try to discover:

1. The reason for your anger

2. The feeling underneath the anger

3. How the current situation connects with your past

4. The belief that caused the anger

HEALTHY WAYS OF DEALING WITH YOUR ANGER

The following models have been used successfully by many people to manage anger constructively. See which model works for you.

The assertive model.

- Identify the specific *behavior* in the other person that upsets you.

- Decide if the issue or behavior is worth fighting over.

- Pick a time that is convenient for both you and your partner and express your desire for a discussion.

- Express your point of view using an assertive model of giving feedback. Example: *When:* "When you take time away from me by talking on the phone with your friends . . ." *The effects are:* "I feel hurt and angry." *I would prefer:* "I would prefer it if you'd tell her you'll call her back later or if you would limit the call to only a few minutes."

- Negotiate a resolution to the problem once you feel the other person understands the issue and your feelings. For example, perhaps you and your partner can agree that she will limit her phone calls when you and she are actively involved with one another (e.g., talking, eating, cuddling on the couch) but that she should feel free to talk as long as she wants when you are in separate rooms or are involved in separate activities.

- Make up. Let go of your anger and allow yourself to forgive your partner. Forgiveness involves acknowledging that the other person cannot be perfect. While you may never completely approve of your partner or the way she behaves at times, you can accept the reality that she is who she is and that more than likely her actions are not deliberate attempts to hurt you. Ideally, both you and your partner will at least try to change some behaviors to avoid future conflict over the same issue, but you can't expect your partner to change who she is for you.

- Ask yourself what you learned about yourself and your partner from this process.

The cognitive model.   The cognitive model is based on the work of experts such as Ellis, Burns, and Freeman. It centers on the following concept:

Unhealthy anger is often triggered by irrational, narcissistic, and unrealistic expectations or beliefs that we have about other people, the world, and ourselves in general. Examples of such beliefs include:

- I must do well and be approved of—otherwise I'm no damn good.

- Those that I associate with must treat me considerately, kindly, and respectfully—otherwise they are no damn good.

- The conditions under which I live (family, employer, etc.) must be exactly the way I want them to be—otherwise it's catastrophic.

By challenging/changing the irrational beliefs that caused your anger, you may find that you tend to become and stay angry less often.

TECHNIQUES FOR MANAGING AND PREVENTING ANGER

The following techniques have also proved highly effective in managing and preventing anger:

- Give up shoulds and wants that are narcissistic or otherwise dysfunctional.

- Acknowledge anger but learn constructive ways of releasing it.

- Practice distracting techniques such as leaving the situation, taking constructive action, counting to ten, saying the word "calm" to yourself.

- Work on becoming more tolerant of others.

- Don't take yourself so seriously. Use humor and see the absurdity of the situation.

- Be your own critical parent: "I'm acting like a narcissistic two-year-old. I need to grow up."

- Practice empathy skills: "Walk in the other person's shoes."

- Practice reframing (thinking of the situation in an entirely different way): "He must be pretty insecure to have done this to me. He's really pathetic."

- Address depression or other problems that are being masked by anger/rage.

- Read books on anger management.

- Use imagery: "Imagine the worst possible scenario, let yourself feel the anger, and then imagine all that you will do is express your point of view without becoming aggressive or otherwise inappropriate."

- Practice forgiveness, not the acts, but the people.

- Practice behavioral techniques such as assertiveness training, active listening, use of positive reinforcement when the other person responds appropriately.

- Look for other pleasures in life when you feel angry or deprived.

- Practice gratitude.

THE PAIN UNDER YOUR ANGER

Underneath your anger, your need to control, your need to blame, your impatience with and intolerance of others' weaknesses is a great deal of pain. It is the pain you experienced as a child when you were neglected, abandoned, abused, victimized, or bullied. In order to stop your abusive behavior, you'll need to uncover this pain.

The reason those who are weak, afraid, vulnerable, or incompetent bother you so much is they remind you of a denied and rejected part of yourself. When you were a child you felt weak, afraid, and vulnerable, but there may have been no one there to comfort you. Your parents may have been too busy to notice you needed comforting, or you may have reached out for comfort only to be rebuffed with comments like "You're too big to get on Mommy's lap" or "Big boys (or girls) don't cry. Be a man (or woman)." Facing your vulnerable feelings all alone may have felt too frightening, and so you built up a defensive wall to hide behind. To the outside world, you may have appeared to be strong and confident, but this was only a facade to cover up your real feelings of vulnerability. You may have become so good at pretending to be strong and invulnerable that you even fooled yourself. Soon you forgot what your real self was like.

The only time you are reminded of these softer feelings is when you experience them in someone else. But this reminder is not a welcome one. It doesn't feel good—in fact, it may be quite painful emotionally (although often on an unconscious level). You may become angry with the person who reminds you of these feelings. You hate yourself for feeling them and hate the other person for having them. You see your real self reflected back at you, and you don't like what you see.

In order to break down the protective wall that you built around yourself, you may need to seek the assistance of a caring professional who will provide a safe environment in which you can revisit your childhood.

MANAGING YOUR STRESS AND YOUR AROUSAL

Many people become emotionally, verbally, or physically abusive because their arousal level is high. In order to reduce your arousal level, you need to learn some general relaxation techniques. I've recommended some books on stress reduction at the end of the book, but here are a few suggestions to get you started:

1. Focus on a word or image that will relax you. For example, say the word "Calm" to yourself over and over. Visualize a scene that is relaxing to you (the ocean, the mountains).

2. Distract yourself.

3. Get involved with a creative activity, especially one that involves using your hands.

4. Learn and practice meditation or yoga.

5. Practice deep breathing.

Although all the above ideas and strategies for releasing anger and stress can be quite beneficial, many abusive partners need outside help when learning to deal more constructively with their anger. I strongly recommend either anger management courses or individual or group psychotherapy.

Step Seven: Identify Your Triggers and False Beliefs

Although it can be said that some people have "abusive personalities," most people become abusive because one of their triggers or hot buttons was pushed. Triggers are suppressed or repressed fears, insecurities, anger, resentments, or regrets that cause automatic and often intense emotional reactions when activated. These intense reactions can be abusive in themselves, can be experienced as abusive by your partner, or can, in turn, trigger abusive reactions within you. By identifying the specific situations, actions, words, or events that trigger these emotional reactions, you can begin to anticipate and manage them better and avoid some of your abusive behavior.

COMMON TRIGGERS FOR ABUSIVE PARTNERS

- *Being ignored or rejected.* Often those who become abusive are triggered when they feel ignored or rejected. This is most likely due to the fact that they were neglected or abandoned when they were children.

- *Envy.* Some are triggered by feelings of envy. Whenever someone close to them has something good happen to them, it makes them feel bad about themselves. This may trigger memories of being a less-favored child or of having a parent who ignored their needs.

- *Shame.* Those who were heavily shamed as children or adolescents are often triggered by any treatment or attitude from others that appears to be disapproving, critical, judging, or rejecting.

HARRISON: IF I FEEL BAD, YOU SHOULD, TOO

Often an abusive partner strikes out at his mate because he is feeling bad about himself. He may do it as a way of fending off shame or guilt at something he's done or almost as a way of saying, "I feel bad about myself, so you have to feel bad, too." This often happens when an abusive partner has a mate who tends to be cheerful, who is well liked, or who is highly accomplished. This was the case with Harrison:

> My partner, Brad, is one of those cheery types of people, and it drives me crazy. I'll come home from a bad day at work, and there he is twittering around the house, singing and being cheerful. It really bothers me. It's bad enough that I've had a rough day, but to go home and be faced with all that cheeriness feels like he's rubbing it in my face. I always get angry with him and say something horrible to him, and of course this always brings him down—which is exactly what I wanted to do. But then he always looks so devastated and so confused, and I end up feeling bad that I was so cruel. This doesn't seem to stop me the next time, though.

My suggestion to Harrison was that the next time he had a bad day at work he not go directly home. Instead, I suggested he go for a long walk or go to the gym for a game of racquetball, where he could work off some of his anger and frustration before going home. If that didn't work and he was still in a bad mood, I suggested he call home first and warn Brad that he is in a bad mood. With that forewarning, Brad could choose to leave the house for a while or to stay out of Harrison's way.

These strategies seemed to work fairly well, but I also suggested to Harrison that he look into himself to discover why he was in a bad mood so often at the end of the day. We talked about what was going on at work, and it turned out that Harrison had a controlling and arrogant boss who set unreachable goals for the company and then blamed his staff when they fell short of his goals. "I don't think he's ever given me credit for anything I've done right, only criticism for the things that go wrong," Harrison explained to me, his face red with anger.

This sounded eerily familiar to me. If I wasn't mistaken, Harrison had used the exact phrases "He never gives me credit for anything I did right. All he did was criticize me when I did something wrong," when referring to his father. Harrison originally started therapy with me because he wanted to work on his relationship with his father, who had rejected him when he discovered Harrison was gay. This had just been the last in a series of rejections all through Harrison's childhood.

When I reminded Harrison of how often he'd used these same words in reference to his father, he was stunned. "Oh, my God. I'm working for my father!" he exclaimed, shaking his head back and forth in disbelief. Why didn't I see this before? No wonder I'm always in a bad mood."

Our session, and the insights he'd achieved because of it, catapulted Harrison to take some action. Within weeks he began looking for another job, and while it took some time to find the right one, just knowing he was leaving made him feel like he had gained some real control over his own life. And although he still had some bad days, because of his new insight, he was able to talk about his feelings with Brad instead of dumping them on him.

Unfortunately, most people are unaware of the feelings that cause them to become emotionally abusive. Your anger journal can help you identify your triggers and your false beliefs and help you gain insight into your behavior.

- *Keep a log of each incident of emotional abuse.* Ask yourself, "What is it about me that caused me to respond in that manner?"

For example, you may find that one of the things that triggers your anger is when things seem unfair or when you feel you have been treated unfairly. Instead of constantly becoming upset over this, it might be far better to work on accepting the fact that there is inequity in the world and concentrate on developing coping skills when you are treated unfairly.

SUGGESTIONS AND STRATEGIES FOR SPECIFIC TYPES OF ABUSE

Control/domination.   The best advice I can give those of you who need to control or dominate your partner is this: You feel you need to control your partner because you feel out of control yourself. The more control you have of yourself, the less control you will need to have of your partner (and others)—therefore, work on gaining real control of your life.

Negativity/criticism.   If you have a tendency to be negative and to only notice your partner's mistakes, oversights, and inadequacies, try this exercise at the end of each day.

EXERCISE: *An Attitude of Gratitude*

1. Before you go to sleep at night, think about the good things that happened that day. If you start to focus only on the things that went wrong, bring your mind back to the things that went right. As one of my clients shared with me, "This really helped me to get some perspective. My tendency is to only remember the things that went wrong, the things that didn't go the way I wanted them to go. But when I stopped myself and said, 'Wait, there has to be some good,' it reminded me of how often things work out and go smoothly."

2. Think of at least three things that your partner did that were either caring, considerate, or thoughtful toward you or someone you care about (such as your parents or your children).

3. Now think of at least three reasons to be grateful for your partner. For example, "I'm grateful because she is still with me," "I'm grateful he's stopped drinking," "I'm grateful that she's so patient."

Unreasonable expectations.   This type of abuse is caused by focusing more attention outside yourself than you do on yourself. Start paying more attention to what you are doing or not doing to make the relationship work. Start focusing more on changing those things about yourself that keep you from meeting your expectations of yourself.

Possessiveness.   We cannot own or possess another person. The more you attempt to hold your partner close to you, the more he or she will pull away—it's a law of nature. We humans, like all creatures, need to have our freedom. We need to be able to have free choice about whether we want to be close to someone, not to be forced to be close when we don't feel like it. When our partner tries to force us to be close when we don't feel like it, we not only pull away and begin to feel like a caged animal, but we begin to resent our partner. The following are some examples of possessive behavior:

- Frequently asking your partner if he loves you

- Frequently telling your partner you love her with the expectation that she will tell you the same

- Frequently telling your partner that you know he doesn't love you or doesn't love you as much as you love him (unless you play a game with this and it is mutual, e.g., saying, "I love you more than you love me," in a playful way)

- Insisting on a hug or kiss when your partner doesn't feel like it or when she is busy with something or someone else

- Insisting on having sex when your partner doesn't feel like it

- Assuming that your partner doesn't love you if he won't have sex with you

- Trying to make your partner feel guilty if he or she doesn't want to have sex as often as you do

- Wanting to know where your partner is and what she is doing at all times

- Constantly accusing your partner of being unfaithful

- Checking up on your partner to make sure he isn't cheating on you

- Hanging all over your partner at a party or gathering so that everyone knows she's with you

EXERCISE: *Stop Pulling at Your Partner*

To prove the validity of the idea that the more you pull at your partner, the more she or he will pull away, try these strategies for a week.

1. The next time you feel compelled to pull at your partner—either by asking if he loves you, by pressuring him for sex, or by calling him to make sure he's at home—restrain yourself. Remind yourself of the way he has negatively reacted to this pressure in the past. If you need reassurance that he loves you, think about one of the ways that he has shown he loves you recently.

2. If you are normally the one who initiates sex and you are unhappy because your partner doesn't like to have sex as often as you do, make a commitment to yourself that you will not initiate sex for a month. I know this is a long time, but it is necessary in order to relieve your partner of the feeling that she is constantly being pressured for sex. A month's time will also give your partner a chance to miss having sex with you and free her up to be able to be the one who initiates it.

If you have been emotionally abusing your partner by holding on too tight or by trying to possess her or him, you will need to work on two major issues: your self-esteem and your trust. We'll discuss how you can improve your self-esteem in chapter 12, "Continuing to Recover." As for trust, the best advice I can give you is that trust has more to do with you than with your partner. If you trust yourself to take care of yourself under any and all circumstances, you don't need to worry about whether you can trust your partner or not.

RECOMMENDED FILMS

This Boy's Life

Radio Flyer

Mommie Dearest (an example of emotional and physical abuse by a controlling mother)

CHAPTER 7

Action Steps
for the Abusive Couple

Control is the ultimate villain in destroying intimacy.
We cannot share freely unless we are equal.
JOHN BRADSHAW

Respect ... is appreciation of the separateness of
the other person, of the ways in which he or she is unique.
ANNIE GOTTLIEB

Experiencing emotional abuse or neglect in childhood severely limits a person's ability to maintain healthy relationships in adulthood. One emotionally abusive relationship, especially if it is with a parent or other caretaker, a sibling, an authority figure such as a teacher, an employer, or an intimate partner can affect all future relationships. Those with a history of emotional abuse experience severe handicaps in relationships, including a fear of intimacy or commitment, a fear of abandonment, a tendency to blame others or be extremely critical, and either a tendency to be clingy and possessive or aloof and self-absorbed. They also tend to view their partner more as an enemy than an ally and to focus far more on what their partner does wrong in the relationship than what she does right.

Those who have been emotionally abused in childhood are drawn to each other like moths to a flame. Each is bent on reinventing childhood relationships, either out of a desire to resolve them or simply because they are drawn to what is familiar. With both parties lacking in the ability to maintain a healthy relationship, these couplings are destined to be problematic. Most often we find that one partner takes on the role of the abuser while the other takes on the role of the victim, but even when no one plays the role of the abuser, dysfunctional responses by one or both partners can make the relationship extremely difficult.

In addition to working on your individual problems and your part in the abuse, you and your partner must work together to stop the abuse that has been destroying your relationship. This chapter provides you the structure and the opportunity to do just that. By working together on the common goal of stopping the emotional abuse in your relationship, you will strengthen your bond with one another and increase the likelihood that you will be successful. Even though you will each need to continue your individual work, your work as a couple is just as important if you plan on staying together.

This chapter is specifically written for you couples who emotionally abuse each other—either because you constantly push each other's buttons, because one partner has begun retaliating against the abuse of the other, or because you have both been emotionally abusing each other since the beginning of the relationship. It can also apply to situations in which one abuses and the other doesn't, but if this is the case, make certain that you both remain clear that the abusive partner is solely responsible for his or her abusive behavior.

In order to get the maximum benefit from this chapter, I encourage you and your partner to read it together and to do the suggested exercises together. This will serve as the closest thing possible to couples counseling, with the added bonus that you will be working on the abusive aspects of your relationship specifically.

As I did in the two previous chapters, in this chapter I present a step-by-step program for you and your partner to follow.

Not every couple will be ready to begin the program at the time of the first reading. You and your partner may choose to return to this chapter after finishing the entire book or after you have each completed more of your individual work. Just knowing this chapter is available when you are ready may be a comfort to each of you.

Stop Blaming Each Other

Before you begin this chapter and the work it will require, you must agree to stop blaming each other. If you can agree that you each play a role in the emotional abuse and/or that you have each emotionally abused one another, then there is no need to continue rehashing who did what to whom. Blame is different from responsibility. When we continually blame someone, we stay stuck in the problem instead of focusing on the solution. It is also important to realize that blaming someone is different from requiring the other person to take responsibility for his actions. There will be an opportunity later on in the chapter for each of you to take responsibility for your actions and to apologize for the hurt you caused each other. For now, instead of maintaining an adversarial position, you must begin to view each other as allies in a cause—that cause being the salvaging of your relationship.

The same holds true of those situations in which only one of you emotionally abused the other. The partner who was abused must be willing at this point to stop blaming her partner for abusing her. This does not mean that you must forgive your partner at this time, nor that you need to forget what he has done. It just means you agree to stop bringing up the abuse—that you stop throwing it in his face, so to speak—and that you agree to move on in the relationship. This doesn't mean, however, that you stop bringing abusive behavior to your partner's attention.

Partners who share the fact that they have each had an emotionally abusive past can be tremendously instrumental in healing each other. Through a series of exercises, I will teach both of you how to have empathy toward each other and specific ways you can support and encourage each other's healing. Once you have gained the kind of understanding that empathy can bring, both of you will be more able to lower your defenses and begin to rebuild trust in each other.

Defending ourselves is ultimately what emotional abuse is all about. The person who is being emotionally abusive is actually defending himself or herself from one of the following:

- Vulnerability
- Shame/embarrassment
- Admitting he was wrong
- Appearing weak
- Fear
- Guilt

Once you are able to lower your defenses with each other and to show how you really feel, you will be able to stop viewing your mate as the enemy and start seeing each other as a true partner. Then, instead of mindlessly repeating the same old patterns over and over, you can begin to interrupt your usual patterns and discover new, healthier ways of dealing with each other.

QUESTIONNAIRE: *Assessing Your Relationship*

Before you begin the program, I suggest you assess the expectations each of you has and determine whether or not you each believe you can save your relationship. To aid in this process, I have provided a quiz that I suggest you each take, either in separate rooms or at separate times. Once you've each completed the quiz, you can compare notes.

1. Do you hold out much hope that your relationship can improve?

2. Do you hold out much hope that there can be an end to the emotional abuse in the relationship?

3. Do you have hope that your partner can change her behavior?

4. Do you have hope that you can change yours?

5. Do you believe your partner is willing to do what is necessary to heal his past?

6. Are you willing to do what is necessary to heal your past?

7. Do you have hope that you and your partner can change the dynamics in the relationship that caused the abuse?

8. Do you believe your partner is committed to changing the dynamics in the relationship?

9. Are you willing to commit to changing the dynamics?

10. Are you willing to stop blaming your partner for all the problems in the relationship?

11. Do you believe your partner is willing to stop blaming you for all the problems?

If you or your partner answered seven or more of these questions with yes, the prognosis for your relationship becoming far more healthy is very good. Seven or more yes answers indicates that you have a lot of faith in both yourself and your partner to turn your relationship around, and this faith can influence the outcome. This does not mean that just by believing you can change the relationship, you will make it happen; it will take a great deal of work on both of your parts. But it does indicate a positive outlook and a belief that both you and your partner are willing to do the work required, and this is very positive, indeed.

If you or your partner answered the majority of questions with no, it indicates that you do not have much hope that your relationship can really change or that you don't have much faith in either your own or your partner's willingness to do the work required to change. If this is the case, I urge you to sit down with your partner and discuss your feelings and your reservations. If either or both of you have already given up hope that you can stop the abuse, then there is little reason to go on trying to save the relationship. You might be better off being very honest with each other and ending the relationship right now.

The Program

Step One: Share Your Histories

The first thing you will need to do is to learn more about one another's histories and to examine your relationship closely to see how your histories dovetail—or merge. You learned how important your childhood history is and how your individual histories set you up for an abusive relationship in chapter 4. Since it is highly likely that both of you were either neglected, abandoned, or emotionally, physically, or sexually abused as children, knowing each other's history will help you recognize the origins of your behaviors and attitudes. This does not mean that understanding why your partner has been abusive should excuse his behavior. But knowing the origins of the other's abusive behavior will help you to bond with one another in a more significant way and develop more empathy for each other.

EXERCISE: *Develop Empathy for Each Other*

This exercise will help you to develop more empathy for one another and to better understand and respect each other's triggers. If you haven't already done so, sit down together and share your childhood histories. Even if you shared your stories when you first got together, it is important to do so again since you are hopefully far more aware of your history and how it has affected you after reading this book. Here are some suggestions for how to go about it:

1. Set aside sufficient time to share your entire story with your partner. Your story does not need to be a chronological retelling of your entire childhood but should include all the following:

   • Any experiences of neglect

   • Any experiences of abandonment

   • Any experiences of abuse—emotional, physical, or sexual abuse

   • Any other experiences that you feel set you up to be in an emotionally abusive relationship (e.g., the fact that one parent emotionally abused the other, etc.)

2. It is usually best for one person at a time to tell his or her story (unless you want to set aside an entire weekend for the sole purpose of sharing your stories). It is simply too time-consuming and too emotionally draining for both of you to try to tell your stories in one night, for example. Also, when only one person

shares at a particular time, it makes it easier for the other partner to devote his or her full attention to listening and being there for his or her partner.

3. If you're the partner who is not sharing, your job is to listen as closely as you can to what your partner is saying. If you'd like to, and it doesn't seem too distracting, you can take a few notes. Try to listen with what is called "an open heart," meaning that you suspend all judgment about your partner and that you listen as empathetically as possible. Try to put yourself in your partner's place, imaging what she was feeling at the time.

4. As your partner shares his or her story, listen without interrupting or breaking in to say that the same thing happened to you or how awful it is that this happened. Just listen. If your partner breaks down and cries, hold him. And it certainly is appropriate when there is a break in the conversation for you to say something about how bad you feel that this happened to your partner. Just don't interrupt his flow of speaking and thinking to do so.

5. If either one of you is uncomfortable sharing his or her story verbally, you can write down your stories and let your partner read what you've written.

6. After you've each had a chance to share your stories, sit down together and discuss your reactions to the sharing. Again, set aside enough time for this so that you don't feel distracted or rushed. Include in your discussion all the following:

- Your emotional reaction to each other's stories—including how it made you feel to realize that this happened to your partner

- The similarities and differences in your past experiences

- Any connections either of you made concerning what happened in your childhood and what has occurred in your present relationship

- Any similarities either of you see between your parents and your partner or your original abusers and your partner

Don't let this turn into a situation where one of you starts to psycho-analyze the other. If your partner does not see the connection that you are making, let it drop. You can't force her to recognize patterns.

EXERCISE: *How Did Your Parents Interact?*

Another aspect of sharing your histories is to discuss how your parents treated each other. In addition to replicating the way we were treated as children, we often repeat the ways our parents interacted with each other. The following questionnaire will help you identify any patterns you may have established based on your parents' treatment of each other. I recommend that you each answer the questions separately and then discuss your results.

1. Did your parents discuss problems rationally, or did they tend to blow up at each other?

2. Did they express emotions easily, or did they hold in their feelings?

3. Did one or both of your parents tend to blame each other for their problems?

4. Did your parents fight often?

5. Did one or both of your parents give each other the silent treatment?

6. Did one or both of your parents yell at each other?

7. Did your parents punish each other?

8. Did one or both of your parents emotionally abuse each other?

Step Two: Discover and Acknowledge Your Part in the Problem

This step is a natural outcome of sharing your histories with one another. For example, if you were emotionally abused by a supercriti-cal parent who had unreasonable expectations of you, and you have repeated this pattern in your relationship with your partner by constantly finding fault in everything he does and by never being pleased, it is important that you acknowledge how this has contributed to the problems in the relationship. Even though your partner may have contributed to the problems by being passive-aggressive (expressing anger in underhanded, passive ways) and deliberately doing things that will anger you, you need to recognize and acknowledge that if you hadn't been so demanding, he might not have been so passive-aggressive.

Even if the only thing you did to contribute to the abuse was to be too complacent, giving in to your partner's demands even though they were unreasonable, or blaming yourself for your partner's problems, you need to acknowledge this to yourself and to your partner. This does not mean that you take responsibility for your partner's abusiveness, however. That is totally your partner's responsibility, no one else's.

In order to prepare for this step, I encourage each of you to spend time considering the following issues:

- What do I do to contribute to the problems in the relationship?

- What are my expectations of a relationship? Are they realistic?

- What can I do to improve the relationship?

EXERCISE: *Take Responsibility for Your Part in the Abuse*

As you did in the previous step, set aside a time when you can each take responsibility for your part in the emotional abuse. Make sure you provide sufficient time and that you are not disturbed. I suggest you follow this format:

1. Sit facing each other as you each take turns acknowledging your part in the emotional abuse. Try to maintain eye contact as much as possible.

2. When it is your turn, be as specific as possible. For example, if you feel your part was the fact that you made fun of your partner in front of others, belittled his attempts at being romantic, and questioned his masculinity—then say this. If you feel your part in the emotional abuse was the fact that you never forgave her for being attracted to another man and used her indiscretion as an excuse to berate and belittle her constantly, tell her this. If you feel that the fact that you refuse to ever be pleased with your partner no matter how hard he or she tries, admit this to your partner.

3. When it is your partner's turn to acknowledge his part in the emotional abuse, listen with an open heart and don't interrupt. Even if your partner does not say what you want to hear or leaves something out, do not say anything. Try to remember how difficult it is for some people to admit their faults and weaknesses, and if you know that your partner is one of these people, give him credit for what he is able to admit.

4. When your partner is finished, let him know that you appreciate the fact that she was willing to acknowledge his part. If he is the type of person who has a difficult time admitting when he is wrong, let him know that it took a lot of courage to do so.

5. If your partner neglected to acknowledge a behavior or attitude that you feel is emotionally abusive or that contributed to the emotional abuse in the relationship, let him know that you think he left something out that you feel needs to be acknowledged. Depending on the situation, he may tell you that he wants more time to think about it, or he may ask you what it is. If he needs more time, by all means give it to him. Remember, if this was a very difficult step for your partner, he may have been as vulnerable as he is capable of being at the moment. Once he has recuperated from the stress of this step, he may be better able to delve a little deeper inside himself to find the fault you were referring to. It will be far more meaningful and powerful for both of you if he is the one to come up with it instead of you telling him.

   If he asks you what you mean, take this as a sign that he is ready to hear it, and by all means tell him. Just make sure you don't get into an argument over whether he does or does not have this particular attitude or behavior. If he protests or challenges you in any way, simply tell him that this is the way you perceive things and agree to disagree for the time being. Then suggest that you stop there but that you'd appreciate it if he'd think about what you've said at a later time.

Step Three: Apologize for Past Hurts and Agree to Move On

Begin this process by each making a list of all the ways you have emotionally abused your partner. If you need help in doing this, refer to chapter 2 for a list of emotionally abusive behaviors and attitudes. Take as much time as you each need to make your list and make sure that it is as complete as possible.

When you have completed your respective lists, set up a time to share your lists with each other. In situations in which only one partner was abusive, I suggest the abusive partner go first. As with the previous steps, make sure you set aside sufficient time and that you are not disturbed. Taking turns, each partner should follow these instructions:

1. Facing your partner, begin by making a statement such as "I am truly sorry for the things I have done or said that have hurt you or that have contributed to the problems in our relationship. I'd like to read you a list of the specific things I've done that I know were hurtful to you or damaging to our relationship."

2. One by one, read each item from your list.

3. After you have read an item, look up and look directly into your partner's eyes and apologize by saying, "I'm sorry" or "Please forgive me."

Step Four: Discover and Discuss How Your Issues Collide

It is not only important for you each to acknowledge and take responsibility for your part in the emotional abuse but for you to understand how your respective problems feed off each other. The following example will illustrate exactly what I mean.

DEBORAH AND JACOB: INSECURE AND DISTANT

My client Deborah has always been very insecure in her relationship with Jacob. From the very beginning, she wanted to know all about Jacob's past, especially his previous girlfriends. Although he didn't have anything to hide, Jacob felt that his past was his business and found Deborah's questions intrusive.

Jacob complained that from the moment he came home from work, Deborah started asking him questions about how work went. Jacob resented the questions, feeling once again that Deborah was being intrusive, and so he wouldn't answer her or would give only evasive answers. This only made Deborah suspicious. She began to wonder if he was having an affair with someone at work.

Because she is insecure about her appearance, Deborah was always on the lookout to make sure Jacob didn't get within range of other women. When they went to a party, she stayed beside him the entire evening, fearing that if she left his side another woman would snatch him away from her. Jacob reported that he felt like he couldn't breathe around Deborah and didn't even like going to parties anymore because he never felt free to talk to new people when he was around her. When the telephone rang and Jacob answered it, Deborah hovered close by in order to hear the conversation. This really bothered Jacob because he felt like he didn't have any privacy.

As time went by, Jacob began resenting Deborah more and more for what he perceived as intrusive and demanding behavior. "I wish she'd get off my back," he shared with me. "I can't stand her constant questioning and her possessiveness. It makes me want to run as far away from her as I can get."

Deborah, on the other hand, described Jacob as withdrawn, indifferent, and sarcastic. "It's like pulling teeth to get him to tell me anything. He doesn't open up about how he's feeling or what he wants or anything. And God forbid he ever tells me he loves me. No wonder I'm so insecure."

As it turned out, both Deborah and Jacob were being emotionally abusive to each other, and yet neither was doing so consciously or intentionally. To make matters worse, their respective behaviors intensified each other's responses. Deborah's insecurity was causing her to be overbearing, suspicious, possessive, demanding, and emotionally suffocating. In response, Jacob had become more and more evasive, withdrawn, and withholding. Deborah's reaction to his withdrawal was to become even more demanding, agitated, and argumentative. And instead of being able to let Deborah know how smothered he felt and to insist she provide him some space and that she honor his boundaries, Jacob either withdrew even more or lashed out in sarcastic remarks. When he did this, Deborah would become sullen and sarcastic in return.

Deborah came into the relationship as an insecure person. Jacob entered the relationship as someone who was very private and somewhat distant. There were good reasons for each of their behaviors, both stemming back to their childhood. Deborah was insecure because her mother was unable to emotionally bond with her when she was a child. Jacob was distant because his father was emotionally distant from him when he was growing up. The important thing here is to realize that although they each entered the relationship with their own issues, their interactions with one another intensified their individual problems. Had Deborah been with a partner who wasn't quite as distant as Jacob, her insecurities might not have been as big a problem. Had Jacob become involved with someone who shared his need for privacy and space, his tendency to be distant would likely not have reached the proportions that it eventually did. This is how patterns dovetail, how couples end up pushing each other's buttons and exacerbating each other's problems.

Step Five: Share Your Triggers

As mentioned earlier in the book, sometimes emotional abuse occurs in a relationship because each partner is pushing the buttons of his or her mate. Usually this happens without either partner ever realizing what is going on. For this reason, it is important for you to share your "buttons" or triggers with each other.

LEONARD AND MAGGIE: A MOTHER WHO WAS TOO LOOSE AND A FATHER WHO WAS TOO STRICT

When Leonard was a child, his mother never had time for him. A single mother, she worked all day, and in the evening she went out to bars to meet men, leaving him with a babysitter. "I never knew what man I'd find in my mother's bed when I got up in the morning. Now, whenever my wife wants to go out with her friends at night, I freak out. I ask her not to go, and she accuses me of not trusting her and of trying to smother her. We always get into a big fight and say horrible things to each other. But it's not that I don't trust my wife, it's just that my buttons get pushed. I'm flooded with memories of my mother, and I begin to feel incredibly insecure. I also freak out if I think she looks cheap in any way. If her skirt is too short, I'll say something about it, and this always makes her really mad. My mother used to look like a tramp when she went out, and I know this is what it's about. But Maggie thinks it's the trust issue again."

Incredibly, Leonard had never told Maggie about his experiences with his mother when he was growing up. "It's just not the kind of thing a man talks about, you know. I don't want to sound like I'm a whining victim or something. My wife has already lost respect for me because of my insecurities."

I encouraged Leonard to share the information about his mother with Maggie and, specifically, to share his triggers with her. I explained that unless she knows about his buttons she will continue to push them without realizing it, and they will continue to argue and name-call. He was reluctant at first, but eventually he followed my advice and had a talk with his wife, sharing his history and his buttons.

Maggie was very understanding and relieved to discover the source of Leonard's insecurity. In turn, she shared with Leonard that her father had been unreasonably strict with her and that her buttons were pushed when she thought he was trying to control her as her father had. She even confessed that she sometimes insisted on going out with her friends just because she didn't want to be controlled by Leonard—even when she didn't really want to go.

Once all this was out in the open, things began to change in their relationship. They agreed to be sensitive to each other's triggers and to tell each other when their buttons had been pushed. This seemed to work beautifully for them. While Leonard still felt insecure when his wife went out, he didn't freak out as much. Instead he told her his buttons were pushed, and she became less angry and more understanding of his reaction. She even found that once she understood that Leonard wasn't try-ing to control her, she actually didn't feel like going out as often. The last time I talked to Leonard, he and his wife were getting along much better.

Step Six: Set Boundaries and Limits

In every relationship each partner has certain behaviors that are off limits—behaviors that are unacceptable to her or him. These may be behaviors that act as triggers, behaviors that go against an individual's moral code, or simply behaviors that make her or him uncomfortable. Unfortunately, partners don't always share with each other exactly what these behaviors are. Instead, they have one argument after another; one upset after another each time one of them crosses the boundaries of the other. The same is true for not sharing what their limits are. For example, it might be okay with you if your mate flirts a little when you are at a party. But it isn't okay if he flirts with someone you don't like, someone you consider to be after him, or someone you think is cheap. If you tell your partner it's okay to flirt or communicate this message to him nonverbally (by not getting upset or laughing it off when you catch him, for example) but then get mad when he flirts with someone who is "off-limits," he's bound to feel confused and angry. But if you are clear as to what your limits are—in this case, who is off-limits—he is much more likely to honor them, and if he doesn't, he certainly will understand why you are upset.

EXERCISE: *Getting Clear about Your Boundaries and Limits*

1. On a piece of paper, each of you makes a list of your partner's behaviors that are unacceptable to you; behaviors that upset you, behaviors that push your buttons, or behaviors that are morally unacceptable. For example, your list might include such things as being unfaithful, talking negatively about you to others, making fun of you in front of others, looking through your private papers, or opening your mail.

2. Make another list of what your personal limits are regarding your partner's behavior. For example, you may think it is okay

for your partner to drink alcohol, but because your mother was an alcoholic, you become upset if she drinks more than two drinks. It may be okay if your husband goes to a topless bar at lunch with his friends, but it is not okay if he goes to a strip club where the women become completely nude.

3. At an appropriate time, sit down together and share your lists. Take turns explaining why you have the boundaries and limits you have and ask your partner if she or he will honor these boundaries and limits.

Step Seven: Agree to Disagree and to Walk Away

From my experience working with clients, I have found that those who become abusive tend to believe that in order to be loving and supportive, their partner needs to agree with them. Those who are abused often agree with this belief. But this belief encourages both abusive and victimlike behavior. In order to have an emotionally healthy relationship, there must be space in your relationship for disagreements without one or both partners feeling unloved or unloving. You do not need to force your partner to see things your way, nor do you need to struggle to change your views or perceptions as a sign that you love your partner. You each have a right to your opinions.

You've no doubt heard the expression "Agree to disagree." It is a popular saying precisely because it works. It means that when you have reached an impasse, it is far more productive to simply say, "We aren't going to agree on this so let's drop it," than to keep hammering away at each other in the hopes that one of you will change your mind.

There are also times when the most constructive thing you can do is to walk away. If one or both of you is so angry with your partner that you can't stop calling him names or berating him for his behavior, the best thing to do is to leave the room or the home, if necessary. After you have cooled off, you may want to sit down and discuss your problem rationally, but until then, it is best to stay away from each other. The same holds true if you are on the receiving end of your partner's wrath. You don't have to sit there and take it just because he is dishing it out. Get up and leave—for his sake as well as for yours.

Often the healthier you become, the less you need to remain locked in the past. As each partner completes his or her unfinished business, dramatic changes can occur in each of your personalities. This, in turn, can result in each of you no longer reacting in the same ways toward each other and to no longer needing to pull at each other to get your unmet needs met by your partner.

RECOMMENDED FILMS

The War of the Roses (a vivid portrayal of an emotionally abusive couple)

Four Seasons (an hilarious yet poignant view of couples in transition)

CHAPTER 8

When Your Partner
Has a Personality Disorder

Women are taught to enhance other people
at the expense of the self, men are taught to bolster the self,
often at the expense of others. It's hard to get it all in balance.

HARRIET LERNER, PH.D.,
The Dance of Intimacy

In addition to one or both partners repeating patterns from the past, emotional abuse is sometimes caused by the fact that one or both partners have a personality disorder. What is a personality disorder? According to the DSM-V, *The Diagnostic and Statistical Manual of Mental Disorders* (which is used by mental health professionals to help determine psychological diagnoses), a personality disorder is an enduring pattern of inner experience and behavior that deviates markedly from the expectation of the individual's culture, is pervasive and inflexible (unlikely to change), is stable over time, and leads to distress or impairment in interpersonal relationships.

In addition to the inability to have successful relationships, those with a personality disorder suffer from disturbances in self-image, ways of perceiving themselves and others, appropriateness of range of emotion, and difficulties with impulse control. There are ten types of personality disorders, some of which can cause a person to exhibit behavior that can be experienced as emotionally abusive.

There are two personality disorders that stand out from the others because those who suffer from them will almost always create an emotionally abusive environment when they are in an intimate relationship. These disorders are Borderline Personality Disorder (BPD) and Narcissistic Personality Disorder (NPD). While other personality disorders and mental illnesses can cause a person to at times become emotionally abusive, they are not *characterized* by emotional abuse as are these two disorders. (Two noted exceptions to this rule are those who suffer from Antisocial Personality Disorder, which I described earlier as an abusive personality, and Paranoid Personality Disorder—which is characterized by a pervasive distrust and suspiciousness of others. These people are almost always emotionally abusive in their relationships, and on an ongoing basis. But those who suffer from these personality disorders are often unreachable, even by professional psychotherapists, and are certainly not going to be helped by a self-help book. Even though BPD and NPD are serious disorders, those who suffer from them are not beyond help.)

I have also singled out BPD and NPD because they—more than any other personality disorders or mental illnesses—are thought to be primarily *caused* by emotional abuse or neglect in childhood. While all personality disorders have a combination of causes—parental upbringing, personality and social development, and genetic and biological factors—BPD and NPD appear to consistently have emotional abuse at their core.

Another reason for my focus is that BPD and NPD are considered by many to be the personality disorders of our time. The sheer numbers of people suffering from these disorders has caused a great deal of focus on them, including a great deal of research as to their cause. Still another reason for the focus on BPD and NPD is the fact that those with BPD tend to become attracted to those with NPD and vice versa. This frequent coupling creates one of the most common types of emotionally abusive relationship.

In this chapter I will define and describe these two personality disorders and illustrate how each is manifested and how each is experienced as emotional abuse by the other partner. I will also provide questionnaires to help you determine whether your partner may have one of these two disorders. I will then offer concrete advice and strategies that partners can use to help them maintain their sanity and to work toward eliminating the most damaging emotional abuse in the relationship.

Please note that the majority of those suffering from Borderline Personality Disorder are women and the majority of those with Narcissistic Personality Disorder are men. There has been much speculation as to why this is so, including the idea that males in almost every culture are discouraged from expressing their emotions openly (with the exception of anger) and are severely stigmatized when they act in any way that can be construed as weak. Therefore, most males are more likely to hold in their emotions and to build up strong defensive walls to protect themselves from getting hurt by others. This defensive wall is characteristic of Narcissistic Personality Disorder. Females, on the other hand, are given permission to express their more vulnerable feelings, such as pain and fear, but discouraged from expressing anger. They are more likely to turn their anger in on themselves and consequently suffer from low self-esteem, overwhelming shame, and depression as a result. These three symptoms are characteristic of those who suffer from Borderline Personality Disorder. Throughout the book I have been changing back and forth from using the male pronoun to the female pronoun. In the next two chapters, however, I will primarily use "she" when discussing borderline individuals and "he" when discussing narcissistic individuals. Keep in mind this does not mean there are no male borderlines or female narcissists, however.

Determining Whether Your Partner Suffers from Borderline Personality Disorder

Those involved with a partner who has BPD or who suffers from strong borderline traits often do not realize they are being emotionally abused. They may know they are unhappy in their relationship, but they may blame themselves or be confused about what is causing the continual disruption in their relationship. They are often blamed for the relationship problems or made to feel that if they would only be more loving, more understanding, more sexual, or more exciting, their relationship would improve. To the contrary, it is often the case that a partner of a borderline is actually codependent or dependent, causing him to be extremely patient and willing to put up with intolerable behavior.

Partly because they are constantly being blamed for things they did not do, those involved with borderline individuals often come to doubt their own perceptions or their sanity. Often accused of behaving, thinking, or feeling in ways that upset their partner, they tend to adapt a careful style of living that authors Paul Mason and Randi Kreger call "walking on eggshells." Many come to believe that they are not only the cause of their relationship problems but the cause of their partner's emotional problems as well.

QUESTIONNAIRE: *Does Your Partner Suffer from Borderline Personality Disorder?*

The following questions, adapted from *Stop Walking on Eggshells* by Paul Mason and Randi Kreger, will help you determine whether your partner suffers from Borderline Personality Disorder or has strong borderline traits.

1. Has your partner caused you a great deal of emotional pain and distress?

2. Have you come to feel that anything you say or do could potentially be twisted and used against you?

3. Does your partner often put you in a no-win situation?

4. Does your partner often blame you for things that aren't your fault?

5. Are you criticized and blamed for everything wrong in the relationship or everything that is wrong in your partner's life, even when it makes no logical sense?

6. Do you find yourself concealing what you think or feel because you are afraid of your partner's reaction or because it doesn't seem worth the hurt feelings or the terrible fight that will undoubtedly follow?

7. Are you the focus of intense, violent, and irrational rages, alternating with periods when your partner acts normal and loving? Do others have a difficult time believing you when you explain that this is going on?

8. Do you often feel manipulated, controlled, or lied to by your partner? Do you feel like you are the victim of emotional blackmail?

9. Do you feel like your partner sees you as either all good or all bad, with nothing in between? Does there seem to be no rational reason for the switch in his or her perception of you?

10. Does your partner often push you away when you are feeling close?

11. Are you afraid to ask for things in the relationship because you will be accused of being too demanding or told there is something wrong with you?

12. Does your partner tell you that your needs are not important or act in ways that indicate that this is how she or he feels?

13. Does your partner frequently denigrate or deny your point of view?

14. Do you feel you can never do anything right or that his or her expectations are constantly changing?

15. Are you frequently accused of doing things you didn't do or saying things you didn't say? Do you feel misunderstood a great deal of the time, and when you attempt to explain, does your partner not believe you?

16. Does your partner frequently criticize you or put you down?

17. When you try to leave the relationship, does your partner try to prevent you from leaving by any means possible (e.g., declarations

of love, promises to change or get help, implicit or explicit threats of suicide or homicide)?

18. Do you have a hard time planning activities (social engagements, vacations) because of your partner's moodiness, impulsiveness, or unpredictability? Do you make excuses for her behavior or try to convince yourself that everything is okay?

If you answered yes to more than half of these questions, especially questions 9 to 18, your partner likely has traits associated with Borderline Personality Disorder. As you can see from this list, many of the above behaviors have already been described in this book as emotionally abusive (e.g., constant criticism, unreasonable expectations, constant chaos, emotional blackmail, gaslighting). What you were probably unaware of was that many of these abusive behaviors are also symptoms of a personality disorder. While it is impossible to diagnose someone without seeing them, I can say with a great deal of certainty that if your partner thinks, feels, and behaves in many of these ways, she probably suffers from BPD. For more information on the characteristics of BPD, refer to the next chapter and to the books recommended at the end of this book.

Twin Fears—Abandonment and Engulfment

At the core of all these feelings and behaviors are the twin fears of abandonment and engulfment. Those who suffer from BPD or have strong borderline tendencies almost always experienced some form of abandonment when they were an infant or child. This abandonment may have been physical (e.g., the hospitalization of a parent, the death of a parent, being put up for adoption, being left in a crib for hours at a time) or emotional (e.g., having a mother who was unable to bond with her child, being an unwanted child whose mother neglected her, having a detached and unloving father). This physical or emotional abandonment causes the borderline individual to be either extremely afraid of being rejected or abandoned in an intimate relationship and having to feel the original wounding all over again, or to be distant and detached as a way of defending herself from the potential pain of intimacy. In many cases, the borderline individual actually vacillates from one extreme to the other. At one point in time, she may herself be emotionally smothering—desperately clinging to her partner, demanding a great deal of attention, begging her partner to never leave her. At another point in time, perhaps only hours or days later, the same person can be overwhelmed with the fear of being engulfed. She may become distant and withdrawn for no apparent reason, or she may push her partner away by accusing him of not loving her, of being unfaithful, of no longer finding her attractive. She may even accuse him of being too needy.

This vacillation between clinging behavior and rejecting behavior is actually quite common in those with BPD. Over the course of a relationship, the most typical pattern that emerges is that a borderline individual will fall in love very quickly and will push for instant intimacy. She may seem to have few, if any, boundaries—insisting on seeing her lover every day, sharing her deepest, darkest secrets, even pushing to marry or live together right away. But once she has captured her partner's heart and received some kind of commitment from him, a typical borderline individual may suddenly become distant, critical, or have second thoughts about the relationship. She may stop wanting to have sex, saying that she feels they had sex too early and didn't get to know one another in other ways. She may suddenly become suspicious of her partner, accusing him of using her or of being unfaithful. She may begin to find fault in everything he does and question whether she really loves him. This distancing behavior may even verge on paranoia. She may begin to listen in on her partner's phone calls, check on his background, or question past lovers.

This behavior on the part of the person suffering from BPD may cause her partner to question the relationship, or it may make him so angry that he distances from her. When this occurs, she will suddenly feel the other fear—the fear of abandonment—and she will become needy, clingy, and "instantly intimate" once again. For some partners, this vacillation may be merely perplexing, but for many it is extremely upsetting. And in some cases, it will cause the partner to want to end the relationship. When this occurs, there will no doubt be a very dramatic scene in which the borderline individual may beg for him to stay, threaten to kill herself if he doesn't, or even threaten to kill him if he tries to leave her.

Even though many of the typical behaviors of a person suffering from BPD are clearly emotionally abusive (e.g., constant chaos, constant criticism, unreasonable expectations), often the relationship becomes mutually abusive because the borderline partner pushes her partner to his limit, and he ends up acting out in frustration and anger. This kind of vacillating behavior is very difficult for most people to cope with, and few come away from the situation without losing their temper or resorting to abusive tactics themselves. When someone is sobbing and clinging to your legs as you try to walk out the door, it is difficult to squelch the desire to either gather them up in your arms or kick them away. If you gather them up in your arms and promise to never leave, it will be difficult for you to ever respect your partner again. You may stay, but you will never see her as an equal again, and this will be an open invitation for you to become emotionally abusive toward her. If you push her away, you may be accused of being physically abusive. Or she may become so enraged with you for rejecting her that she physically attacks you and you are forced to defend yourself. If you are a man, you'll have a difficult time explaining why you kicked or hit an innocent woman. If you really lose your temper and hurt her, you may end up staying with her out of guilt, but you're very likely to repeat your abusive behavior the next time she frustrates you.

Strategies to Help You Cope
and to Stop the Emotional Abuse

1. Acknowledge What You Are Getting
Out of Being in the Relationship

Women and men who become involved with a partner who suffers from BPD soon discover that their partner is a deeply unhappy person. Many learn that their partner had a desperately unhappy child-hood, often suffering from either physical or sexual abuse or severe neglect and abandonment. Under the circumstances, it is natural for you to want to be a positive influence in your partner's life and to somehow make up for the severe pain and loneliness she has experienced. Unfortunately, this may have lead you to put up with unacceptable behavior and to swallow your anger and ignore your own needs. This is what is commonly referred to as codependent behavior on your part (codependents typically avoid their own problems by focusing on those of someone else).

You are not helping a partner with BPD by subordinating your own needs and by putting up with unacceptable behavior. In fact, this enables or reinforces inappropriate behavior on the part of your partner. With no negative consequences for their actions, they have no motivation to change.

2. Identify Your Partner's Triggers

Borderline individuals tend to react spontaneously and sometimes intensely to certain situations, words, or actions—triggers. Knowing what your partner's triggers are can help you avoid some conflicts. Since perceived abandonment is a huge trigger for those with BPD, know ahead of time that by setting limits, you will likely be perceived as shutting her out. Your need for time away from the relationship will likely be perceived as you pulling away from her or even of you ending the relationship. Knowing this may help you to anticipate her reaction, be more sensitive to her feelings when she reacts, and help you to stay detached and not get sucked into her drama. Of course, you cannot avoid all her triggers all the time, and you must keep in mind that your partner's behavior is her responsibility, not yours. See chapter 9 for a list of common BPD triggers.

3. Try to Find Patterns in Her Behavior

Some people suffering from BPD are actually quite predictable if you know what to look for. For example, notice the circumstances surrounding her outbursts, depressions, or bouts with anxiety. Were there factors such as the time of day, the presence or absence of alcohol (in you and in her), or the presence of a specific person? Behavior that is predictable can be much easier to handle than behavior that seemingly comes out of nowhere. Taking the time to know your partner and her moods will help you to understand her better, avoid conflicts, and help you stop taking her outbursts personally.

4. Determine Your Limits and Set Appropriate Boundaries

Refer to chapter 5 for information on how to do this.

5. Get a Reality Check

If you become confused about whether or not you are guilty of the behavior or attitude that your partner is accusing you of, check it out with close friends or family members. While it is not usually advisable for partners in a relationship to involve others in their domestic problems, in your situation it may be the only way you can stay clear about what is the truth about you and what is a projection or fantasy on your partner's part. Since borderline individuals can also be very perceptive about others and may be the only people who are willing to tell you the truth about yourself, it can be even more confusing.

For example, your partner may complain to you that you are insensitive to her needs and too focused on yourself. You may not feel that this is true since you spend a great deal of time trying to make her happy, but after hearing this complaint over and over, you might come to doubt your perceptions. It is time for a reality check. It's quite possible that you are rather self-focused, since it is common for those who suffer from BPD and those with NPD (characterized by self-absorption) to become involved with one another. But it is also possible that your partner is projecting (attributing her own denied qualities onto you) or confusing you with her parent(s). Of course, you can't always depend on your friends or family to always tell you the truth, but if you let them know it is important and that you would appreciate their honesty, they will likely tell you how they really perceive you. While you might be different with your friends and family than you are with your partner, more than likely they have observed you in many different situations and with previous lovers, and you can probably trust their perception of you.

6. Mirror Your Partner's Projections Instead of Taking Them In

Those who suffer from BPD tend to project their own feelings onto others, particularly their partners. Many partners tend to absorb these projections and soak up their pain and rage. Mason and Kreger, the authors of *Stop Walking on Eggshells,* call this "sponging." Instead of acting like a sponge, try acting more like a mirror—reflecting your partner's painful feelings back to her or him.

7. Disengage If Your Limits Aren't Observed or If You or Your Partner Is Losing Control

If your partner is unable to or refuses to honor the limits you have set or if a situation arises that threatens to get out of hand, the best thing you can do is to emotionally or physically disengage from her. Don't stubbornly continue to assert your point of view when you can see that it is triggering your partner or causing her to become enraged. In her emotional state, she will not be able to really hear you or take in your perspective anyway, and if you persist, she is likely to resort to name-calling, character assassination, or suicidal threats. And don't feel obligated to continue a discussion that has eroded into an argument just because your partner wants to continue it. Here are some suggestions for ways to disengage:

- Change the subject or refuse to continue the discussion.
- Say no firmly and stick to it.
- Leave the room or the house if necessary.
- If the discussion or argument occurs on the phone, hang up and refuse to answer if she calls back.
- Stop the car or refuse to drive until your partner has calmed down.
- Stop seeing your partner for a while.
- Suggest you continue the discussion in your therapist's office.

There will be times when none of these suggestions work, when your partner has completely lost control. Your suggestion to table the discussion or your attempt to walk away may be interpreted as rejection or abandonment, and your partner may become enraged, attempt to prevent you from leaving, or threaten suicide. In these situations, you should stop trying to handle the situation yourself. If your partner is in therapy, call her therapist. If she is not, call a crisis line. If she threatens violence toward you or herself, call the police.

Borderline Personality Disorder is a serious personality disorder. Many of those suffering from the disorder don't just threaten suicide; they actually go through with it. And some can become extremely violent if they feel provoked. It is very important that you seek outside help from a competent mental health professional if your attempts at coping with the situation and stopping the emotional abuse seem to upset your partner to the point that she threatens your life or hers.

8. Make a Distinction between the Things You Can Control and the Things You Cannot

No matter how hard you try, a partner with BPD may not respond as you would like during any particular emotional exchange, discussion, or disagreement. This is beyond your control. What is within your control is how you choose to react to the situation, whether you do all you can to take care of yourself in the relationship, and whether you do your part in helping to eliminate the emotional abuse in your relationship.

9. Work on Your Own Issues

If you are codependent, join CODA (Codependents Anonymous), read books on codependency, or enter therapy to work on your issues. If you have control issues, particularly if you have the need to make everyone happy, work to discover the origin of this need so you don't continue to take responsibility for your partner's happiness. You may focus on the needs of others in order to avoid your own unresolved issues, you may feel it is up to you to make others happy because this was the message you received from your parents, or you may have an investment in avoiding your own unhappiness. If you have low self-esteem, enter therapy to discover the causes and to develop ways to build up your self-confidence and improve your self-image so you will be in a better position to depersonalize and deflect your partner's criticism.

10. Don't Blame All Your Problems in the Relationship on Your Partner's BPD

Before you conclude that your partner's strong reaction is merely a symptom of her disorder, ask yourself if your behavior would have caused others to be upset. If you and your partner are going through a particularly difficult time, such as when she is feeling especially insecure, ask yourself if your own behavior or attitude could be contributing to the situation. If your partner accuses you of something, before writing it off as her typical blaming and criticizing, ask yourself if there is any truth to what she is saying. Those with BPD can be very intuitive, and many are extremely sensitive to cues such as body language and tone of voice. Some are even capable of picking up on something someone is feeling before they are aware of it. Being honest with yourself and with owning up to how you are truly feeling will help your partner to trust you and may defuse a potentially explosive situation.

Remember that you both play a part in the problems in your relationship. By acknowledging how your behavior may have contributed to the problem, you can act as a healthy role model to your partner. Don't, however, take on more than your share of responsibility. As much as you don't want to blame your partner for everything based on her problems with BPD, you also don't want to fall into the trap of allowing your partner to blame you for all the problems in the relationship.

Narcissistic Personality Disorder

Narcissism has not received as much attention as other psychological disorders, and yet it is often the cause of abusive behavior and the core problem of many that suffer from addictions. In fact, it has been called the most hidden disorder of our time. Most people think that narcissistic individuals are those who have extremely high self-esteem and who think too highly of themselves. But ironically, those suffering from

Narcissistic Personality Disorder (NPD) or who have strong narcissistic tendencies have extremely low self-esteem.

According to Dr. James Masterson, a leading expert on narcissism, on the surface, the narcissistic individual is brash, exhibitionistic, self-assured, and single-minded, often exuding an aura of success in career and relationships. Narcissists often seem to be the people who have everything—talent, wealth, beauty, health, power, and a sense of knowing what they want and how to get it.

In spite of his air of self-sufficiency, the narcissistic individual is actually more needy than most people. But to admit that he is needy, to admit that a person or a relationship is important to him, forces him to face feelings of deficiency. This, in turn, will create intolerable emptiness, jealousy, and rage inside him. To prevent this from occurring, he must find a way to get his needs met without acknowledging his needs or the person who meets them. He accomplishes this by viewing people as objects or a need-fulfilling function.

The term *narcissist* comes from the Greek myth of Narcissus, who stared endlessly at his own reflection mirrored in a lake. Unable to pull himself away from the contemplation of his own beauty, he eventually starved and fell into the water, never more to be seen.

The narcissist has no desire to develop his genuine self—he is in love with his false self—the self that wants to deal only with the pleasant, happy, beautiful side of life. This fixation cuts him off from a full range of life experiences and emotional responses such as anger, jealousy, and envy. This reluctance to face the disturbing side of life is characteristic of the person who suffers from narcissism. For this type of person, there is a segment of life which is not conscious, but that is hidden and unavailable.

The narcissistic individual remains aloof from other people and tends to have only transient social relationships. Because he cannot acknowledge that he needs others, he is almost incapable of feeling true gratitude. Instead, he wards off this feeling by demeaning the gift or the giver. He can be charming when he wishes to impress others and does give the perfunctory "thank you" when it is required socially, but his words are not deeply felt.

With his spouse and family, the narcissistic individual does not even pretend to be grateful. They belong to him and are supposed to meet his every need. Not only will his spouse and children's efforts to please him not be appreciated but they can always count on his criticism when what is offered is beneath his standards.

A person suffering from narcissism will tend to either choose a fellow narcissist as a partner or someone who feels inadequate, invisible, and needs to hide in a relationship. This suits him just fine since he doesn't want to recognize the existence of another person. In his book, *Trapped in the Mirror: Adult Children of Narcissists in Their Struggle for Self,* Elan Golomb, Ph.D., explains:

> Often, her mate is the child of a narcissist, already indoctrinated to regard exploitation and disregard as love. Others lured by the narcissistic aura are those in whom healthy childhood exhibitionism has been repressed.... If the parent puts the child to shame for showing off, the need for attention gets repressed into the unconscious. Repression means that the need is not satisfied and continues to press for expression in the adult without her being aware of it. The repressed adult may select an exhibitionistic mate to achieve vicarious satisfaction.

As long as nothing infiltrates his cocoon, the narcissistic individual will not be aware of any serious personality problems. He thinks he has it all, and those who know him will agree, since he has carefully selected them to be part of his world and thereby bolster his view of himself.

In spite of his aura of grandiosity and his bubble of self-sufficiency, the narcissistic individual is extremely thin-skinned. He constantly takes offense at the way people treat him (e.g., they don't treat him with enough respect, they don't appreciate him enough) and frequently feels mistreated. This may be the only clue that there is something wrong with him, but don't be fooled—the person with NPD is suffering from a serious psychological disorder. While the narcissistic individual may not feel the emptiness in his life, his behavior and attitude cause suffering in all those with whom he has intimate contact. Typically, those who suffer from NPD or who have strong narcissistic traits only seek treatment when they fail to live up to their own expectations of greatness or when their environment fails to support their grand illusions. At this time he will likely become depressed and seek psychotherapy to ease the pain.

QUESTIONNAIRE: *Is Your Partner Suffering from Narcissism?*

1. Does your partner seem to be constantly wrapped up in himself—his interests and projects—and have little interest in what is going on with you? Even when he does take an interest, is it short-lived?

2. Does your partner like to be the center of attention? Does he become bored or rude when someone else has the floor? Does he tend to bring the conversation back to himself?

3. Does she seem to feel she is entitled to special treatment from you and others?

4. Does he seem to lack empathy and compassion for other people? Does he seem to have particular difficulty feeling other people's pain, even though he expects others to feel his?

5. Does your partner feel that his opinions and beliefs are always the right ones and that others (including you) really don't know what they are talking about?

6. Does he think he is smarter, hipper, more attractive, or more talented than almost anyone else?

7. Does he seem to have an inordinate need to be right, no matter what issue is being discussed? Will he go to any lengths to prove he is right, including browbeating the other person into submission?

8. Is your partner charismatic, charming, and/or manipulative when she wants something, only to be dismissive or cold after a person has served his or her purpose?

9. Have you come to distrust your partner because you have frequently caught him in exaggerations and lies? Do you sometimes even think he is a good con man?

10. Does he often appear to be aloof, arrogant, grandiose, or conceited?

11. Can he be blisteringly insulting or condescending to people, including you?

12. Is he frequently critical, belittling, or sarcastic?

13. Does your partner become enraged if he is proven wrong or when someone has the audacity to confront him on his inappropriate behavior?

14. Does he insist upon being treated a certain way by others, including waiters and waitresses in restaurants, store clerks, and even by his own wife and children?

15. Does she frequently complain that others do not give her enough respect, recognition, or appreciation?

16. Does he constantly challenge authority or have difficulty with authority figures or with anyone who is in a position of control or power? Is he constantly critical of those in power, often insinuating that he could do better?

17. Does your partner seldom, if ever, acknowledge what you do for him or show appreciation to you?

18. Does he instead seem to find fault with almost everything you do?

19. Even when he is forced to acknowledge something you've done for him or a gift you've given him, does he somehow always downplay it or imply that it really didn't meet his standard?

20. Does your partner focus a great deal of attention on attaining wealth, recognition, popularity, or celebrity?

If you answered yes to more than half of the above questions, your partner may be suffering from NPD or may have strong narcissistic personality traits. For more information on this disorder, refer to the next chapter and to the books recommended at the end of this book.

Strategies to Help You Cope and Stop the Emotional Abuse

It is important when dealing with a narcissistic individual or someone with strong narcissistic traits to keep remembering that he is not a very conscious human being, especially when it comes to his own behavior. Although much of his behavior can be experienced as emotionally abusive (e.g., his arrogance, his dismissive attitude, his need to be right), he isn't necessarily trying to make you feel bad about yourself. In fact, the primary goal of the narcissist is to make himself feel good, even at the expense of others. His inattentiveness, his brashness, and his insensitive comments may seem as if he is deliberately trying to hurt you, when in reality, most of the time he frankly could care less about how you feel. Most narcissistic individuals are oblivious to others and to the feelings of others. The only time you become important is if you upset the status quo in any of the following ways:

- He needs you in some way or wants something from you.

- You confront him.

- You threaten to change things.

- You threaten to end the relationship.

For this reason it is important not to take what a narcissistic individual says or does personally. This, of course, is a very difficult task. But if you can try to remember that in a narcissistic individual's world, he is the center of the universe and everyone else is but a mere satellite revolving around him, it might help. This doesn't mean he doesn't have feelings or that he isn't capable of caring about others, but it does mean that his needs will always come first.

The only time most narcissistic individuals deliberately try to hurt others is when they themselves feel criticized or threatened in some way (e.g., if you dare to question their ability or knowledge, if you tell them they are wrong about something, or if you challenge their authority). This is when you will feel their full wrath. Narcissistic individuals can cut you to your core in seconds by using just the right words that can wound you the most.

Here are some other suggestions and strategies to help alleviate a great deal of the emotional abuse that can occur in a relationship with a narcissistic person:

- Recognize that someone with NPD has a tremendous need for personal space. If you insist on too much closeness, he will feel smothered and will lash out at you in order to push you away.

- If he becomes critical of you, call him on it immediately. The more you allow him to criticize you, the more he will disrespect you and the more he will continue to criticize you. Narcissistic individuals only respect those they feel are their equal. While they may seek out relationships in which they can feel superior and in which they can control the other person, these people are mere puppets to them. In order for a narcissistic individual to truly care about another person, he must respect her.

- Begin to recognize his tendency to criticize as a sign that he:

  1. Needs some space from you.

  2. Is feeling critical of himself.

  3. He is testing you to see whether you are his equal.

  Confront him about his criticalness, ask him if he needs more space, and certainly don't buy into his criticism by asking questions or arguing with him.

- If you have a complaint, state it clearly and strongly. Don't beat around the bush don't try to be "sensitive" and say it subtly. This will only enrage him. And don't whine. Narcissistic individuals hate it when people whine or act like a victim, and they lose all respect for them when they do.

- When you have a complaint, follow it with a clear statement of how you would like him to change. For example, say something like this: "I don't like the way you dismissed my comment as if it had absolutely no merit. My opinions are as valid as yours."

- Refuse to allow yourself to be charmed or used by your partner. Only do what you really feel like doing and don't allow yourself to be talked into anything you don't really want to do.

- Take more responsibility for making sure you get a chance to talk. Instead of sitting patiently while he goes on and on about himself or his projects, tell him you'd like to share something that happened to you. If he refuses to stop talking, say something like "I've been listening to you now for quite some time. I'd appreciate it if you'd give me a turn to talk." If this still doesn't work, say something like "I'm tired of listening to you and not being heard. I'm going to go now" (or "let's go").

- Realize that while he can dish out criticism, he can't take it, especially if it involves pulling his covers—exposing the vulnerabilities and weaknesses under his facade. In fact, even constructive criticism is experienced as a deep wounding in the narcissistic individual. This feeling of being wounded is so profound and so specific to narcissistic individuals that there is a psychological term for it—"narcissistic wounding." When you suggest or point something out to him, don't be surprised if he takes it as a criticism and reacts very strongly. He may lash out at you, he may huff out of the room, or he may give you the silent treatment. You may be able to help the situation by saying to him at a later time, "I didn't mean to hurt your feelings. I was only trying to make a suggestion," or "I'm sorry if I hurt your feelings, I was only trying to point something out that might help you."

- In spite of this sensitivity, you must stop the narcissistic individual from abusing you in any way. Even though he may not have intended to hurt your feelings, even though he may react very negatively at the time, confronting him is the only way to stop his abusiveness and the only way to gain or retain his respect.

- If he does make a positive change in his behavior, be sure to acknowledge it. Don't belabor the point since doing so may cause him to feel too vulnerable and his pride may rise up, causing him to be angry with you. Just acknowledge the change briefly and thank him for making it.

Unfortunately, once a narcissistic individual loses respect for you, it may be nearly impossible to regain it. It depends on how much you've allowed him to control you or abuse you in the past, how much whining and groveling you've done, and how much you've allowed him to see your neediness and vulnerability. If he shows no signs of respect for you whatsoever—he sighs and rolls his eyes when you talk, he laughs at you when you try to stand up to him, he challenges you to try to live without him—then there is little chance of ever regaining his respect, and the relationship will continue to be an abusive one. Your best bet is to work on gaining enough strength to end the relationship. If you choose to stay, all you can do is cut off his aggressiveness and abusiveness by confronting it at the moment and work on building a strong enough sense of self that your partner cannot erode your identity.

Above all, seek professional help to assist you in overcoming your anger and shame—shame at not being loved, shame at having accepted his humiliation for so long, and shame at what you have submitted to and undergone.

Should You Tell Your Partner That You Suspect He or She Has a Personality Disorder?

After reading this chapter and discovering that your partner may suffer from a personality disorder, you may feel eager to share this information with him or her. This is understandable since you probably feel relieved to learn that there is a reason for your partner's behavior, and you may assume that your partner may feel relieved to learn it as well. But unfortunately, this is usually not the case. Most partners become angry and defensive, and some respond with such shame and despair that they try to hurt themselves.

It is usually best if a person learns about their disorder from a therapist, not from their partner. The only exception to this rule is if your partner is actively seeking answers to why he or she is acting and feeling the way he or she does. If you do share this information with your partner, make sure you do so in a loving and caring way.

One of my goals for this chapter is to humanize these two personality disorders, since they have both been demonized by the media and even by some in the professional community. Many people view those suffering from personality disorders as freaks who are beyond help. This is absolutely not true. Those who suffer from Borderline Personality Disorder or Narcissistic Personality Disorder suffer from an illness as surely as those with depression or schizophrenia and many are victims of emotional, physical, or sexual abuse as children. Since the descriptions and the behavior of those who suffer from both BPD and NPD seem so negative, those diagnosed with these disorders tend to feel stigmatized. For this reason, it is important to realize that these disorders are something that people have, not something they are.

Understanding that your partner has a personality disorder will explain a great deal. It doesn't excuse his or her behavior, but it makes sense out of it. By understanding the disorder and the probable cause of the disorder, some partners can gain the necessary empathy that will be required in order for them to try to work out the problems in the relationship. For others, of course, it will mean you now have a legitimate reason to leave the relationship, and in some cases, this is probably the best option.

Learning that your partner has a personality disorder doesn't give you an excuse to stop working on your own issues and taking responsibility for your part in your relationship problems. This is especially true because partners of those with a personality disorder often have a personality disorder themselves.

When You Both Suffer
from a Personality Disorder

It is quite common for those with a personality disorder to be highly attracted to each other. The most common and problematic combination—Borderline Personality Disorder with Narcissistic Personality Disorder—occurs for a couple of reasons. First of all, the root cause of both BPD and NPD are often essentially the same—severe neglect and abandonment, emotional abuse, and often physical and sexual abuse in childhood. In fact, it is not uncommon for a person to have both BPD and NPD tendencies. Those suffering from BPD and NPD or those who have strong tendencies in these directions are, in many ways, like kindred spirits who recognize each other across a crowded room. We can often recognize and empathize with the pain our partner endured more than we can our own.

Second, even though both people in these couplings suffered the same neglectful, abusive childhoods, they often reacted to and coped with their suffering in radically different ways. The borderline individual is overwhelmed with her unmet needs and constantly tries to get them met in other people. She often creates a chameleonlike identity by taking on the qualities and characteristics of those she admires. The narcissistic individual denies he has any needs, retreats inside himself, and creates a facade of self-sufficiency. The person with BPD will admire the narcissistic individual's seeming independence and self-reliance, and the person suffering from narcissism will recognize his own vulnerability and neediness in the borderline and will, in an odd way, admire this in her.

One of the reasons why this combination is so problematic is that the person suffering from NPD is commonly very self-absorbed and self-centered and is often lacking in the ability to empathize with others. The person suffering from BPD sets and maintains little or no boundaries and tends to overempathize with others. In this situation, the person with BPD will continually feel wounded by the fact that the person with NPD pays little or no attention to her and doesn't seem to care how she feels. The person suffering from narcissism, in turn, will feel outraged at the borderline individual's insistence that he pay attention to her and will attempt to bully her into submission. Since the partner with BPD looks to others for identity, having few real opinions, values, or boundaries of her own, she typically acquiesces, doubting her perceptions more and more as time goes by.

In a situation where both of you have a personality disorder it will be necessary for each of you to understand both your own issues and the issues of your partner in order for the relationship to work. With this new understanding and with the specific coping skills I teach in the book, it is possible for you to eliminate the emotional abuse in the relationship.

RECOMMENDED FILMS

Fatal Attraction (although extreme, it does portray one type of borderline partner)

Malice (another extreme example that shows how narcissistic people will sometimes do anything to achieve wealth or status)

The Talented Mr. Ripley (shows a male borderline individual taking on the identity of a male narcissist)

CHAPTER 9

When Your Abusiveness Stems from a Personality Disorder

Although the world is full of suffering,
it is also full of overcoming it.

HELEN KELLER

In this chapter I offer step-by-step guidance for how those with Borderline Personality Disorder or Narcissistic Personality Disorder can work toward curbing those characteristics and tendencies that are emotionally abusive to their partner, as well as how they can begin to better take care of their own needs in a relationship. Although the chapter was written specifically for someone with these disorders, as mentioned in the earlier chapter, I also encourage your partner to read it in order to better understand the unique problems someone with a personality disorder must face.

Both BPD and NPD have a stigma attached to them, but there are many people who suffer from these disorders. In fact, they are considered by many to be the personality disorders of our time. This may be due to the fact that so few of us grew up in a two-parent family, to the fact that more and more single mothers are raising children while at the same time having to earn a living, or to the fact that all forms of child abuse have been increasing over the years. It is generally believed that these personality disorders are caused, or at least exacerbated, by inadequate parenting, parental neglect, abandonment, and/or child abuse.

To add to the stigma that these two personality disorders carry, there has been very little public education concerning them, and consequently, what little information the public is privy to is usually misinformation. For example, we casually use the word "narcissist" to describe someone who seems to think only of himself or herself, someone who has an extremely high opinion of himself or herself, or someone who often pays a great deal of attention to his or her appearance and thinks he or she is extremely attractive. But the truth is that the person with NPD or narcissistic tendencies has developed a facade of extreme confidence to hide tremendous feelings of inadequacy.

When word got out that the woman who relentlessly pursued her ex-lover in the movie *Fatal Attraction* suffered from BPD, borderline individuals came to be associated with stalking and violent, sadistic behavior. While some people who have extreme versions of BPD can be violent, and some do stalk past lovers, the majority of borderline individuals do not engage in such behavior.

After reading the previous chapter, some of you may suspect or feel certain that you, too, suffer from a personality disorder. Others have known already. Today more health care providers are sharing this diagnosis with their patients, and in the past ten years, there have also been many books written for the layperson on the subjects of BPD and NPD and websites have been created specifically for those suffering from these disorders.

For those of you who suspect you suffer from BPD or NPD but still aren't certain, the information and questionnaires offered in this chapter may help. Of course, in order to be absolutely certain, you will need to be diagnosed by a qualified health care provider. Information on how to find such a person will be provided at the end of the book.

Do You Suffer from Borderline Personality Disorder?

My philosophy is that it is better to know something than to not know. It is better to know if you suffer from a disease or disorder than to go along blindly, acting as if nothing is wrong—particularly if you are causing your loved ones to suffer. The sooner you know what is wrong with you, the sooner you can get the help you need. According to the DSM-V, Borderline Personality Disorder is characterized by a pervasive pattern of instability of interpersonal relationships, self-image, and affects (moods) and marked impulsivity beginning by early adulthood and present in a variety of contexts, as indicated by five or more of the following:

1. Frantic efforts to avoid real or imagined abandonment. *Note:* Do not include suicidal or self-mutilating behavior covered in number 5 below.

2. A pattern of unstable and intense interpersonal relationships characterized by alternating between extremes of idealization and devaluation.

3. Identity disturbance: markedly and persistently unstable self-image or sense of self.

4. Impulsivity in at least two areas that are potentially self-damaging (e.g., spending, sex, substance abuse, shoplifting, reckless driving, binge eating). *Note:* Do not include suicidal or self-mutilating behavior covered in number 5 below.

5. Recurrent suicidal behavior, gestures, or threats, or self-mutilating behavior.

6. Affective instability due to a marked reactivity of mood (e.g., intense episodic dysphoria, irritability, or anxiety usually lasting a few hours and only rarely more than a few days). (Dysphoria is the opposite of euphoria. It's a mixture of depression, anxiety, rage, and despair.)

7. Chronic feelings of emptiness.

8. Inappropriate, intense anger or difficulty controlling anger (e.g., frequent displays of temper, constant anger, recurrent physical fights).

9. Transient, stress-related paranoid ideation or severe dissociative symptoms.

Please refer to the previous chapter for a questionnaire that will help you further determine whether you may suffer from this disorder or from borderline tendencies.

How Borderline Personality Disorder Can Lead to Emotionally Abusive Behavior

Those who suffer from BPD or strong borderline tendencies most often become emotionally abusive due to their tendency to project or transfer their own feelings, behaviors, or perceived traits onto others. Projection is a defense mechanism that we all use from time to time, but those suffering from BPD use it in excessive ways. Because they tend to be overwhelmed with self-criticism, self-loathing, and self-blame, and because they often cannot contain these feelings without dire consequences (deep depression, self-mutilation, or suicide attempts), borderline individuals tend to project their feelings of self-hatred outside themselves onto others. This can cause them to be extremely critical or judgmental of others, particularly those closest to them. Because they feel like there is something wrong with them, they accuse others of being inadequate and incapable. Often, their self-hatred comes out as verbal abuse, constant criticism, or unreasonable expectations.

Those suffering from BPD also accuse others of having feelings and thoughts that really belong to them. They often project their self-hatred by experiencing others, particularly their partner, as being disapproving of their actions or judgmental or critical of aspects of their personality. This can cause them to become almost paranoid, constantly assuming their partner is criticizing them when he or she is merely stating a preference or opinion.

The following are some examples of typical borderline projections:

- You think I'm too stupid to understand (I'm afraid I'm too stupid to understand).

- You don't think I'm pretty (I don't think I'm pretty).

- You don't think I did a good job (I don't think I'm capable of doing things right).

- You think I'm too impatient with the kids (I'm afraid I'm too impatient with the kids).

- You spend too much time at work so you won't have to be around me (I don't want to be around me so why would anyone else?).

Because people with BPD feel so innately bad about themselves, they cannot imagine how someone could love them. This can cause them to demand constant reassurance and proof of their partner's love and to become extremely jealous and possessive. They often demand all their partner's attention and accuse him or her of being unfaithful when there is absolutely no proof that any such infidelity has occurred.

CHELSEA: THE POT CALLING THE KETTLE BLACK

Projection also works in another way. If you suffer from BPD, you may accuse your partner of doing something that you are actually doing. For example, Chelsea often complained to her friends about her husband, Randall. She'd go out to lunch with a girlfriend and spend most of the time talking about how much Randall neglected her, how he worked late almost every night and was then too tired on the weekends to go anywhere with her. But this didn't stop her from worrying about what Randall told his friends and family about her. "I'll bet all you do is complain about me to your mother every time she calls," she'd accuse Randall. When she called her husband at work and his secretary answered, she'd accuse him of turning his secretary against her. "Why else is she so cold and formal with me?" she'd grill Randall. "You must have told her negative things about me to make her dislike me the way she does."

In addition to projection, if you suffer from Borderline Personality Disorder or have strong borderline traits, there are many other aspects of your personality that can lead to abusive behavior. These personality traits include:

- *Inappropriate, intense anger or an inability to control your anger.* This includes frequent displays of temper or sudden outbursts, constantly being angry, getting into physical fights.

- *A need to control your partner and your environment.* Those who suffer from BPD need to feel in control of other people because they feel so out of control of themselves. In an attempt to make your world more predictable and manageable, you may order your partner around, require him to do things a certain way, insist on being the one in charge, or try to "make him over."

- *Intense fear of rejection or abandonment.* This may cause you to be extremely possessive, jealous, and controlling or to react in extreme, sometimes outrageous ways, such as bursting into a rage when your partner tells you he is going on a business trip or desperately clinging to a girlfriend who is threatening to end the relationship.

  This same fear of abandonment may cause you to be hyper-vigilant—looking for any cues that might show you that your partner doesn't really care about you. If and when your fears seem to be confirmed, you may erupt in a rage, make outrageous accusations, seek revenge, or engage in some kind of self-destructive act.

- *A tendency to alternately idealize and devalue a person* or to view a person as either "all good" or "all bad." As long as you feel your partner is paying enough attention to you, appreciating your efforts and behaving in ways that cause you to respect him, you will likely perceive him as "all good." But as soon as he rejects you, disapproves of something you've done, or does something that you disapprove of, you may suddenly see him as "all bad." This may cause you to belittle or berate him—sometimes in front of others (character assassination)—or to threaten to leave him (emotional blackmail).

- *Feelings that vary dramatically from moment to moment* (e.g., being flooded with emotion or being numb to your feelings, which can manifest into total silence or explosive screaming). This fluctuation of feelings is magnified greatly by the next personality trait:

- *A tendency to forget what you felt prior to the present.* This amnesia surrounding emotions prevents you from remembering past experiences and from appreciating that pain is temporary and can be survived. Whatever feeling-state you are experiencing at the moment seems to last forever, and you can't recall ever feeling differently. As a result, your last encounter with your partner may be recalled as the whole of your relationship. You forget all the good times you've had with your partner and may threaten to end the relationship based on one bad incident. With this black-and-white quality of feelings, disappointment often turns to rage, which may be directed at others in fits of temper or physical attacks. (Rage may also be turned against the self in the form of self-abuse, self-injury, or suicidal threats or behavior.)

- *Your feelings may become so intense that they distort your perception of reality.* You may imagine others are deliberately persecuting you, including your partner. You may accuse your partner of plotting against you with others or of deliberately trying to upset or undermine you, when in reality, he or she has merely let you down.

- *You may resort to using* alcohol, drugs, binge eating, impulsive sexual encounters, compulsive shopping, gambling, shoplifting, or other behaviors as a quick fix for painful, seemingly endless emotions, such as loneliness and anger. Under the influence of alcohol or drugs you may become emotionally or even physically abusive to your partner.

- *Emotional blackmail.* You may threaten to end the relationship, move out of the house, or kick your partner out of the house whenever there is a fight or disagreement. While you may change your mind as soon as you cool down, your threats take a toll on your partner and on your relationship. Those suffering from BPD also threaten to hurt or kill themselves in order to get their partner to take them back or to get their way.

- *Unpredictable responses.* Because of an inconsistent sense of self, you may also seem to set up no-win situations for your partner. You may react one way to your partner's behavior one time and an entirely different way the next. Or you may ask your partner to treat you a certain way and then, when he does, you may get angry with him for it. In this way, you keep your partner completely off balance since he or she cannot predict how you will react, and he may grow to feel that no matter what he does, he'll be wrong.

- *Constant chaos.* Your insecurity, accusations, jealousy, posses-siveness, emotional outbursts, and depression create constant chaos and drama in the relationship. You start fights, become depressed and cry for hours; then you want to make up as if nothing had happened and beg your partner to take you back. You hate your partner one day and love him the next. You may alternately cling to your partner out of a fear of abandonment and push your partner away out of a fear of being smothered. Those with BPD or borderline tendencies often experience a great deal of anxiety, a constant nervous feeling or the feeling that there is a whirling cyclone going on inside them. This feel-ing of anxiety is so uncomfortable that they create drama as a way to distract themselves from it. Other BPDs prefer to create upheaval in their lives rather than be forced to face the horrible feelings of emptiness they might otherwise experience.

- *Constant criticism and continual blame.* You may criticize your partner as a way of creating distance so you can ward off feel-ings of engulfment, or you may criticize as a way of coping with abandonment fears. You may feel defective at a very core level and fear that your partner will one day discover this and reject you completely. Therefore, you find fault in him as a way of deflecting his judgments and criticism. If he's the one who is always wrong, you can't be. You may also criticize your partner for things you yourself are guilty of (projection).

- *Gaslighting.* Although it is not necessarily your intention, your behavior can cause your partner to question his or her own sanity. You forget you said or did something and then deny it when your partner brings it up. You have an emotional outburst and then deny it ever happened (it is quite common for those suffering from BPD to dissociate while in a rage). Even when you realize you've done something, such as when you catch yourself being inconsistent, you may be too ashamed to admit it. You may even try to portray your partner as the one who is mixed up or even imply that he's crazy.

How You Can Begin to Change Your Emotionally Abusive Behavior

Changing your behavior when you suffer from BPD or strong borderline traits won't be easy. It isn't as if you can simply *will* yourself to change. Much of your abusive behavior is unconscious, based on strong defense mechanisms. Even when you are consciously aware of your abusive behavior, it may feel at the time that it is the only thing you can do to protect yourself (e.g., verbal abuse) or to hold on to your partner and your relationship (e.g., lie, manipulate). For some of you, especially those who suffer from a more extreme version of BPD, professional psychotherapy may be the only way you can make the kind of substantial changes to your personality that will interrupt your abusive patterns. Please refer to the back of the book for suggestions on how to find the appropriate treatment and the right therapist. For others, particularly those who suffer from a milder form of BPD or who have only borderline tendencies, the following suggestions can help you begin to change your behavior immediately.

1. Admit You Have a Problem

The first step will be for you to become more aware of your abusive behavior and of the effect it has on your partner (and others). This can be an extremely difficult task in itself, and it will take a leap of faith on your part as well as tremendous courage. You will need to ask those closest to you to give you feedback about your behavior. This step, of course, makes the assumption that you can believe what those close to you will tell you—more specifically, it assumes you can trust their perceptions and judgment. This poses quite a dilemma. Since you likely have difficulty trusting your partner, how in the world can you trust what he says about your behavior? Since you already feel that others misperceive you and misjudge your actions, how can you trust their perceptions of you?

Although your partner can certainly have distorted perceptions around some issues—particularly those issues that pertain to his or her own background—when it comes to your abusive behavior, your partner's perceptions are probably closer to the truth than yours. While this statement goes against everything I have ever told clients who don't suffer from Borderline Personality Disorder, it does apply to those who do. Unfortunately, those who have BPD frequently experience distortions in their perceptions, particularly in terms of how they view themselves in relationships. While they can be extremely sensitive and perceptive when it comes to other people, they aren't able to perceive themselves as accurately. It is also common for those suffering from BPD to dissociate when in a rage or when they are under a great deal of emotional stress, causing them to be unaware of their abusive behavior.

EXERCISE: *Get Feedback from Others*

1. Ask your partner to write a list of your behaviors that are most hurtful to him.

2. Ask your partner to explain why each behavior is particularly hurtful.

3. Ask her or him to describe those behaviors on your part that could be described as "abusive" and, if possible, to explain why he or she views them that way.

4. You may also wish to ask your close friends for similar feedback. Keep in mind that your friends may or may not experience the full force of your abusiveness since you may be on your

good behavior with them or you may not feel threatened by them—meaning you may not fear either being abandoned by them or smothered by them. Be careful about asking family members for feedback, since your disorder likely stems from your family dynamics and there is even some evidence that BPD may be at least partly genetic. This means it is likely that some members of your family also suffer from BPD and also have distorted perceptions. Family members are not likely to be that objective about you, anyway. They may either be far too critical or far too accepting of your behavior.

2. Face the Truth about Your Childhood

Although there is no absolute consensus as to the cause of Borderline Personality Disorder, most experts agree that there is definitely an environmental factor. Most people suffering from BPD share one factor in particular—abandonment. This abandonment can either be physical or emotional in nature and can stem from any or all of the following circumstances:

- An insufficient bonding experience with a primary caretaker, particularly the mother
- The long-term absence of one or both parents
- The loss of a parent either through death or divorce
- An insufficient, inappropriate, or negative relationship with the father
- Parental neglect
- Rejection or ridicule from parents, siblings, or peers

In addition, many, but not all, borderline individuals also experienced emotional, physical, or sexual abuse—or all three.

3. Identify Your Triggers

Those who suffer from BPD or who have strong borderline tendencies tend to react similarly to certain behaviors and attitudes from others. When a person is triggered, he or she reacts spontaneously and intensely, often without realizing what caused the reaction. The following is a list of the most common triggers for those with BPD:

- *Perceived abandonment.* Because of your fear of abandonment, you are probably acutely sensitive to any hint of perceived abandonment, and you likely react powerfully and sometimes violently to it. For example, even the slightest hint of disapproval from your partner can trigger powerful feelings of rejection.

- *Being criticized.* When you feel criticized, you are likely to react very intensely. This is true for several reasons. First of all, when you are criticized you likely become overwhelmed with shame. Shame is different from guilt in that it makes the person feel that their entire being is wrong or bad as opposed to guilt, which reminds us that committing certain acts are wrong. The second reason is closely related to the first. Those suffering from BPD tend to see things in all-or-nothing terms. When they are criticized, it makes them feel "all bad." Third, criticism feels like rejection to BPDs and can therefore trigger a fear of abandonment. It goes like this—if you don't like something I've done, it means you don't like me and that you are going to abandon me.

- *Feeling that others are unpredictable or inconsistent.* Although borderline individuals are often unpredictable and inconsistent themselves, they have a tremendous need for consistency and predictability, especially from those close to them. When they perceive a person as being inconsistent or a person or situation as being unpredictable, this causes them to be fearful and anxious. This is likely due to the fact that those who suffer from BPD did not receive the consistency they needed from their parents, especially their mothers. In order for a child to develop a strong sense of self, she must have what is called *object constancy*. This particular trigger can, in turn, trigger a fear of abandonment since unpredictability often goes hand in hand with rejection or abandonment.

- *Feeling invalidated or dismissed.* Because borderline individuals have not developed a strong sense of self, they are especially sensitive to comments or attitudes that are invalidating or dismissive. Comments like "You're overreacting" or "You shouldn't feel like that" may seem like they deny your feelings and thoughts. Even though there are many times when you may be overreacting or reacting inappropriately, these types of invalidating comments are in themselves inappropriate.

- *Envy.* Borderline individuals are often triggered when someone else receives special recognition. They become overwhelmed with feelings of envy and may become depressed or act out in order to draw the attention to themselves. This can happen during celebrations when all the attention is focused on someone else or even during a crisis when someone else needs support.

- *Travel or moving.* Those with BPD tend to respond well to structure and predictability. When this is disrupted, they can become disoriented. Moving to a new home or town or even going on vacation can trigger feelings of insecurity and fear.

- *Having every reaction attributed to their disorder.* If you have been diagnosed with BPD, you can be triggered when someone else attributes everything you do to BPD.

Knowing your triggers can provide you with a great deal more control of your borderline tendencies. For example, if your trigger is abandonment or rejection, don't set yourself up for it by leaving plans open. When you and your partner are making plans for an activity, make sure you get a clear commitment from him concerning both the event itself and the timing. While other people may be comfortable with "Let's wait and see how we feel" or "I'll pick you up around eight," you are not. You need to know from your partner that a plan is definite, otherwise you set yourself up for feeling abandoned or rejected if he decides not to go. And you need to know exactly what time he will pick you up or what time you will meet so you don't end up standing around waiting—feeling anxious, irritated, enraged, or worse, abandoned. Getting clear commitments from your partner won't guarantee that you are never disappointed at last-minute changes or that you will never be kept waiting, but it will certainly help. If you have a partner who is unable to commit to a certain time or who is consistently late even when he or she does commit, it is time to make other arrangements. The following example shows you what I mean.

Danielle and Lana: Better Never Than Late

[This is what Danielle told me:] I travel a lot for business, and my partner, Lana, always volunteered to pick me up at the airport. I really appreciated it, and it always made me feel loved by her. But she was always late. I'd stand outside looking at every car that approached that looked like hers, and every time it wasn't, I'd feel a sense of loss. I'd keep looking at my watch, feeling more and more panicked as time went by. By the time she was fifteen minutes late, a horrible feeling of abandonment would come over me. I'd feel like a little lost child in a big city. I'd become desperate, pacing back and forth, my heart pounding. When she'd finally show up—sometimes an hour late—I'd be so enraged with her that we'd end up having a big fight and I'd break up with her.

I told my therapist about this situation, and she suggested that I stop having Lana pick me up. At first, I argued that I liked her picking me up, that it made me feel loved. But she reminded me that I might initially feel loved, but by the time Lana finally gets there, I'm feeling very unloved.

4. Admit Your Abusive Behavior to Your Partner

It will be extremely difficult for you to admit to your abusive behavior for several reasons. First, because you already feel unlovable and because you fear abandonment, you don't want your partner to know there is anything wrong with you or that you've done anything wrong. Your unconscious reasoning may be like this: "If my partner discovers I'm not perfect, he's going to reject me. Therefore, I can't admit I have a problem. It's better to make him think the problem lies with him."

Second, you probably judge yourself as harshly as you judge others. And just as you see others in all-or-nothing, black-and-white terms, you see yourself in the same way. If you admit to yourself and your partner that you have been abusive, you are likely to see yourself as "all bad" and fear that your partner will do the same.

Third, if you suffer from Borderline Personality Disorder, you also tend to suffer from pervasive shame—the feeling that you are worthless, flawed, and defective. Admitting that your behavior is sometimes abusive may trigger what is commonly called a "shame attack"—an overwhelming feeling of being exposed as the defective, evil person that you feel you are at your core and feeling isolated, empty, and alone in the world as a result of it. Nevertheless, it is still important to let your partner know that your behavior has been abusive. Refer to chapter 6 for more information about how to go about doing this.

5. Reach Out for Help

As I wrote earlier, many people suffer from Borderline Personality Disorder without realizing it. Many people go their entire lives without knowing why they feel and behave as they do, and most never receive any help for their problems. Others seek help for related problems such as eating disorders, alcohol or drug abuse, or compulsive shopping or gambling. Some seek help for depression and suicidal attempts. But few seek help because they are abusing their partner. In fact, most people who suffer from BPD believe they are the ones who are being abused in their relationships. By admitting that you are, in fact, being emotionally abusive to your partner, you will be exhibiting a great deal of integrity and courage. Not only will you possibly be saving your relationship but the help you get will save you as well. You've no doubt sensed for a long time that there is something terribly wrong with you. After all, you've been in emotional pain most of your life. You've experienced a constant feeling of emptiness inside that you've tried to fill up with food, alcohol, or relationships. You've been in a constant state of either anxiety or depression.

It is especially important to reach out for help if you are experiencing chronic or severe depression. You cannot just will yourself out of depression. By its very nature, depression takes away your will and your motivation, and it distorts your perception. You may need medication, at least temporarily, especially if you feel suicidal. More important, you need someone to talk to, someone who is not involved personally in your life, someone who can provide an objective perspective.

You will also need the help of a professional to help you identify and express your emotions. The most common defense is *intellectualization*. When we intellectualize, we seek reasons to explain, analyze, censor, and judge our feelings. We tell ourselves that certain feelings are bad or wrong and therefore we shouldn't feel them. Or we tell ourselves that feelings are childish and that those who express them openly are foolish. But while our emotions can sometimes be unpleasant, confusing, untimely, and even disruptive, they are as natural as any body function and as necessary. You undoubtedly need help to work past your tendency to intellectualize your emotions and help to begin allowing yourself to express your emotions in constructive ways.

Strategies for Specific Borderline Behaviors

- *To stop possessive, clinging, harassing behavior.* Keep a photo of your partner or loved ones close by, and when you become insecure in their absence, take a long look at the picture. Do the same with love letters written by your partner. This will provide you with what is referred to as *object constancy* and will help you to feel more secure and trusting of your partner.

- *To stop losing yourself in the relationship.* Take time away from the relationship. For example, one client shared with me, "I feel quieter inside when I'm away from George. Whenever I'm around him I feel chaotic inside. But when I get away, it's like I can breathe. I can hear myself think. I need to take mini-vacations from him from time to time just to find myself again. I don't know if I'll ever be able to have myself and be in a relationship at the same time, but I sure know time away helps."

- *To curb your tendency to be critical or judgmental.* The next time you feel critical of your partner or children, make sure you aren't trying to push him away because you are feeling engulfed or feeling critical of yourself and projecting it onto others. Before you say anything negative, write in your journal, take a walk, or just let some time pass—and possibly with it your mood.

- *To curb your tendency to need to be in control.* Instead of trying to control others, focus your energy on gaining control of yourself. The best way to do this is by identifying and monitoring your emotions, identifying your needs, and setting your boundaries.

Do You Suffer from Narcissistic Personality Disorder?

You may have reason to believe that you suffer from Narcissistic Personality Disorder, either from reading the information on narcissism in the previous chapter or because someone, possibly your partner, may have told you that you fit the description. If this is true for you and you haven't read the previous chapter, I suggest you do so now. The following questionnaire will also help.

QUESTIONNAIRE: *Do You Have Narcissistic Personality Disorder?*

1. Do you feel you are special or that you have special talents or gifts that others do not possess?

2. Do you feel you are entitled to special treatment or recognition?

3. Do you secretly feel you are better than most people (e.g., smarter, more attractive, more talented)?

4. Do you become easily bored with people when they talk about themselves?

5. Do you tend to think that your feelings or your opinions are more important than those of others?

6. Does it hurt you deeply if your talents, accomplishments, or physical attributes are not recognized or appreciated?

7. Do you feel deeply insulted if you are ignored or not acknowledged?

8. Have you been accused of being overly self-focused or self-centered?

9. Have you been accused of being conceited or of being egotistical?

10. Do you often fly off the handle or become enraged at the slightest provocation and often without really knowing why?

11. Do you lose respect for others when you discover they are less intelligent, successful, powerful, or together emotionally than you had first thought?

12. Do you have difficulty identifying or empathizing with others, especially with their pain?

13. Do you find that you are often envious of what others have accomplished or accumulated?

14. Do you tend to focus more on what you don't have than what you do?

15. Do you frequently feel that your efforts and accomplishments are being ignored, minimized, or that you are being passed over for special recognition, promotions, awards, and so on?

16. Are you able to walk away from relationships fairly easily once someone has insulted you or hurt you?

17. Is one of your major goals in life to become successful, famous, wealthy, or to find "perfect" love? Do you feel like a failure or feel depressed because you haven't reached your goal?

18. Do you feel like you don't really need other people all that much, that you are fairly self-sufficient?

19. Are most of your friendships based on a mutual interest, or on the fact that you both have a strong desire to become successful, famous, or wealthy?

20. Do your relationships tend to be short-lived? Are you close to someone for a while but find that over time they no longer serve a function in your life?

If you answered more than five questions with a "yes," especially if they were questions 10 to 20, you may suffer from Narcissistic Personality Disorder.

According to the DSM-V, Narcissistic Personality Disorder is characterized by the following:

- An inflated sense of self-importance

- Fantasies of unlimited success, fame, power, beauty, and perfect love (uncritical adoration)

- Exhibitionism (a need to be looked at and admired)

- A tendency to feel rage with little objective cause

- A readiness to treat people with cool indifference as punishment for hurtful treatment or as an indication of the fact they have no current use for the person

- A tendency toward severe feelings of inferiority, shame, and emptiness

- A sense of entitlement accompanied by the tendency to exploit

- A tendency to overidealize or devalue people based largely on a narrow focus or an inability to empathize

How Narcissistic Personality Disorder Leads to Abusive Behavior

If you suffer from NPD or have strong narcissistic tendencies, your behavior and attitude toward others is often experienced as abusive, even though you may not intentionally try to hurt anyone. Those with NPD are often oblivious to others and to how their behavior affects them. This doesn't make your behavior and attitude any less hurtful or damaging, however, and often it is your careless disregard toward others that hurts the most. The specific behaviors and attitudes manifested by a narcissistic individual that are most hurtful to others include:

- Negating the feelings, ideas, and opinions of others

- Sarcastic remarks and put-downs

- A general attitude of arrogance and condescension toward others

- A tendency to be dismissive of others, especially if he or she does not respect them

- Being overly critical and judgmental of others

- Unreasonable expectations; never being pleased

Although most of their abusive behavior is unconscious and unintentional, at times those suffering from NPD can be deliberately abusive. Generally speaking, the impulse to emotionally abuse is set in motion either when the relationship becomes too symbiotic or when a partner is somehow found lacking. Too much closeness terrifies a narcissistic individual and so he criticizes or imposes control on his partner in order to hold her at bay. By accusing her of being too demanding or invasive, he can keep her at a safe distance. By asserting control and dominance over her, he can keep her in a dependent or one-down position. The narcissistic abuser also works at keeping his partner off balance so he can avoid having to make the emotional commitment that he so desperately fears. The unspoken message is "I don't love you," but it remains indirect and hidden so his partner won't leave. But neither can she feel safe and secure in the relationship. She is always in a state of confusion, constantly asking herself, "Does he love me or not?"

When a person suffering from narcissism experiences disappointment in his partner, this can also set abuse in motion. A typical narcissistic individual often becomes intensely attracted to someone in a short amount of time and will tend to idealize his partner, viewing her as more beautiful, talented, popular, or giving than she actually is. When this idealization wears off, he may become so disappointed that he loses any respect he once had for her. This lack of respect is expressed through belittling, dismissive, or sarcastic comments or put downs, and a blatant lack of consideration.

When the person suffering from narcissism is faced with the inevitable ending of a relationship—either because he is unable to ignore the fact that the relationship is a failure or he is interested in someone else—he will inevitably become abusive. Unable to accept responsibility for the failure of the relationship or for his attraction to someone else, he must make his partner responsible—in his own mind and in hers.

In some cases, it is not a question of the narcissistic individual *becoming* abusive but of his previously hidden abusive nature being revealed. In order to justify his desire to end the relationship, his partner must be forced to behave in unacceptable ways so that she can then be invalidated. In the situation where the narcissistic partner is attracted to someone else, he must turn his previous partner into a scapegoat and project everything bad onto her in order to idealize the new love object and establish a new relationship.

How You Can Begin to Change Your Emotionally Abusive Behavior

1. Admit You Have a Problem

This will undoubtedly be very difficult. In fact, it may be the most difficult thing you will ever have to do. Believe me, I know. There came a time in my life when I had to admit to myself that I have some very clear narcissistic tendencies. It occurred during the writing of my book *The Emotionally Abused Woman*. As I listed the symptoms of narcissism, I was amazed to find that I recognized myself in the description of the disorder.

It should have come as no surprise to me since I come from a long line of narcissists. My mother and several of her brothers suffered from the disorder, as did her mother. But for some reason, I imagined I'd escaped from our family curse. I should have known that it is not that easy to do. Having been raised as the only child of a narcissistic mother, there was no way I could escape my destiny, no matter how hard I tried. As Elan Golomb wrote so eloquently in *Trapped in the Mirror*:

Each narcissistic parent in each generation repeats the crime that was perpetuated against him. The crime is nonacceptance. (The narcissist is more demanding and deforming of the child he identifies with more strongly, although all his children are pulled into his web of subjectivity.) How can he accept offspring who are the product of his own unconsciously despised self? His attitude is a variant of the Groucho Marx Syndrome: "I would not join any club that would have me as its member," here transposed into "I would not love any child that would have me as its parent." The child has rejection as its birthright.

Even though it is difficult to imagine, those suffering from Narcissistic Personality Disorder have an even worse reputation than those who suffer from Borderline Personality Disorder. Calling someone a narcissist is considered an extremely derogatory word. To be a psychotherapist with narcissistic tendencies was especially humiliating, although I have come to realize I certainly am not alone. And neither are you. We are said to live in the age of narcissism, and because of this, few of us are entirely free of its traits. We see our narcissism reflected in the label "the Me Generation," and in such popular expressions as "What's in it for me?" and "taking care of number one." Our society worships beauty—especially beautiful bodies—as well as external things such as power, status, and money.

As difficult as it will be for you to admit your narcissistic traits, this is what you will need to do if you are going to stop your abusive behavior and possibly save your relationship. As long as you avoid admitting the truth, you will continue to be abusive, and you will continue damaging your partner and your relationship.

2. Face the Truth about Your Childhood

When we look behind the self-important, self-absorbed, egotistical, "me-first" behavior of the person suffering from narcissism, we almost always discover a person whose early, *healthy* narcissistic needs (for attention, affection and respect, as well as the need for food and shelter) were not met. Some of you reading this book already know the roots of your problem. You remember well the neglect or abuse that you experienced at the hands of one or both of your parents. But others have been so good at covering up their hurt and anger that they have little or no memory of how their parents treated them. Fortunately (and unfortunately), you can almost always recognize shadows of your parents' behavior in your own. If you are domineering and tyrannical toward your partner and/or children, you can almost guarantee that this is the way your were treated as a child. If you are distant and aloof with your partner, you need only look to your parents for the reason.

3. Begin to Let Down Your Defenses

If you are like most people with narcissistic traits, you have probably built up a fairly strong defense system to protect yourself from pain, doubt, and fear. Perhaps you learned early on in life that you couldn't depend on others, that you were essentially alone in the world. You may have had to toughen up after years of neglectful or abusive treatment from your parents or other caretakers. You may have determined early on that in order to reach your goals, you needed to block out all other distractions, including your own emotions. Only by looking behind these defenses will you be able to get to the roots of your problem and come to terms with your parents' abusive behavior.

In order to achieve success, recognition, financial gain, or adoration—prizes that those with NPD or with narcissistic tendencies value more than the average person—you probably had to work hard. You had to keep your eye on the prize and not get distracted by other things (relationships, petty problems, your emotions and those of others). That kind of focus creates a certain kind of person: someone who doesn't give up easily, but also someone who doesn't reach out for help easily; someone who is tough, but perhaps a little too tough when it comes to his own feelings and the feelings of others.

Discovering that you have emotionally and possibly even psychologically damaged your partner and/or your children and that you have risked losing your family because of it has undoubtedly put a chink in your armor and caused you to feel more vulnerable than you are used to feeling. This crack in your facade can be the first glimpse you have had to your real self. Ironically, your newly experienced vulnerability—the feeling that you are now exposed for all the world to see, that all your weaknesses are now visible—is the very thing that can save you. It is the very thing that will allow you to admit that you need help.

4. Reach Out for Help

Narcissistic Personality Disorder is a serious psychological disorder that requires professional treatment. If you have a full-blown version of this disorder, you will not be able to recover without the help of a qualified psychotherapist. Treatment will not be easy because it will require you to admit that you have human failings like everyone else. It will require you to face the truth about how you have caused those closest to you to suffer—namely, your partner and your children. You will also need to recognize your need for other people. At the same time, you will need to recognize that just because you need other people, it does not mean they will necessarily supply your needs. Most important, it will require you to once more experience the feelings of being a helpless and manipulated child who sustained considerable damage at the hands of selfish or unloving parents or other caregivers. You will need to begin to recognize the emptiness of a life compulsively controlled by the need for admiration and achievement.

But as difficult and painful as the process is, the rewards are many. You will uncover your authentic self underneath your cold mask of superiority. You will gain the ability to feel compassion and empathy toward others and yourself. You will gain the ability to feel real, genuine gratitude toward others and toward life in general. And you will grow to appreciate leading an ordinary life, one with real joys and sorrows, not the false pleasures of a fantasy life filled with distorted mirrors.

My Personal Program
for Overcoming Narcissistic Tendencies

It will take time to overcome your narcissistic tendencies and to reap the benefits of long-term therapy. In the meantime, you can begin to make some changes right now. The following suggestions are based on what worked for me and many of my clients:

1. Catch yourself in the act when you begin to criticize your partner. Ask your partner to tell you each and every time she feels criticized, belittled, or made fun of, and then, when she does so, thank her for the reminder. Realize that your need to criticize comes from either your own self-hatred, your need to push your partner away, or your need to maintain control over your partner.

2. Instead of talking about yourself as often, start listening—really listening—to your partner when he or she is talking. Ask more questions and take a real interest in what he or she has been doing. It will be difficult at first. You may find yourself bored or easily distracted. When this happens, you'll need to will yourself to focus on what your partner is saying. You will undoubtedly slip back into monopolizing the conversation from time to time, but with continued effort you can make real changes that your partner will appreciate immensely.

3. Admit your need for people, especially your need for your partner and children. Notice how much better you feel when you and your partner are getting along and how wounded you feel when you don't feel included, acknowledged, and admired. Make the assumption that your partner and children probably feel the same way when you don't include, acknowledge, and admire them.

4. Instead of focusing only on your own needs, try focusing on the needs of others, particularly the needs of your partner and children. Think of ways to show them how much you appreciate them.

5. Ask your partner to tell you the ways that you have been abusive or hurtful and really listen to her when she does. Ask her how your behavior affected her. Try putting yourself in her place and imagine how it must have felt to be treated the way you have treated her.

6. Apologize to your partner for the way you have treated her in the past and show her that you mean to make significant changes in your behavior.

7. Start appreciating the good things in your life, especially the good things your partner brings to your life. Begin to practice gratitude every day. For example, every morning, think of five things to be grateful for. Or, at the end of the day, instead of keeping yourself awake by obsessing about your career or your looks, think back over the day and find at least five things to be grateful for.

8. Begin to appreciate the simple beauty of life. Slow down, take long walks, and appreciate nature.

RECOMMENDED FILMS

Girl, Interrupted (realistic account of a young borderline individual)

Wild Iris (an excellent portrait of a narcissistic mother and how it affects both her daughter and grandson)

PART THREE

WHERE DO YOU GO FROM HERE?

CHAPTER 10

Should You Stay or Should You Leave?

*You never know what is enough
unless you know what is more than enough.*

WILLIAM BLAKE

The decision whether to continue your relationship or to end it will undoubtedly be a difficult one. Unless you are with someone who exhibits an abusive personality—someone whose road through life is strewn with people they have wounded or irreparably damaged—it is difficult to know when it is time to leave and when there is still a chance for some real change in the relationship. The information, exercises, and questionnaires in this chapter will help those of you who are undecided to determine whether you should stay or leave.

Good Reasons to Stay

There are both good and bad reasons to stay. The following is a list of some of the good reasons:

- You or your partner have admitted to being abusive and have begun to take some of the steps outlined in either chapter 5 or 6.

- You or your partner have admitted to being abusive and have begun working with a psychotherapist or started marital or couples counseling.

- You have made it clear to your partner that you will no longer tolerate abuse of any kind, and he or she responded by curbing his or her tendency to be abusive.

- You have begun to use some of the strategies suggested in this book, and your partner seems to be responding by not being as abusive or not being abusive as often.

Of course, even when you both commit to working on the problem or to seeking professional help, it is always possible that one or both of you will continue to be abusive without any sign of stopping. In these situations, the abused partner may need to end the relationship in order to prevent further damage to his or her self-esteem and sanity. This was the case with James: "I hated to admit it, but even after months of trying, Nicole was not changing. I know she tried, but before long she was back to her old ways. She needs professional help and she refuses to get it. I love her and I don't blame her because I know she has serious problems, but I'm just no longer willing to put up with the abuse."

Unless those who suffer from personality disorders such as BPD and NPD get professional help, most will fall back into their old ways of relating to their partner, no matter how hard they try to the contrary.

QUESTIONNAIRE: *Intimacy, Sharing, and Respect*

The above reasons for staying are particularly good ones if you and your partner have a basically healthy and rewarding relationship in other respects. A healthy relationship is one in which the following three components are present: intimacy, sharing or mutuality, and respect.

The following questions will help you evaluate the quality of your relationship, including how much intimacy, sharing, and respect you experience with one another:

1. Do you and your partner share emotional and sexual intimacy?

2. Is there a sense of equality and give-and-take in your relationship?

3. Do you and your partner treat one another with respect?

4. Do you feel there is more honesty than dishonesty between you?

5. Do you believe you bring more joy than pain to each other's lives?

6. Do you feel that your intentions are good when it comes to how you treat each other?

7. Do you feel you and your partner basically wish each other well?

8. Do you and your partner have much in common?

9. Do you share the same hopes and dreams?

10. Do you feel you and your partner understand each other?

If you can answer yes to the majority of these questions, then it is likely that the emotional abuse that exists in your relationship is a result of bad habits rather than an intention on either of your parts to deliberately undermine, control, or destroy your partner. By continuing to enforce your boundaries with one another, either you or your partner or both of you will soon be able to break the bad habits that have interfered with your relationship functioning in a more positive way.

If you are only able to say yes to half of these questions, it is likely that your individual histories are interfering with your ability to be intimate, caring, and/or respectful to one another. By continuing to follow the programs I have outlined in the book, especially by completing your unfinished business, you will likely find that your levels of intimacy, honesty, and respect for one another increase.

If, on the other hand, you cannot answer at least three of these questions with a yes, especially numbers 1 to 7, then it is likely that either you or your partner has a need to undermine, dominate, or control or to use your partner as an outlet for your anger. This means that change is not likely to occur in the relationship, especially not without professional help.

You May Still Need to Leave

Sometimes even those couples who share intimacy, equality, and honesty need to end the relationship. Even those who acknowledge the abusiveness in the relationship and actively work on discovering and respecting one another's triggers and boundaries sometimes continue to make each other unhappy. This does not mean that either partner is a bad person or that either should be blamed for the relationship ending. It just means that you have come to the conclusion that considering each of your issues, it is best if you end the relationship and go on with your lives separately.

Some couples discover that their individual histories pose too great an obstacle to maintaining a mutually healthy, fulfilling, loving relationship. While some may be able to accommodate one another's needs without causing themselves too much pain, others may become clear that their needs are not now, nor will they ever be, compatible and that to continue the relationship will only cause continued emotional distress. For example, due to a history of being emotionally smothered by a parent, one partner may need a great deal of emotional and physical space. But when he or she takes this space, it may trigger memories of abandonment and rejection for the other partner.

Good Reasons to Leave

The following are good reasons why you should seriously consider either ending the relationship or separating from your partner until things change:

- Your partner refuses to admit he is being abusive.

- Your partner refuses to get help for her abusive behavior.

- You made it clear to your partner that you will no longer tolerate abuse of any kind, but he or she has continued to be abusive.

- You and/or your partner have not been willing to follow through on the exercises, and you continue to abuse one another.

- You and your partner have both followed the strategies in the book, but you continue to push each other's buttons and to abuse one another.

- You are unwilling to admit that you are being emotionally abusive to your partner.

- You are unwilling to follow the suggestions in the book or to seek professional help, and you continue to abuse your partner.

When You Definitely Need to Leave

If any of the following circumstances exist in your current relationship, it is absolutely essential that you end your relationship as soon as possible:

1. *If your children are being emotionally, physically, or sexually abused by your partner.* If your partner is overly controlling, domineering, critical, or rejecting of you, it isn't too much of a stretch to realize that he or she is going to treat your children the same way. Unfortunately, most nonabusive partners try to fool themselves into believing otherwise. But the truth is that it is rare for these types of abusers to confine their criticism and controlling behavior to their spouse. A person who is critical, demanding, rejecting, and difficult to please generally treats everyone in his life in a similar way, especially those closest to him. Don't continue to be blind to the way your partner treats your children or to make excuses for his or her behavior. If you can't walk away from the abuse, get professional help. Therapy will help you build up your self-esteem and gain the courage to do what you know is right for you and your children. Remember that you are who you are today primarily because of the way your parents (or other caretakers) treated you. Don't continue the cycle of abuse by exposing your children to the same unacceptable behavior you grew up with.

   If your children are being physically or sexually abused by your partner, it is vital that you get the children away from him, even if you are not strong enough to leave yet. Each day your child is exposed to such violence, major harm is being done to your child's mind, body, and spirit.

2. *If you are emotionally, physically, or sexually abusing your children.* The fact that you are reading this book tells me that you don't want to continue your behavior. You now know where your abusive tendencies come from, and you certainly don't want to continue treating your children the same way you were treated as a child. For the time being, the most loving thing you can do for your children is to separate yourself from them for their protection. This may mean leaving your children with your partner and you leaving the house. Or it may mean sending your children to live with friends or relatives (as long as it isn't the same person who abused you) while you and your partner get help. Either way you will be doing everyone a tremendous favor. Unless you show good will to your children in this way, they will likely never forgive you for the harm you inflict upon them, and you will never forgive yourself.

   Once you have received the help you need, you can be reunited with your children. Believe me, you will earn their respect and gratitude when they learn why you left them. And you will gain self-respect you never thought possible, knowing you cared about your children enough to give them this gift.

3. *If you are afraid you are going to abuse your children.* If you haven't begun to abuse your children but have had strong desires to do so, this is your chance to break the cycle of abuse once and for all. Reach out for professional help. A good therapist will help you find ways to release the pain, anger, fear, and shame that are compelling you to strike out at others. And depending on how close you've come to harming your children, seriously consider separating yourself from them until you have received the help you so desperately need. You're not a bad person, just a desperate person who is out of control of herself and her emotions. Do the right thing.

4. *If your children are being damaged by the emotional abuse between you and your partner.* It's one thing to decide to stay in an

emotionally abusive relationship if children are not involved and an entirely different one if they are. Those in emotionally abusive relationships often believe that because their children are not witnessing physical abuse or fighting between their parents, they are not being harmed. But when one or both parents are emotionally abusive, children can sense the tension, fear, anger, and hostility that permeate the home environment. This tension and hostility causes children to feel insecure, frightened, and off balance.

You may think your children are too young to understand what is being said between you and your partner, but even the smallest of children know when one parent is being disrespectful, critical, or demeaning toward the other. Even the youngest child understands when one parent makes the other feel humiliated or inadequate. Older children pick up on the disrespectful, abusive attitude of one parent toward the other and feel they must take sides. They either feel anger and hatred toward the parent who is being abusive or they lose respect for the abused parent and begin to mimic the abusive parent.

The longer the emotional abuse continues in your relationship, the more your children will be affected. Not only are they being damaged in the present by witnessing abusive behavior, but you are providing them poor role models and setting them up to be either victims or abusers. (Many children who become bullies or victims of bullies in school witnessed emotional or physical abuse in their own homes.) Unless you and your partner are actively working on stopping the abuse—either by reading this book and working the programs, or by working with a professional therapist—you are sacrificing the emotional health of your children by choosing to stay together.

5. *If your partner is physically abusing you or is threatening to do so.* Many people start out by emotionally abusing their partner and work their way up to physical abuse. The more emotional abuse you take, the more permission your partner feels he or she has to become even more abusive, including physically abusive. As your partner's anger intensifies and as the relationship deteriorates, he or she may resort to physical violence as a way of gaining control.

If he or she has already hit you, even if it was "just a slap," you are in danger. The same holds true of behaviors such as pushing, shoving, pinning you down, or holding you captive against your will. All of these behaviors indicate that your partner has lost control of himself or herself and are danger signs for you. In some cases, it may indicate that your partner has become mentally unstable. Don't fool yourself. If he has become violent with you once, he will do it again, and the next time it will be worse. Don't accept the excuse that he was drunk or high. He hit you because he has a problem. Drinking or using drugs may exacerbate his problem, but it is not the cause. Neither should you allow your partner to use the excuse that she has an emotional problem such as Borderline Personality Disorder. While it is true that those with this disorder can become out of control and physically violent, this is still no excuse. She needs to take responsibility for her behavior by seeking the professional help she needs.

If your partner refuses to seek professional help, I advise you to separate from her until she does so. Otherwise, every day you stay in this relationship you are endangering your emotional and physical well-being, and possibly your very life.

6. *If you have reached a point where you are becoming physically abusive.* If you are being emotionally abused, you may have become so frustrated and angry that you have reached a breaking point and have begun to act out your anger in a physical way. If this is the case, you could hurt your partner seriously next time or push him into hurting you. Either way, it's time to leave.

If the emotional abuse in your relationship has escalated into physical abuse, you are likely to do it again, and the next time it will be worse. Even if you only slapped or pushed your partner, unless you get professional help, you are putting your partner in more danger as each day goes by. If you are afraid to seek professional help, explore other options in your community. Check your local papers or yellow pages to see if there are anger management courses available. Or see if there is a support group in your area for violent or potentially violent people.

If you honestly feel that you are not an abusive person by nature but that your partner has pushed you into becoming violent, then the best thing for both of you is for you to end the relationship. Even if your partner suffers from a mental or emotional disorder of some kind, you are not helping either of you by staying.

7. *If you have begun to fantasize about harming or killing your partner.* If you have reached this point, you feel trapped and believe there is no way out of your abusive relationship. But it is important to realize that this is a symptom of the emotional abuse you have been suffering—it is not reality. The reality is that there is a way out. You will need to get professional help in order to gain the courage and strength to leave, or if you are afraid for your physical safety, you need to contact the police or a battered woman's shelter. In either case, you need to realize that there is certainly a better way out than risking being in prison for the rest of your life or being overwhelmed with guilt for the rest of your life because of the physical harm you caused your partner.

8. *If you are seriously questioning your sanity.* If your partner is using gaslighting techniques on you (e.g., denying that things have occurred, telling you that you are imagining things, or accusing you of being crazy) and you are beginning to distrust your own perceptions, it is time to leave the relationship. The longer you stay, the more you will doubt yourself and your sanity, and the more your mental health will be jeopardized.

9. *If it has become clear to you that your partner does not respect you.* If you are in a relationship with someone who devalues you, looks down on you, or doesn't recognize your worth, there is little or no hope for the relationship. It's time to leave.

When You Are Resisting Leaving

Sometimes we know we should leave but are unable to do so. We know the relationship isn't going to get any better, know that the abuse is only going to get worse, even know that we are in physical danger or are in danger of losing it and hurting our partner—and yet still be unable to leave.

This is what a reader emailed me: "I know the solution should seem easy enough . . . I should just get out. But I find I am in this mental state of resistance, and I'm not sure why. As silly as it may sound, I feel as though I need a "reason" to divorce him, a reason to tell others. The problem is that he doesn't abuse my kids—just me—and I feel selfish for taking the kids away from their father. My kids have told me they don't want to leave their father all alone, and frankly, neither do I. I feel sorry for him. I filed for divorce two months ago, but I still can't get up the courage to leave."

I strongly urged this woman to seek professional psychotherapy in order to gain the courage to leave, and I urge you to do the same if you are in a similar situation and find yourself resisting what you know must be done. There are plenty of reasons to leave, even if your partner is not physically abusing you or the children, the most important reason being that your children are being negatively affected by observing the emotional abuse that is going on in the household. It's not about what you tell others; it's what you tell yourself. If you have such low self-esteem that you can't understand that you deserve to be treated better, you need to work with a professional therapist who can help you build up your self-esteem.

Trust and Forgiveness

Many of you reading this book have no doubt discovered that your love for each other has been able to survive the emotional abuse, and some have even discovered that it is quite possible to not only stop the abuse but to deepen your relationship in the process. Unfortunately, for many, once emotional abuse has become part of a relationship, it is very difficult to move forward without fear, resentment, or anger continuing to pollute your relationship. Once someone has been victimized by his or her partner, it is difficult not to live in fear that it will occur again. This fear may inhibit you from letting your guard down and opening your heart up to your partner. You may be so on guard that you do not feel safe enough to be vulnerable—either emotionally or sexually.

In order to move past the abuse and move forward in your relationship, you must both be willing to trust and to forgive. This is a tall order for anyone. It takes time to rebuild trust, and it can try the patience of both of you when you realize that the trust is just not there. The survivor will tend to become impatient with herself, thinking that she should be past it by now, and the previously abusive partner may begin to feel that he is constantly being punished for things he did in the past and not being given a chance to prove himself.

Although it is important for you survivors to work at rebuilding your trust in your partner, it is far more important that you trust yourself. If you trust yourself to take care of yourself—meaning that you trust yourself to speak up if your partner ever crosses the line and becomes abusive again—then you both can relax in the relationship and let time show you whether your partner has, in fact, stopped his abusive ways. The same holds true if you are the previously abusive partner.

It is also important for the survivor to be able to forgive. If you cannot forgive your partner for having emotionally abused you in the past, your anger and resentment will make it impossible to move forward. While you have every reason to be angry about the abuse, you need to take responsibility for finding constructive ways of releasing your anger. Otherwise your anger will continue to seep out, creating a wedge between you and your partner and triggering defensiveness and anger from him. Your partner can't be expected to tolerate your anger indefinitely, nor is it fair to expect him to.

Forgiving is different from forgetting. Certainly you can never forget how your partner treated you, nor should you. Remembering the abuse will keep you on your toes and strengthen your resolve to never allow it to happen again. But when you forgive, you say to your partner that you are willing to give him or her another chance, that you recognize we all have our issues and that we can't expect perfection from one another.

Unfortunately, some survivors will discover that they are unable to rebuild trust in their partner or are unable to forgive their partner for the abuse, even though they have given themselves time to do both. If this is the case, it will be important to admit this to yourself and to your partner. Once this reality is faced, one or both of you may come to realize that it is time for the relationship to end.

Survivors also need to forgive themselves for allowing the abuse to continue. There is no need for you to continue to chastise yourself for being so passive or weak or foolish—whatever labels you've put on yourself. You put up with the abuse for the same reason your partner abused you—because you were abused or neglected as a child.

CHAPTER 11

Preventing Emotional Abuse in the Future

Freedom is what you do with what's been done to you.
JEAN-PAUL SARTRE

In this chapter we will focus on ways in which both partners can prevent emotional abuse in the future, whether you decide to stay in your current relationship or to end it. For those abused partners who choose to end their current relationship, I provide tips on how to spot a potential abuser in the future, how to take it slow and get to know a potential partner before committing to a relationship, and how to communicate a clear message that you will not accept abusive behavior, including how to set adequate boundaries and limits. For the abusive partner, I will present information on how you can prevent future abuse by changing certain behaviors and how to choose a partner who is your equal and is therefore less likely to put up with abusive behavior. I'll also provide strategies to help individuals and couples break the cycle of abuse and avoid becoming emotionally abusive parents.

For the Abused Partner

In this section, we'll focus on several issues of importance to the abused partner, including preventing future abuse in your relationships,

227

taking a hiatus from relationships, spotting a potential abuser, and continuing to set boundaries and limits.

Preventing Abuse in Your Current or Future Relationships

Whether you stay with your current partner or enter a new relationship, you will need to continue your efforts to identify and confront abusive behavior if you are going to prevent future abuse. The following suggestions will help keep you on track:

1. Pay attention. You don't need to be hypervigilant, but you do need to be cognizant of how your partner treats you on a daily basis. If you begin to let things slide with a new partner or allow him to talk to you or treat you in an abusive way, or if you allow a previously abusive partner to revert back to her previous controlling ways, you will send the message that you will allow yourself to be abused in the future.

2. Trust your perceptions and honor your feelings. At this point, you are able to determine when your partner is being deliberately cruel, even if he says he's just kidding. You can tell when her questioning of you is just a way to control you. And you can tell when your partner's facial expressions and comments are insinuating that you are crazy, stupid, or inadequate. The more you trust your perceptions, the less confused you will be and the better able you will be to take care of yourself.

3. Continue to speak up. You need to speak up each and every time your partner becomes abusive; otherwise you're sending the message that it is okay.

Take a Hiatus from Romantic Relationships

For those of you who have ended your relationship, the best advice I can give you as to how to avoid future abuse is to take time off from intimate relationships for a while. You'll need time to recover from the wounds of your previous relationships, time to work on completing your unfinished business with your original abuser, and time to discover who you are outside a relationship. If you jump right into a new relationship due to your fear of being alone, you can almost guarantee that you will once again become attracted to an abusive partner. I've seen this time and time again with my clients. Those who took the time to heal and to rediscover themselves were much less likely to enter another abusive relationship, but those who got involved right away with a new partner almost always ended up being re-abused.

EXERCISE: *What You Will and Will Not Put Up With*

Before you even consider starting a new relationship, you will need to get clear about what you are and are not willing to accept in terms of a partner's attitude and behavior. In chapter 5 we discussed the importance of setting limits and boundaries by stating to a partner what you are no longer willing to put up with. But it is equally important that you set limits and boundaries with yourself. The following sentence completion exercise will help you gain some clarity about this.

- Spend some time reviewing your previous relationships, especially the aspects that were abusive and the behaviors you put up with but shouldn't have.

- With this in mind, complete the following sentences.

  I won't have a relationship with someone who_____.

  I will only choose partners who_____.

Continue completing these sentences until you feel satisfied that you have covered all the bases and until you feel strong and determined.

Examples:

I won't have a relationship with someone who constantly talks about himself.

I won't have a relationship with someone who criticizes me.

I will only choose partners who treat me as their equal.

I will only choose partners who are open to constructive feedback.

Take It Slow and Get to Know Your Partner

In order to establish a healthy, lasting relationship, one based on intimacy, sharing, and respect, you need time—time to get to know the other person, time for him to get to know you, and time to determine whether you are compatible.

Many emotionally abusive partners are initially quite charming. Don't let yourself be fooled again. Take time to get to know the *real* person, not the superficial, beginning-of-the-relationship persona that we all project. This will only be revealed through time, as layer after layer of defensiveness is stripped away, and the other person's false self melts away.

Learn How to Spot an Abuser

Most abusive partners exhibit similar behaviors and attitudes and have very similar personality traits. By being able to spot these behaviors, attitudes, and traits you can avoid becoming involved with another abusive partner. Be on the lookout for:

- Poor impulse control
- Low self-esteem
- Selfishness and narcissism
- Being needy and demanding (of your time, attention, etc.)
- Alcohol abuse or drug use; alcoholism or drug addiction
- A history of being abusive (emotionally, physically, or sexually) as an adult or older child
- A history of mental illness
- Dependent personality (unable to support self financially, emotionally)
- Personality disorder (especially Borderline Personality Disorder or Narcissistic Personality Disorder)
- Antisocial behavior (does not believe in or abide by society's rules, has own set of rules that seem to accommodate his or her desires)

- Being aggressive, demanding, abusive

- Needing to feel powerful and in control

- Being preoccupied with sex, needing to have sex daily or several times a day; masturbating compulsively

- Poor social skills; difficulties developing adult social and sexual relationships

Talk Openly about Your Expectations in a Relationship

In addition to taking it slow and really getting to know a potential partner, it is important to talk openly about your expectations of one another. The following example should act as a warning against entering a relationship blindly.

From the time Tammy and Carlo got married, Carlo began to dominate and control her. "He started ordering me around, and he expected me to mind him as if he was my father instead of my husband," Tammy said. "He wasn't like that when we were dating. Believe me, I wouldn't have married him if he were. When I confronted him about it, he told me that now that I was his wife he had different expectations of me—that it may have been okay for me to be so independent when we were dating, but not as his wife. I don't know where he got such an idea. Carlo's father is dead, so I didn't get a chance to see how his father treated his mother."

Tammy confronted Carlo in a joint session with me, telling him that she was not willing to put up with his treatment of her and explaining to him how his behavior hurt her. She made it clear that unless he changed his behavior and his expectations, she was going to have to end their marriage. Carlo was unwilling to hear that his behavior was abusive, and his pride prevented him from seeking therapy for himself. Tammy then focused on gaining the strength and courage to end the marriage.

"I don't want to end my marriage," she shared with me. "I love Carlo, and I wanted it to work out for us. But I'm simply unwilling to be treated like this. I'd rather end it now, before he beats me down so much that I don't have the strength to leave."

Had Tammy discussed her expectations of marriage with Carlo and talked openly with him about what he expected, she might have discovered his controlling attitude and his beliefs about the role of women in a marriage.

Continue to Set Limits and Boundaries

Even if you manage to spot potential abusers and only enter into relationships with nonabusive partners, this does not mean you will be immune to abuse. Even healthy partners can become abusive if they are not given appropriate limits and boundaries. If you have a tendency to lose yourself in relationships by becoming too enmeshed in the life of your partner, giving up your own activities and friends, and focusing too much attention on your partner and your relationship, work on maintaining a separate life and a separate self. Determine how much involvement you can handle before you start to "disappear," and set your boundaries accordingly. By using the following questions as a guide, you can begin to set emotional boundaries that are healthy for you:

- How much intimacy can I tolerate before I start to feel smothered?
- How much time can I spend with my partner before I start to feel uncomfortable or start to lose myself?
- How much can I share about myself before I feel I have shared too much?

Continue to Work on Yourself

In order to prevent future abuse, you will also need to continue working on becoming the most assertive, independent person you can be. Don't fool yourself into thinking that it was all your partner's fault and that if you choose a different type of partner next time, you have nothing to fear. If you are a dependent type of personality who is drawn to "take control" types of partners, you are bound to slip right back into unhealthy ways of relating that will encourage abuse.

An acquaintance recently told me, "I like strong, powerful men, men who take charge. I don't like making decisions. I'd rather be with someone who will make the decisions for me." I could hardly believe my ears. She was recently out of an abusive marriage with an extremely controlling man, and I knew she had an attraction to controlling men. What I was surprised about was that she wasn't embarrassed in the least about the fact that she preferred to be dependent. I was even more surprised that she hadn't yet made the connection between her desire to avoid responsibility and her tendency to be abused.

If you are going to avoid abusive relationships, you need to learn to make your own decisions. You need to learn to speak your mind and get over your fear of offering your opinions and stating your preferences. You'll need to realize that your thoughts, your ideas, your perceptions, and your needs are as important as anyone else's.

If you are a woman, refer to my book *Loving Him without Losing You* for more information on how to learn to make decisions, speak up, and state your preferences, as well as how to go slow in the beginning of a relationship and how to avoid losing yourself in relationships.

For the Abusive Partner—
Catch Yourself in the Act

No matter what your individual issues are, all abusers tend to engage in certain predictable behaviors that lead up to them becoming abusive. The following is a list of such behaviors:

- Focusing outward instead of inward (projecting, criticizing, judging)

- Being out of touch with what you really feel

- Thinking only of how a situation makes you feel (lack of empathy)

- Having a tendency to want to control situations and people

- Having a tendency to obsess and ruminate about things

If you work on extinguishing these behaviors in addition to completing your unfinished business, you will stop being emotionally abusive. The following suggestions will help you begin to change these behaviors and to catch yourself in the act before you become abusive.

- When you begin to focus on what your partner is doing wrong, focus instead on what is going on inside of you.

- Ask yourself—What am I really feeling under all that anger and criticism?

- Try putting yourself in your partner's place the next time you are upset with her. Imagine how she is feeling.

- Recognize that your partner is separate from you and therefore has a right to have different reactions and opinions about things, to be in a different mood than you are in, to have different tastes from yours, and to make choices that you might not make. Realize that you cannot control anyone else. Even if your partner allows you to control her, the price you pay for her compliance is the loss of her love. No slave ever loved his master. No prisoner ever loved his jailer. There is no room for true love or devotion in the heart of someone who is scrambling for their life every day. There is only room for hatred and dreaming of the day when they will finally be free.

- Recognize that your feelings of anger probably have more to do with you than they do with your partner. Instead of ruminating about what your partner has done or how she or he has upset you, take a look at your personal history for answers to why you are so upset.

- When you discover that you are too invested in changing your partner's mind or in getting her to do something, disengage. If you continue to push, you are likely to say things you will regret later. Get some space from your partner or the situation, and remind yourself of what is really important—such as maintaining your relationship.

EXERCISE: *FEEL*

As you can see, all these suggestions have to do with getting in touch with what you are feeling. As a simple reminder, I created the acronym FEEL:

F ocus

E motion

E mpathy

L eave

The next time you feel yourself getting angry or critical of your partner, say the word FEEL to yourself and remind yourself of what each letter means. Then remember to focus on yourself instead of on your partner, pay attention to what you are really feeling under the anger, and have empathy for how your partner is feeling. If none of this works, disengage from the situation and go for a walk.

For Both Partners

The following suggestions apply to both the abused partner and the abusive one:

Go Slow

In order to avoid choosing another abusive partner or a partner who will allow you to become abusive, you must be willing to go slow when it comes to getting sexually and romantically involved. Many who become involved in abusive relationships get involved far too quickly before they have a chance to get to know the other person. This often stems from the fact that they didn't get their emotional needs met in childhood and are essentially looking for someone who will fill up those empty places inside them. As soon as someone comes along who seems caring, all those unmet needs become activated, and there is a powerful push to merge with the other person.

But there are several problems with this. First of all, if you become romantically and sexually involved with someone right away, by the time you finally get to know the person, you are no longer objective and are therefore more likely to be blind to the person's problems and issues. Women, in particular, need to be careful because when they have sex, the chemical oxytocin—a bonding agent—is released, causing them to fall in love and making it difficult to walk away, even when their partner's abusive tendencies begin to surface.

Since you probably know your pattern, be on guard when you meet your type. If you become enormously attracted to someone right away, *beware!* This person is probably a replica of your original abuser. If you feel as though you've known someone all your life, it may be because you have!

Have Equal Relationships

Another important way of preventing future abuse is to make sure you have equal relationships. An equal relationship is one in which each is seen as an equal in the other's eyes. Victims of emotional abuse tend to choose partners who they consider to be more powerful, more accomplished, more intelligent, and so on. Those who tend to become abusive, on the other hand, tend to choose partners who they view as less powerful, less accomplished, less intelligent, and so on.

When you enter a relationship with someone to whom you feel "less than," you essentially give away your power to that person, which sets the tone for the entire relationship. You'll tend to bend over backwards to please him, to give in to him, to keep quiet when you should speak up, to tolerate unacceptable behavior, or to generally allow him to control the relationship.

If you become involved with someone who perceives himself or herself as being more powerful or better than you, she will take advantage by pushing limits, taking you for granted, or trying to dominate you.

If, on the other hand, you are the one who tends to become involved with those who have less power than you, or who you perceive as being "less than" you, you are making a clear statement that you are unwilling to have an equal relationship or that you are afraid to be involved with someone who is your equal. You are making it clear that you need to be the one who is the dominant one in the relationship and that you intend to control the relationship and your partner. This is a clear setup for abuse.

In order to break your pattern—whether it be to choose someone who has more personal power or less—you will need to aim for relationships in which both you and your partner view each other as equals. This doesn't mean you are equal in all respects, but that overall, your strengths and qualities balance each other out.

QUESTIONNAIRE: *Equal or Unequal?*

The following questions will help you decide whether a current or potential relationship is an equal one.

1. Who has more personal power in the relationship? Who do you feel is the stronger of the two in terms of being able to ask for what you want and being able to take care of yourself emotionally?

2. Which of you has the stronger need to be in control? Who usually gets his or her way when choosing what you will do at any given time?

3. Who is more in control of your sexual relationship?

4. Which of you has more self-confidence? Which one feels better about himself/herself?

5. Which of you is more successful in your career?

6. Who makes more money?

7. Would you say one of you feels superior to the other? If so, who?

8. Who would you say loves the other more?

9. Who is more emotionally dependent on the other? Which of you would have a more difficult time going on without the other?

10. Who is more invested in maintaining the relationship?

If you answered "my partner" to most of questions 1 to 7 and "me" to questions 8, 9, and 10, your partner has more power in the relationship. If you answered "me" to questions 1 to 7 and "my partner" to questions 8, 9 and 10, you have more power.

Preventing Your Children
from Being Emotionally Abused

Unfortunately, another way victims of both childhood and adult abuse repeat the cycle of violence is by becoming emotionally abusive toward their own children. If you were emotionally abused as a child or if you have either been the victim or perpetrator of emotional abuse in an intimate adult relationship, you are far more likely to emotionally abuse your children than any other group of people. This is true for all the following reasons:

- It is a natural progression for victims of abuse to take the anger they still inevitably feel toward their abusers out on those less powerful than themselves. This is probably the most potent reason why you must continue to work on your unfinished business with your original abusers and, if appropriate, any unfinished business you have with your previous or current partner. The more you work on releasing your anger in constructive ways, the less likely you will be to abuse your own children.

- We tend to treat our children the way we were treated ourselves. Many survivors of emotional abuse have told me how shocked they were to hear the very words their parents said to them coming out of their own mouths. As my client Morgan told me, "When I was a kid, my father constantly put me down for being a little overweight. He'd call me names like "lard ass," and "buffalo bottom." I hated it and hated him for talking to me like that. His words stayed with me all my life, and because of them, I still feel self-conscious about my body. So when I heard myself calling my daughter those same names, I shuddered in disbelief. I never wanted to hurt my daughter the way I'd been hurt, but somehow the words just tumbled out of my mouth."

  Other parents have found themselves punishing their children with the silent treatment just the way their parents had done with them, becoming overly controlling or possessive the way their parents were, or becoming overly critical of their children just as their parents had done with them.

If you catch yourself repeating your parents' abusive behavior, immediately apologize to your child. Tell him or her that you are sorry, that you didn't mean it, and that you are going to work on never doing it again. And then do just that. Continue working on clearing up your unfinished business and on releasing your anger in constructive ways. If you find that you continue emotionally abusing your children, seek professional help. You don't want your children to suffer as you did, and you don't want them to become either a victim or an abuser.

- Those who are emotionally abusive to their partner tend to also emotionally abuse their children because the same dynamics are at play. They abuse because they are angry, insecure, and full of shame. When these feelings get triggered, they lash out at whoever is closest to them—whether it is their partner or their child. Our children also remind us of ourselves and can act as a trigger, bringing back painful memories. We see ourselves in our children, and if we are full of self-hate and loathing, those feelings will be projected onto our children.

- Those who have been victims of emotional abuse in an adult relationship can also take their anger out on their children, especially if a child reminds you of an abusive partner. This is often the case when an emotionally abused woman has a son or when an emotionally abused man has a daughter.

Your children also need you to protect them from other people who may become abusive toward them. For this reason, you must continue to work on coming out of denial about your own childhood abuse, as well as how much you have been negatively damaged by your partner's abuse. Otherwise, you won't recognize that these same people are abusing your children, even if it happens right in front of your eyes. If you are able to admit the truth about the way your parents or other caretakers treated you when you were a child, you will not be as likely to expose your children to these same people. Unless you have reason to believe that those who abused you have changed (because they have had professional counseling, because they have admitted they were wrong and have apologized to you), don't be foolish enough to think they will not abuse your children in the very same way they abused you.

Strategies to Help You Avoid Emotionally Abusing Your Children

1. Try to accept your children for who they are. Don't set unreasonable expectations for how they should act in public or how they should perform in school or in extracurricular activities. Allow your children to make mistakes and to be kids.

2. Don't look to your children for needs that you should meet elsewhere. Your child should not be your confidante or your best friend.

3. Respect your children and they will respect you. Abusive parents often demand total obedience and demand that their children show them respect at all times. But a parent needs to earn respect, just like everyone else.

4. Maintain appropriate boundaries. Respect your child's privacy by knocking before entering his or her room, by not listening to his telephone conversations, and by not opening his mail. Close the door when you go to the bathroom, and don't barge into the bathroom when your child is in there.

5. Set appropriate limits and administer proper discipline. Don't be afraid to say no to your children or to punish them when they do something wrong (the most effective punishments are time-outs and taking away privileges, not physical punishment). Children who are allowed to walk all over their parents grow up feeling entitled to special treatment from others, disrespecting authority, and lacking proper limits and boundaries.

6. Learn appropriate ways of being affectionate with your children. Physical touch is vital to a child's development. Children need to be held, nurtured, and comforted. If you were deprived of this kind

of nurturing, you may have difficulty giving it to your children, but it is very important that you work through your reticence.

7. Continue working on yourself and on being a good parent. There are numerous parenting classes available and many fine books on parenting. If you find you are becoming abusive, I recommend individual therapy, family therapy, and a group called Parents Anonymous. There you will meet other parents who have been abusive to their children, learn how they were able to stop, and learn effective parenting skills.

8. If you are undecided as to whether you should become a parent given your abusive background, I suggest you read my book *The Parenthood Decision*. It includes questionnaires and information that will help you determine whether you should wait to become a parent or not become a parent at all.

CHAPTER 12

Continuing to Recover

*What lies behind us and what lies before us
are tiny matters compared to what lies within us.*

RALPH WALDO EMERSON

This chapter is for both the survivor of emotional abuse and the abusive partner. In it you will each find strategies and information that will help you continue to recover from both the childhood abuse that you each suffered and the repercussions of having been in an emotionally abusive relationship with someone you cared about as an adult. If you choose to remain in your present relationship, I advise you each to read the entire chapter, including those sections that pertain to your partner. This will enable you to continue to deepen your understanding of one another and to help one another in the recovery process.

Many of you will undoubtedly want to know how long recovery will take. Generally speaking, the longer the abuse occurred—either in childhood or adulthood—and the more intense the abuse was, the longer the process of recovery. The same holds true if you have been emotionally abused by more than one person. The sooner you start on the recovery process, the firmer you are about not allowing abuse to continue, the faster the recovery process will be. This is because each time you allow yourself to be abused, you are re-experiencing the abuse you suffered as a child and are, in essence, being re-abused. For abusive partners, the longer you allow yourself to focus outside yourself and to be abusive, the more shame you pile on yourself and the more you avoid working on your own issues.

True Power Comes from Knowing You Have Choices

The recovery process begins with the first recognition that you have been abused in the past or are currently being abused. In order to continue recovering—either from being abused or from abusing—you must realize that true power comes from knowing you have choices.

If you are the previously abused partner, you must come to the realization that you always have the choice to continue a conversation or to end it. You always have the choice to confront your partner on his or her behavior. You have the choice whether or not you want to do something. And you always have the choice whether to continue or end a relationship.

If you have a history of being abusive, you, too, must remember you have choices. No matter how much you were abused or neglected as a child, no matter how hurt or angry you become, you can choose not to repeat the cycle of abuse. You can choose to take a walk and get away from the situation, you can choose to release your anger in constructive ways, or you can choose to write about your feelings. You can take a deep breath, count to ten, and calmly tell your partner what is upsetting you. Or best of all, you can choose to take your focus off your partner and go inside yourself in order to discover what is really bothering you and why.

Key Issues for Victims and Abusers

There are two key issues that both victim and abuser must address if you are to recover from your abusive patterns: raise your self esteem, and continue to identify and honor your emotions.

Raise Your Self-esteem

Those who were emotionally abused, neglected, or abandoned in child-hood will inevitably suffer from low self-esteem. The same is true of those who were physically or sexually abused. We've heard a lot about self-esteem in the past ten to fifteen years, so much so that we often don't take it very seriously. But in order for you to recover from child-hood or adult abuse, you must work on raising your self-esteem. There is absolutely nothing as important to our psychological well-being as our self-esteem. It affects virtually every aspect of our lives, including how we perceive ourselves and others, how others perceive us, our choices in life, our ability to give and receive love, and our ability and willingness to take action when things need to be changed.

Our self-esteem is how we feel about ourselves; it is our overall judgment of ourselves. If we have high self-esteem, we like and approve of ourselves and we accept ourselves for who we are, including our so-called bad qualities. If we have high self-esteem, it can be assumed that we also have self-love, self-respect, and feelings of self-worth.

Unfortunately, most victims of childhood abuse do not have high self-esteem and therefore do not love or respect themselves, nor can they imagine that anyone else can truly love or respect them. They don't think they deserve to be loved or respected, nor do they feel they deserve to be treated with kindness and consideration. When someone treats them with respect or kindness, they often become uncomfortable and proceed to push the person away, instead becoming attracted to partners who treat them with the disdain, cruelty, or indifference they are more accustomed to and feel they deserve. Those who tend to be abusive may initially become attracted to a partner who treats them with kindness and respect, but once they "have" them they grow increasingly disdainful of such a partner. Although it is an unconscious motivation, they believe that any partner who wants to be with them must have something seriously wrong with her and therefore does not deserve their respect. It's also often the case that loving kindness can become just too painful to either the victim or the abuser because it reminds them so much of what they didn't receive as a child.

How Do You Begin to Raise Your Self-esteem?

The following strategies are applicable for both men and women, victimized partners and abusive ones:

1. Notice how often you are self-critical. When you are self-critical, you are essentially doing the same thing to yourself that your parents or other original abusers did to you—you are re-abusing yourself and damaging your self-esteem. Self-criticism is partly the reason why you allowed your partner to abuse you or why you abused your partner. Pay attention to your self-talk or inner dialogues. Catch yourself whenever you engage in a critical, negative thought about yourself and *stop it!* Ask yourself, "Whose voice am I hearing?" Are you saying the same things to yourself that were said to you by your parents or by a previous abuser? Counter the critical message with something like, "That's not true; I'm not stupid. I just made a mistake." Then replace the negative self-talk with positive, encouraging statements, such as "I'm doing the best I can," or "I'm getting better."

2. Focus on your positive attributes instead of your faults. Self-criticism is damaging enough, but when coupled with a lack of self-praise, it can be devastating to your self-esteem. In addition to being overly criticized as a child, you were also probably seldom praised. The same holds true for those of you who have been emotionally abused as an adult. Now you must begin to turn this around by talking to yourself in ways that are reassuring, approving, and loving. You won't be able to stop your self-criticism right away, but you can balance it with self-praise.

EXERCISE: *Your Weaknesses and Your Strengths*

- Make two lists—one of your weaknesses and one of your strengths.

- If your strengths list isn't at least as long as your weaknesses list, work on thinking of more positive attributes to add to the list.

- Ask a supportive friend to help you if you get stuck.

3. Set reachable goals. Both survivors and abusers tend to set impossibly high standards for themselves. They expect themselves to be perfect, and they are extremely self-critical when they make mistakes or don't meet their own unreasonably high expectations. The only difference is that survivors blame themselves for their perceived failures and abusers tend to blame others.

   The experience of success does wonders for our self-esteem. But in order to feel successful, we need to set goals that are reachable. Set small goals instead of big ones. With each small success, you will build your self-confidence and raise your self-esteem.

4. Stop comparing yourself with others. The problem with comparing yourself with others is that you will either end up feeling *less than* or *better than* others. If you feel less than, your self-esteem will be lowered. Those who have been mistreated in the past often allowed abuse to continue because they felt so bad about themselves that they believed no one else would want them or because their low self-esteem caused them to believe an abuser's accusations or put-downs. Many abusers feel less than others, and this adds to their shame.

   Other people who have become abusive compare themselves with others and end up feeling superior. This gives them permission to mistreat and disrespect others, particularly their partner.

   The next time you find yourself comparing yourself with someone, try telling yourself that he or she is just *different* from you, without placing a judgment value on how she is different. Even if the other person seems to have more than you do or is more accomplished, remind yourself that it doesn't mean she is better than you are or has more worth than you. In fact, many people probably admire you for your attributes. Bolster your own self-esteem by turning your attention to your own good qualities. Also, realize that when we envy someone we are usually seeing an incomplete picture. While this person may seem to have it all, no one has everything. In the end it does all balance out. Instead of envying what others have, decide what *you* want out of life and focus on achieving it.

5. Accept that you and others are both good and bad. Some who were emotionally abused in childhood tried to become all good in an attempt to win their parents' approval and love. Even though this probably didn't work very well, it may have helped them escape the radar screen of their parents' criticism or abuse. As adults, they continued doing what they were told and not making waves in the belief that this is the way to avoid abuse. Unfortunately, for many, their "good girl" or "good boy" act may have actually set them up for abuse as adults. Others who were abused as a child came to believe that they were all bad—as their parents led them to believe. Since they felt it was hopeless to try to be good, they chose to become like their abusers.

Whether you view yourself as all good or all bad, in order to raise your self-esteem and break the cycle of abuse, you must come to understand that we all have both good qualities and bad qualities. No one is a total failure, and no one is a total success. Gently but firmly stop expecting perfection from yourself and others.

6. Begin to nurture yourself. Those who were neglected and abused as children did not receive the nurturing they needed in order to grow up with high self-esteem. Some grew up expecting their romantic partners to give them the nurturing they hungered for, only to be disappointed. But our partners are not our parents, no matter how much we try to make them into parents. No one can make up for the deprivation you experienced, and no one should be expected to. You are the only one who can give yourself the nurturing you need. The more you nurture yourself, the more you will be healed from the devastating damage caused by the emotional abuse to your mind, body, and spirit. Caring for yourself and treating yourself with tenderness will contribute greatly to your positive feelings about yourself and will in turn help raise your self-esteem.

Continue to Identify and Honor Your Feelings

A major part of the damage caused by childhood abuse of any kind is that it causes us to disown our emotions, to push them down until we are no longer aware of them or have lost control of them. Many survivors of childhood abuse live in a state of emotional bankruptcy, "sleepwalking" through life and depriving themselves of any emotionality. Even those who become emotional volcanoes—spewing out their pain and anger at everyone in their path—are often numb to their real feelings of pain, fear, and shame.

By splitting off from your emotional and physical feelings, you may manage to avoid a great deal of pain, but you do so at a great price. You can't cut off your feelings of pain, fear, shame, and anger without also sacrificing your ability to feel such emotions as joy and love. And without access to your emotions, there is a major part of yourself that is hidden from you. This lack of awareness has been one of the factors that has contributed to your either becoming abusive or to your being abused.

An effective way to reclaim all your emotions (pain, anger, fear, guilt, shame, joy, and love) is to begin to pay close attention to your body. Your body experiences a different set of physical sensations for every emotion that you experience. For example, when you are angry, your shoulders may tighten and you may clench your jaw. When you are frightened, you may lift your shoulders and your stomach may tighten or feel all jittery inside. When you feel ashamed, you may feel as if a heavy burden has been placed on your shoulders. Paying close attention to the way your body reacts to emotions will be a major step in reclaiming an important part of yourself.

Both abusers and survivors need to continue to find constructive ways of releasing their anger—the survivor so that he or she will not continue to swallow his or her anger and turn it on himself or herself, the abuser so he or she will not continue to take his or her anger out on his or her partner. Refer to chapter 6 for specific strategies for coping with and releasing anger in constructive ways.

Strategies for the Abused Partner

Those who have been emotionally abused will suffer from many battle scars, even though these scars may be invisible to the human eye. The long-term effects of emotional abuse can include:

- A distrust in your perceptions

- A tendency to be fearful or on guard

- Self-consciousness or fear of how you are coming across

- An inability to be spontaneous

- A distrust of people and in future relationships

- Anger that bursts out unexpectedly

- Sensitivity to anyone trying to control you

Once you are no longer being continually damaged by emotional abuse, many of these long-term effects will diminish in time. Your trust in your perceptions and your spontaneity will gradually return and your tendency to be on guard and self-consciousness will fade. But you will find that your trust in others will not return as readily. If you have chosen to stay with your partner, it may take quite some time before you are able to trust that she will not resume her abusive ways. If you have ended an abusive relationship, it will take quite some time before you are able to trust another person.

This distrust is actually a very healthy reaction. Just because your partner has admitted he has been abusive and has been working on the issues that caused his behavior does not mean that he will not sometimes backslide and return to his old ways of coping. And if you have ended an emotionally abusive relationship, the last thing you need to do is to begin a new relationship right away. Instead, you need to work on your own issues to make sure you don't choose an abusive partner once again. When you do begin to date again, you need to take it slow and get to know the person before getting involved. Allow your distrust to act as a reminder of what you have endured and a warning against making the same mistakes again.

It will also take some time before your anger subsides. Although it can be quite disconcerting to have anger burst out of you unexpectedly, this symptom of emotional abuse is quite natural and actually quite healing. You stored up a lot of anger all those months or years that you were being emotionally abused, and all that repressed and suppressed anger now needs to come out of you. You will need to find appropriate ways to release your anger such as writing a letter to your abusers that you may or may not choose to send, yelling into a pillow, or stomping on aluminum cans. You'll find that if someone tries to control you or if someone (including your current partner) begins to emotionally abuse you in any of the ways we've discussed in this book, your anger will be especially powerful. Instead of being embarrassed or concerned about your anger, begin to view it as a powerful affirmation that you will no longer tolerate such behavior from others.

Your anger can motivate you to take better care of yourself, to pursue goals and dreams you put aside or came to believe you were incapable of. If you can channel your righteous anger, it can inspire you to help other victims of abuse or to ensure that your own children are never abused. If, on the other hand, you use your anger to punish your partner or potential partners or if you turn it against yourself instead of releasing it in positive ways, your anger can destroy you.

If you've chosen to stay with your partner, and he has apologized for past abuse and has stopped abusing you currently, it is unfair to continue punishing him. If you've ended your relationship, other men or women who approach you or date you are not responsible for what your previous partner did and therefore don't deserve your anger. If you find that you have difficulty separating the present from the past or if the acting out of your anger is becoming dangerous to yourself or others, I recommend you seek professional help.

Give Yourself Permission to Feel

All through the recovery process as a survivor of emotional abuse, you will need to focus on identifying, trusting, and expressing your feelings. This is especially important because victims of emotional abuse are often told that they are overly sensitive or that their reactions and feelings are inappropriate. The emotions survivors will undoubtedly feel as a result of the abuse include:

- Shame—at not being loved, at having accepted humiliation, at what you have submitted to and undergone.

- Fear—when someone reminds you of a past abuser, when you catch yourself being abusive, when you enter a new relationship.

- Grief—concerning the loss of identity and self-esteem, concerning the loss of love you once felt toward your partner, the amount of time lost in an abusive relationship, or at the realization that you were not loved.

- Anger—at the abuser for damaging your self-esteem and for making you doubt your perceptions; anger at your original abuser for modeling abusive relationships, for causing you to have such low self-esteem, for setting you up for further abuse.

Self-Care

Many people stay stuck in the past because they refuse to let go and move on. They desperately want to get what they didn't get as a child, and they keep searching for someone to be the good parent they long for. But no one else can fill up the empty spaces inside you, and no one can make up for what you missed as a child. You will now need to give to yourself what you missed— you will need to become your own "good enough" parent.

You began this work by following my suggestions on how to raise your self-esteem. The following suggestions will help you still further in the process. Self-care includes:

- Putting your own needs first at times

- Valuing and respecting yourself, including your feelings and your needs

- Praising yourself

- Nurturing yourself (e.g., give yourself the gift of a massage or manicure as often as possible)

- Asking for what you want and saying no to what you don't want

- Recognizing that you have choices and rights
- Expressing your feelings, needs, and opinions

EXERCISE: *Your Childhood Wish List*

1. List all the things you wish you had received in childhood but did not. This list tells you the things that you now need to do for yourself.

2. Begin today to meet some of these needs. When you have successfully met one, cross it off your list and focus on the next item. Don't get overwhelmed and feel that you have to do everything on the list at once. Take your time and relish the little steps—whether you're able to cross one item off the list a week or one item a month, you're starting to take care of your own needs, and that's what matters most.

Becoming your own good parent, giving yourself the nurturing and caring that you are still so much in need of, is an important part of completing your unfinished business. Once you have done so you will feel less resentful of those in your childhood who deprived or abused you, and you will be less needy and dependent in your relationships.

Recovery for the Abusive Partner

You, too, will need to begin to identify and honor your feelings. While anger, pain, fear, and grief are all important emotions for you to focus on, next to anger, shame is probably the emotion you need to work on the most. Because you were likely rejected and criticized as a child and blamed for whatever went wrong in your family, you developed a great deal of personal shame. Those who were heavily shamed as children react by building a wall or defense system that is so strong that the feelings or reactions of others cannot get through. This wall or defense system is the primary reason many people who become emotionally abusive do not have empathy for others. It's almost as if they cannot afford to pay attention to the feelings of others because there is such potential for them to become overwhelmed with shame when they do.

Part of your unfinished business is to begin to put the unhealthy shame and blame where it belongs—on your original abusers instead of on people in your current life, most particularly your mate. The next time you have a shame attack because someone criticized you, made fun of you, questioned your choices, or blamed you for doing something you didn't do, instead of turning around and putting your shame on those closest to you, connect your shame with how you felt as a child and remember who it was that made you feel that way. Then find constructive ways to express your righteous anger toward those who deserve it.

Stop Taking Things So Personally

Partly due to the tremendous amount of criticism you likely experienced as child, you are probably hypersensitive when it comes to criticism and judgments from others. If your partner merely makes a suggestion that you should buy some new clothes you may interpret it as her saying that you are a slob. If she makes a comment about how tired you look, instead of hearing it as an expression of concern, you may hear it as her telling you you look old.

If you continue to assume that every innocent comment means that there is something wrong with you or that you are being criticized, you will either continue to adamantly defend yourself against a nonexistent attack (and become abusive in the process) or to continue to feel completely worthless. Try taking things at face value instead of assuming that there is hidden meaning in every comment. If someone says something that causes you to doubt yourself or to doubt her intention, ask her to clarify what she meant.

Face Your Fears

Instead of covering up your fear of abandonment or rejection with bravado or with attacks, begin to acknowledge your fears. Everyone experiences fear—it is a very human quality. Pretending you are not afraid only serves to disconnect you from your true self.

Stop Mind Reading

Since you feel so convinced that you are inadequate, flawed, worthless, or bad, you probably assume that others view you in the same way. This belief can cause you to have a tendency to *mind read*—to assume you know what others are thinking. The truth is, your partner and others probably don't perceive you as half as inadequate or flawed as you do. In fact, you've probably been able to fool them quite well with your bravado and the false mask of confidence you project. And the truth is, your partner is probably far more loving and patient with you than you are with yourself.

Judging you is not the foremost priority on everyone else's mind. In fact, in most cases, when you are assuming that others are thinking bad thoughts about you, they are probably not thinking about you at all. If you have been abusive to your partner, believe me, she is far too busy trying to survive and to avoid your wrath to focus on judging you. And others are far too busy with their own lives.

For Both Partners— Finding the Right Therapist

Throughout the book I've encouraged you to seek professional help, whether you are an abusive partner or the partner who has been abused. The following information will help you to find the right kind of help for your particular needs.

I recommend that you be very clear from the very beginning (even with your first phone call) that you would like to work with someone who is familiar with the effects of emotional abuse and has experience working with those who were emotionally abused as a child. Depending upon your personal history, you may also want to ask if the therapist has experience working with others types of childhood abuse, including physical and sexual abuse. If you have been the victim of adult emotional abuse, tell the therapist this and ask if he or she has worked with other survivors. If you have been the abusive partner, ask if the therapist has experience working with abusers. A competent therapist should have no problems answering your questions and providing you with his or her qualifications.

If you believe you might be suffering from Borderline Personality Disorder or Narcissistic Personality Disorder, I recommend that you ask potential therapists if they have experience treating these disorders. It requires special training and education to work with these disorders effectively, and there are several recommended treatment modalities that work most effectively. The most effective short-term treatment is called Cognitive Behavioral Therapy or Dialectic Behavior Therapy (DBT). To locate a clinician who specializes in DBT, contact the following for referrals:

- Behavioral Technology Transfer Group, (206) 675-8558

- For long-term intrapsychic psychotherapy nationwide, contact The Masterson Institute for Psychoanalytic Psychotherapy, (212) 935-1414

Epilogue

As you continue to recover from the wounds of your emotionally abusive childhood, you will discover the great joy of having overcome one of the most difficult obstacles to achieving a healthy relationship. If you are fortunate enough to travel this road with your partner, the two of you can be each other's greatest allies. If you travel the road alone, you'll find that your next relationship will be far healthier than your previous ones. Although recovery will be an ongoing process, this does not mean that you won't be rewarded for your efforts all along the way.

Today I can proudly say that I am no longer an emotional abuser nor am I a victim, and I consider this to be one of my greatest accomplishments. I am certain that if you continue the recovery process, someday you can say the same thing.

I would appreciate hearing how this book has affected you. I am also available for lectures and workshops. You can e-mail me at Beverly@beverlyengel.com or write to P.O. Box 6412, Los Osos, CA, 93412-6412.

References

Unattributed quotes are from interviews conducted by the author.

CHAPTER 2: PATTERNS OF ABUSE

Patricia Evans, *The Verbally Abusive Relationship* (Avon, Mass.: Adams Media, 1992).

Susan Forward, *Emotional Blackmail* (New York: HarperCollins, 1998).

CHAPTER 4: PATTERNS THAT BEGIN IN CHILDHOOD

Judith Viorst, *Necessary Losses* (New York: Fawcett, 1986).

Beverly Engel, *The Emotionally Abused Woman* (New York: Fawcett Columbine, 1991).

Michael Gurian, *A Fine Young Man* (New York: Tarder, 1998).

CHAPTER 6: ACTION STEPS FOR THE ABUSIVE PARTNER

Lewis B. Smedes, *Shame and Grace: Healing the Shame We Don't Deserve* (San Francisco: HarperSanFrancisco, 1993).

CHAPTER 9: WHEN YOUR ABUSIVENESS STEMS FROM YOUR PERSONALITY DISORDER

James Masterson, *The Search for the Real Self: Unmasking the Personality Disorders of Our Age* (New York: The Free Press, 1988).

Elan Golomb, Ph.D., *Adult Children of Narcissists in Their Struggle for Self* (New York: William Morrow, 1992).

Further Reading

EMOTIONAL CHILD ABUSE

Emotional Child Abuse: The Family Curse, by Joel Covitz

Emotional Abuse, by Marti Tamm Loring

Necessary Losses, by Judith Viorst

The Drama of the Gifted Child: The Search for the True Self, by Alice Miller

RECOVERY

Stalking the Soul: Emotional Abuse and the Erosion of Identity, by Marie-France Hirigoyen

Finding the Love You Want, by Harville Hendrix

If You Had Controlling Parents: How to Make Peace with Your Past and Take Your Place in the World, by Dan Neuharth

The Narcissistic/Borderline Couple, by Joan Lachkar

Emotional Blackmail, by Susan Forward

Are You the One for Me? Knowing Who's Right and Avoiding Who's Wrong, by Barbara De Angelis

Adult Children of Abusive Parents, by Steven Farmer

Divorcing a Parent, by Beverly Engel

Toxic Parents, by Susan Forward

RECOVERY FOR FEMALE VICTIMS OF EMOTIONAL ABUSE

The Emotionally Abused Woman, by Beverly Engel

Encouragements for the Emotionally Abused Woman, by Beverly Engel

Loving Him without Losing You, by Beverly Engel

The Dance of Anger: A Woman's Guide to Changing the Patterns in Intimate Relationships, by Harriet Lerner

RECOVERY FOR MALE VICTIMS OF EMOTIONAL ABUSE

The Wounded Male, by Steven Farmer

Wounded Boys Heroic Men: A Man's Guide to Recovering from Child Abuse, by Daniel Jay Sonkin, Lenore E. A. Walker

Flying Boy: Healing the Wounded Male, by John Lee

ANGER MANAGEMENT AND STRESS REDUCTION

The Relaxation and Stress Reduction Workbook, by Martha Davis, Matthew McKay, and Elizabeth Robbins Eshelman

The Big Book of Stress Release Games, by Robert Epstein, Ph.D.

Angry All the Time: An Emergency Guide to Anger Control, by Ron Potter-Efron

The Angry Self: A Comprehensive Approach to Anger Management, by Miriam M. Gottlieb, Ph.D.

Beyond Anger: A Guide for Men, by Thomas J. Harbin

RELATED RECOVERY ISSUES

Boundaries: Where You End and I Begin, by Anne Katherine

Codependent No More: Beyond Codependency, by Melody Beattie

Shame and Grace, by Lewis B. Smedes

The Shame That Binds, by John Bradshaw

Blessings from the Fall: Turning a Fall from Grace into a New Beginning, by Beverly Engel

The Power of Apology, by Beverly Engel

Boundaries and Relationships, by Charles L. Whitfield, M.D.

OTHER FORMS OF ABUSE

The Verbally Abusive Relationship, by Patricia Evans

The Right to Innocence: Healing the Trauma of Childhood Sexual Abuse, by Beverly Engel

The Courage to Heal, by Laura Davis

Getting Free: You Can End Abuse and Take Back Your Life, by Ginny NiCarthy

It's My Life Now: Starting Over after an Abusive Relationship or Domestic Violence, by Meg Kennedy Dugan

BORDERLINE PERSONALITY DISORDER

Lost in the Mirror: An Inside Look at Borderline Personality Disorder, by Richard A. Moskovitz, M.D.

Skills Training Manual for Treating Borderline Personality Disorder, by Marsha M. Linehan

Stop Walking on Eggshells: Coping When Someone You Care about Has Borderline Personality Disorder, by Paul Mason and Randi Kreger

Narcissistic Personality Disorder

Trapped in the Mirror: Adult Children of Narcissists in Their Struggle for Self, by
    Elan Golomb, Ph.D.
*Children of the Self-Absorbed: A Grown-Up's Guide to Getting Over Narcissistic
    Parents,* by Nina W. Brown
The Search for the Real Self: Unmasking the Personality Disorders of Our Age, by
    James F. Masterson, M.D.

Breaking the Cycle

The Parenthood Decision, by Beverly Engel
Your Child's Self-Esteem, by Doroty Corkville Briggs

Websites and Chat Rooms

www.beverlyengel.com
www.powerofapology.com

EMOTIONAL ABUSE CHAT ROOMS

www.healingclub.com
www.thewoundedhealer.com
www.selfgrowth.com
www.about.com
www.joy2meu.com

DOMESTIC VIOLENCE CHAT ROOM

www.thewoundedhealerjournal.com

BORDERLINE WEBSITES & CHAT ROOMS

www.mhsanctuary.com/borderline/
    chatrooms for BPDs, partners, families—also for males suffering from BPD
www.bpdcentral.com/
    for partners of BPDs

Index

abandonment
  in childhood, 52, 53, 66, 67–68, 167, 196
  Borderline Personality Disorder and, 167–69, 188, 191, 196, 197
  fear of, 41–42
abuse, 84–88. *See also* childhood, emotionally abusive; *specific kinds of abuse*
abusers
  admission of abuse by, 116–18
  apologies by, 130–32, 155
  borderline, 186–211
  characteristics of, 120–24, 230–31, 233
  childhood abuse history among, 73, 118–23, 125, 137, 196, 207
  determining who is the abuser, 50–53
  emotions of, 114, 125, 132–44, 252–53
  key issues for, 243–47
  malevolent, 42–43
  mutual, 145–61
  narcissistic, 202–11
  original, 23, 73–74, 96, 99, 127–28, 169
  preventing further abuse, 233–41
  recovery for, 252–54
  reluctance to seek help among, 81
  signs of, 17–20
  stopping, program for, 115–44

  talking to, 86, 101–105, 106, 109–12, 149–61, 179, 180
  unconscious decision to become, 74
  victimization feelings among, 50–53
  victims who become, 23, 41
abusive attitude, 11–12, 20
abusive personality, 56–57
agreeing to disagree, 160–61
alcohol use, 67, 68, 88, 188, 200, 222
alone, fear of being, 91–92, 95
anger
  in borderlines, 188, 190
  dealing with, 124, 132–39, 234, 248
  healthy vs. unhealthy, 133
  journal, 134–35
  male and female patterns of, 76–77, 120
  toward parents, 119, 124
  reasons for, 21–23, 125
  repressed, 97, 98–99, 124, 248
  victims', 249–50, 251
apologizing for abuse, 130–32, 155, 210
arguments, 35, 39
arousal, high levels of, 124, 138–39
authoritarian parents, 70

Behavioral Technology Transfer Group, 255
beliefs, faulty, 134, 139–41
bipolar disorder, 34
bisexuals, 3
blackmail, emotional, 31–33, 192

262